# ALEISTER & ADOLF™

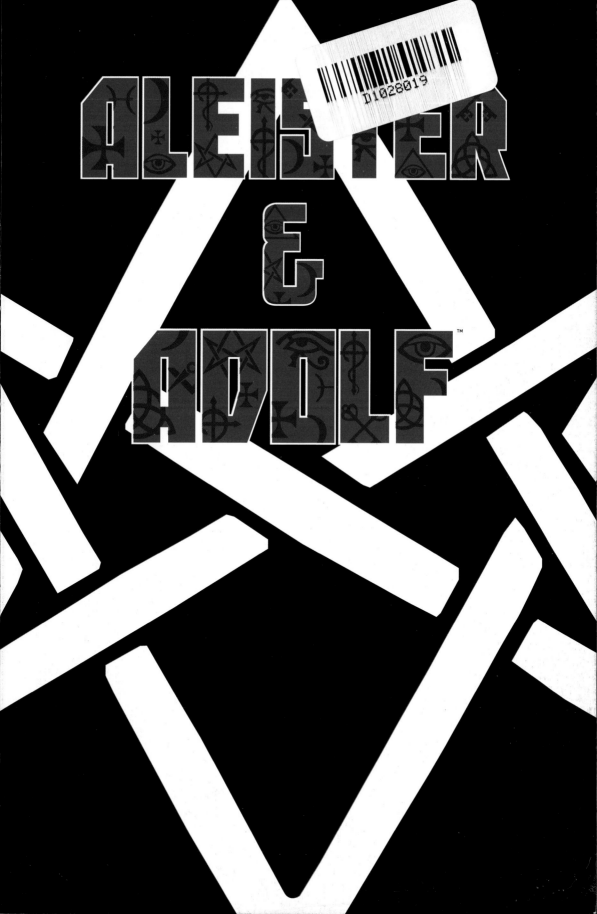

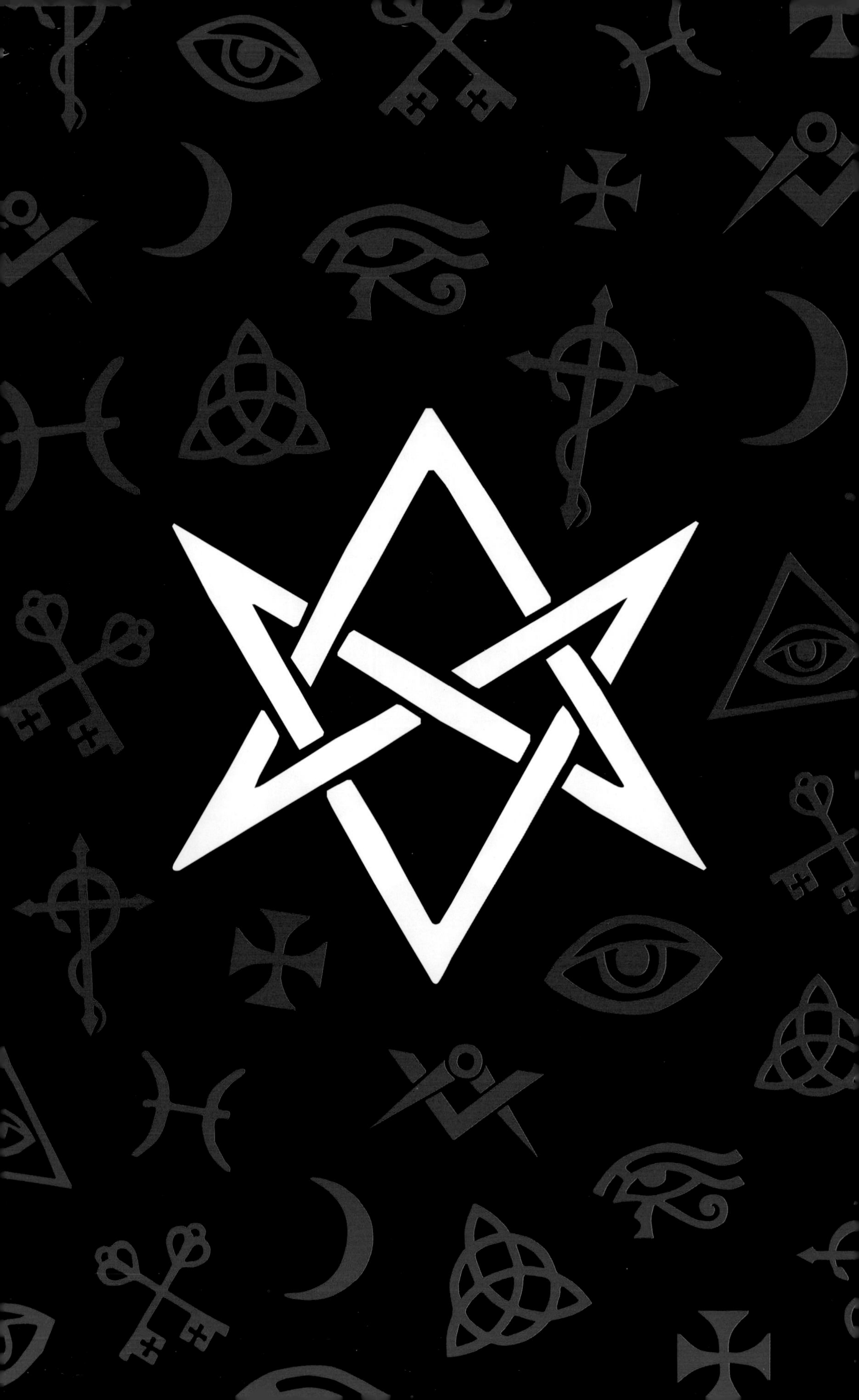

ALEISTER & ADOLF™

**story**
DOUGLAS RUSHKOFF

**art**
MICHAEL AVON OEMING

**lettering**
NATE PIEKOS OF BLAMBOT®

president and publisher
**MIKE RICHARDSON**

editor
**DANIEL CHABON**

assistant editor
**CHUCK HOWITT**

designer
**SKYLER WEISSENFLUH**

digital art technician
**ADAM PRUETT**

Published by Dark Horse Books
A division of Dark Horse Comics LLC
10956 SE Main Street
Milwaukie, OR 97222

DarkHorse.com

To find a comics shop in your area, visit comicshoplocator.com

First hardcover edition: November 2016
First paperback edition: December 2020
Ebook ISBN: 978-1-50672-206-1
Trade paperback ISBN: 978-1-50672-104-0

10 9 8 7 6 5 4 3 2 1
Printed in China

**ALEISTER & ADOLF**

Library of Congress Cataloging-in-Publication Data

Names: Rushkoff, Douglas, author. | Oeming, Michael Avon, artist. | Piekos,
    Nate, letterer.
Title: Aleister & Adolf / Douglas Rushkoff, story ; Michael Avon Oeming,
    art ; Nate Piekos of Blambot, lettering.
Description: First paperback edition. | Milwaukie, OR : Dark Horse Comics,
    2020. | Summary: "The original graphic novel Aleister & Adolf in a trade
    format, with new cover and expanded content"-- Provided by publisher.
Identifiers: LCCN 2020007771 | ISBN 9781506721040 (paperback) | ISBN
    9781506722061 (ebook)
Subjects: LCSH: Graphic novels.
Classification: LCC PN6727.R84 A76 2020 | DDC 741.5/973--dc23
LC record available at https://lccn.loc.gov/2020007771

**Neil Hankerson** Executive Vice President • **Tom Weddle** Chief Financial Officer • **Randy Stradley** Vice President of Publishing • **Nick McWhorter** Chief Business Development Officer • **Dale LaFountain** Chief Information Officer **Matt Parkinson** Vice President of Marketing • **Vanessa Todd-Holmes** Vice President of Production and Scheduling **Mark Bernardi** Vice President of Book Trade and Digital Sales • **Ken Lizzi** General Counsel • **Dave Marshall** Editor in Chief • **Davey Estrada** Editorial Director • **Chris Warner** Senior Books Editor • **Cary Grazzini** Director of Specialty Projects • **Lia Ribacchi** Art Director • **Matt Dryer** Director of Digital Art and Prepress • **Michael Gombos** Senior Director of Licensed Publications • **Kari Yadro** Director of Custom Programs • **Kari Torson** Director of International Licensing • **Sean Brice** Director of Trade Sales

# FOREWORD

Douglas Rushkoff and Michael Avon Oeming's masterful *Aleister & Adolf* peels back the tattooed skin of history to reveal the intricate occult clockwork that secretly drives events and remakes the lives of unsuspecting millions. With the fizzing, urgent pace and page-turning suspense of a Hollywood thriller and the sweeping scope of a postmodern historical novel, *Aleister & Adolf* has some real philosophical meat at its heart, and its provocative themes speak directly to the traumatized, hypnotized inhabitants of the twenty-first-century hallucinosphere.

Rushkoff blends sex magic, death rituals, sigil warfare, and the insidious mind-control techniques of our corporate overlords into a slowly unfolding decades-old mystery, while his pitch-perfect dialogue brings to life a colorful cast that's big enough to include such real-world luminaries as Rudolf Hess, General Patton, and Ian Fleming, the creator of James Bond—warriors all in a shadow conflict, waged in the epic darkness of the collective unconscious. Deploying impeccable historical research, Rushkoff and Oeming lay bare in this stark depiction of World War II and beyond a monumental clash of opposing magical viewpoints; an endless war between sex and death; Eros and Thanatos; Victory and Surrender; the Scarlet Woman and the Black Sun; Crowley and Hitler . . . Aleister & Adolf.

It's the Wickedest Man in the World versus History's Most Evil Dictator in an apocalyptic struggle for the soul of humanity, across a battlefield of storm and symbol! Place your bets! Your ringside seat awaits . . .

—**Grant Morrison**

*March 1, 2016*

Most of the
stuff in this story really
happened. The rest may as
well have. It's all how you connect
the dots. —DR

# MAGICAL WARFARE

### Interview with Douglas Rushkoff by Richard Metzger

*Aleister & Adolf* is a new graphic novel from Dark Horse Comics, the product of the creative pairing of media theorist Douglas Rushkoff—Professor of Media Studies at Queens College in New York—and award-winning illustrator Michael Avon Oeming.

In *Aleister & Adolf* the reader is taken behind the scenes of the capitalist spectacle and inside the boardrooms where corporate-occult marketing departments employ fascist sigil magick developed by the Nazis during WWII in today's advertising logos. A place where the war for men's minds is waged with symbols and catchy slogans. It's a fun, smart read, and you'll be much smarter after you've read it, trust me. And Oeming's crisp B&W artwork is perfectly suited for getting across some often difficult and tricky philosophical concepts. He's a unique talent indeed.

Rushkoff recently told AV Club:
"Swastikas and other sigil logos become the corporate logos of our world. And given that we're living in a moment where those logos are migrating online where they can move on their own, it's kind of important that we consider the origins and power of these icons."

Grant Morrison even wrote the introduction to *Aleister & Adolf*. I mean, how can you lose with something like this?

*I asked Douglas Rushkoff a few questions via email:*

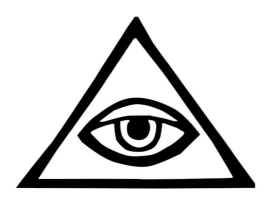

*Dangerous Minds: Where did you find the inspiration for Aleister & Adolf?*

**Douglas Rushkoff:** It's almost easier to ask where *didn't* I find inspiration for *Aleister & Adolf*. The moment it occurred to me was when I was in an editorial meeting at DC/Vertigo about my comic book *Testament*, back in 2005. The editor warned me that there was an arcane house rule against having Jesus Christ and a Superhero in the same panel. Not that I was going to get to Jesus in my story, but the rule got me thinking about other potentially blasphemous superhero/supervillain pairings. And that's when I first got to wondering about Aleister Crowley vs. Adolf Hitler.

But as I considered the possibility, it occurred to me that they were practicing competing forms of magic at the same time. And then I began to do the research, and learned that the premise of my story was true: Aleister Crowley performed counter-sigils to Hitler's. Crowley came up with the V for Victory sigil that Churchill used to flash—and got it to him through Ian Fleming (the James Bond author) who was MI5 at the time.

I've always wanted to do something about Crowley, but I've been afraid for a bunch of reasons. Making him something of a war hero, and contrasting him with a true villain like Hitler, became a way to depict him as something more dimensional than "the Beast."

*Did you think of the ending first? It's a bit like a punchline, isn't it?*

**Douglas Rushkoff:** I didn't think of the ending first. The first thing I thought of was to have a young American military photographer get sent to enlist Crowley in the magical effort. I wanted us to see the story through someone like us—someone more cynical, perhaps—and then get to have the vicarious thrill of being drawn into Crowley's world.

Then, I decided I needed a framing story—just to show how relevant all this creation of sigils is to our world today. So I created a prologue for the story, that takes place in a modern advertising agency: the place where the equivalent of sigil magic is practiced today. I wanted to set the telling of the story within the frame of how corporate sigils are taking life on the Internet today. So the outer frame takes place in the mid-nineties, when the net was being turned over to marketers. The ending is pretty well broadcast up front.

*Aleister & Adolf reminds me a lot of Robert Anton Wilson's Masks of the Illuminatus—which I think is his best book—because it sort of forces its ideas into the reader's head like an earworm that you can't resist. Also, Crowley is a character in that book, too, of course. Do you see it as a bit of a RAW homage?*

**Douglas Rushkoff:** It's a RAW homage in that the story has verisimilitude—it is told in a way where it's absolutely possible for this all to happen. There's no supernatural magic here; it's just the magick of Will. There's the black magic of the Nazis. But however extreme the Nazis, it was real. It's got the reality quotient of *Eyes Wide Shut* or *Apocalypse Now*.

And that's the understanding of sigil magic I got from Bob. It's all very normal. That doesn't mean it doesn't work. Just that you have to participate in its perception. It's just a different way of understanding the connections. So while the protagonist of the story starts off as a disillusioned atheist and ends up believing in magick as Magic, even Crowley (at least my Crowley) tries to convince him not to take it so literally.

I wouldn't understand magick that way if it weren't for Bob. It's embedded in the fabric of reality. It doesn't need to break the rules of reality to work.

*Are you aware of a recent trend among some alt-right types to organize acts of group 4Chan "meme magick"? Some of it's just blatant harassment and bullying over Twitter, but there's actually a sophisticated intent behind some of it. Pepe the Frog has become a hypersigil. I'm not being admiring of it—the idea that certain reichwingers would want start a magical war via social media is alarming to say the least—but the concept is a sound one magically speaking: They've figured out how to amplify their signal's strength like a radio transmitter.*

**Douglas Rushkoff:** There's a real crossover between the alt-right and the occult. I knew a guy writing a book about it, in fact. And remember, it was one of Bush's advisors who once explained that the future is something you create. And there's an any-means-necessary quality to libertarianism that is consonant with chaos magic.

Plus, you're talking about homespun propagandists inhabiting the comments sections of blogs and things. They're not reading Bernays and Lippman. They're waging hand-to-hand battle in the ideological trenches. A bit of NLP, rhetoric, and magic are what you turn to.

The interesting thing here is why the left does not use these techniques. It goes against our sense of what is fair. We know we're "right" and so we want to win with the fact. Sigil magic feels like cheating on some level. So we have to ask ourselves, isn't the full expression of our Will something we want to unleash? If not, why not?

*This isn't the freethinking/pansexual "Generation Hex" types who seemed to be on the horizon a few years ago, but rather like an evil skinheads contingent at Hogwarts.*

**Douglas Rushkoff:** Alas it is not. That's partly because the freethinking pansexuals got a bit distracted by other things. And most of them worked alone. I don't think there were nearly as many, either. That's pretty rarified air. Back in the eighties, there were more kids taking acid in the parking lot at AC/DC concerts than there were in the dorms of Reid College. And likewise—as a result of economics as much as anything—there's more gamergaters throwing sigils online than Bernie Sanders supporters. Sometimes magic gets in the hands of people you'd rather not find it.

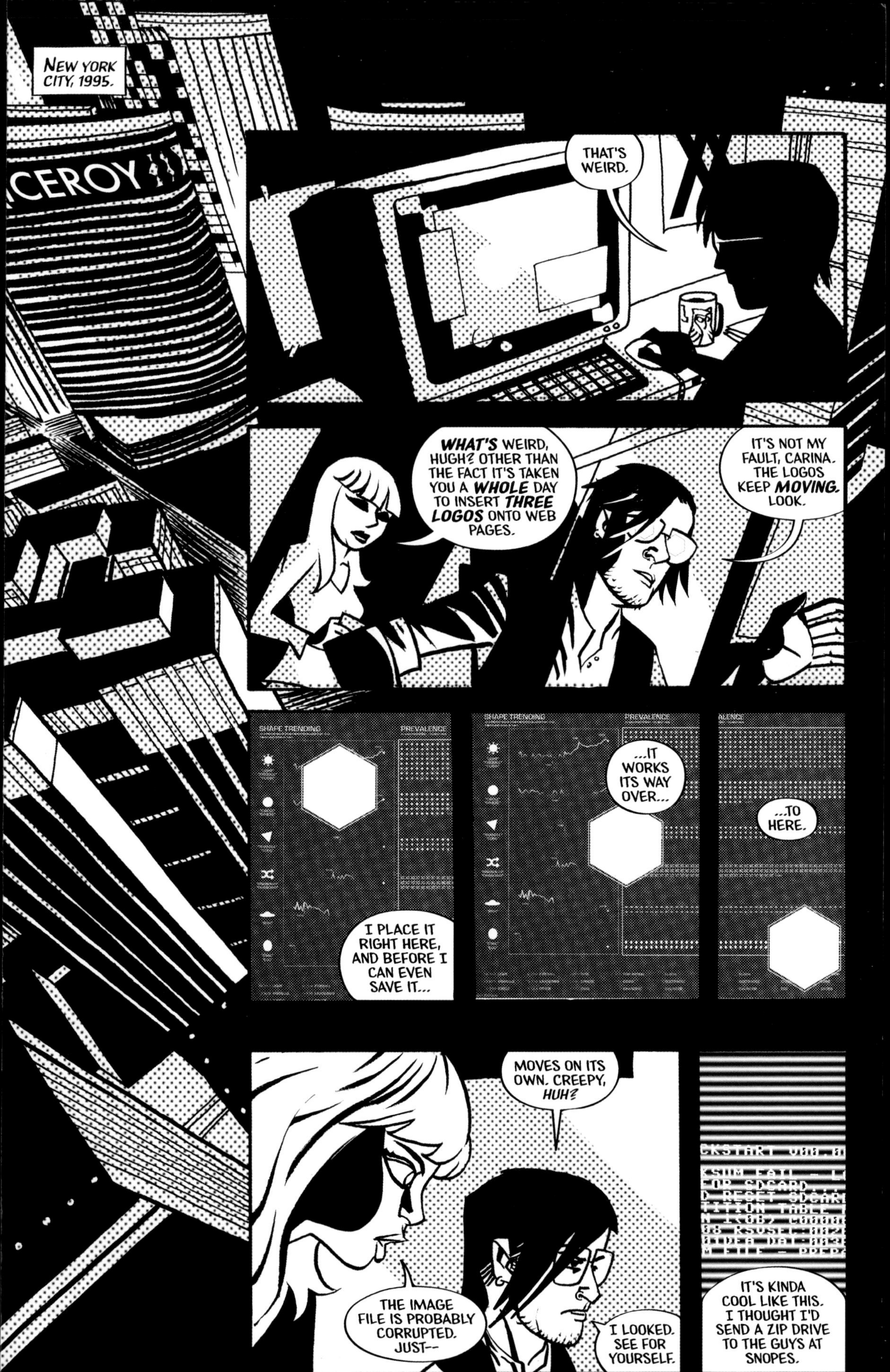
NEW YORK CITY, 1995.
CEROY
THAT'S WEIRD.
WHAT'S WEIRD, HUGH? OTHER THAN THE FACT IT'S TAKEN YOU A WHOLE DAY TO INSERT THREE LOGOS ONTO WEB PAGES.
IT'S NOT MY FAULT, CARINA. THE LOGOS KEEP MOVING. LOOK.
SHAPE TRENDING
PREVALENCE
I PLACE IT RIGHT HERE, AND BEFORE I CAN EVEN SAVE IT...
...IT WORKS ITS WAY OVER...
...TO HERE.
MOVES ON ITS OWN. CREEPY, HUH?
THE IMAGE FILE IS PROBABLY CORRUPTED. JUST--
I LOOKED. SEE FOR YOURSELF.
IT'S KINDA COOL LIKE THIS. I THOUGHT I'D SEND A ZIP DRIVE TO THE GUYS AT SNOPES.

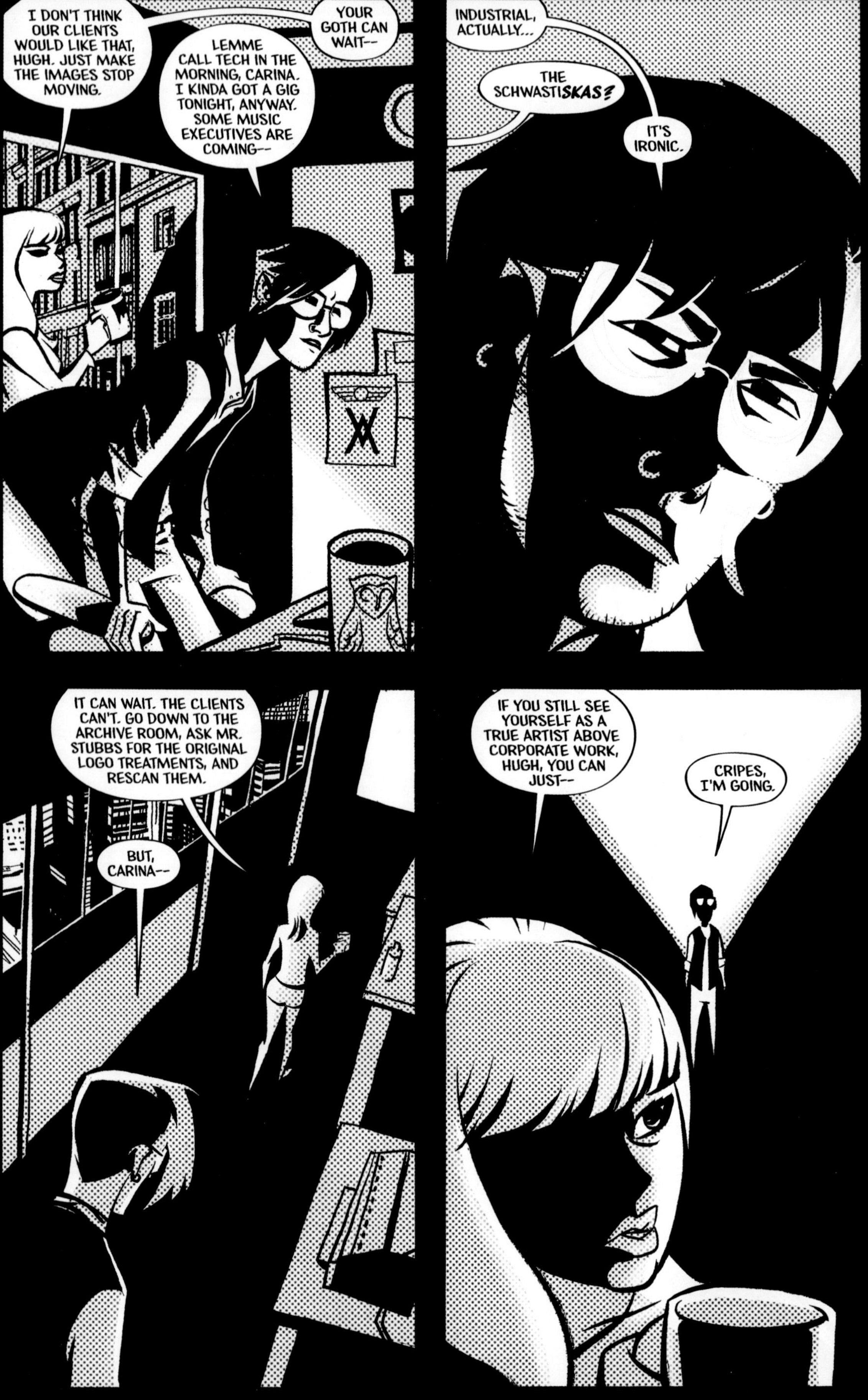
I DON'T THINK OUR CLIENTS WOULD LIKE THAT, HUGH. JUST MAKE THE IMAGES STOP MOVING.
LEMME CALL TECH IN THE MORNING, CARINA. I KINDA GOT A GIG TONIGHT, ANYWAY. SOME MUSIC EXECUTIVES ARE COMING--
YOUR GOTH CAN WAIT--
INDUSTRIAL, ACTUALLY...
THE SCHWASTISKAS?
IT'S IRONIC.
IT CAN WAIT. THE CLIENTS CAN'T. GO DOWN TO THE ARCHIVE ROOM, ASK MR. STUBBS FOR THE ORIGINAL LOGO TREATMENTS, AND RESCAN THEM.
BUT, CARINA--
IF YOU STILL SEE YOURSELF AS A TRUE ARTIST ABOVE CORPORATE WORK, HUGH, YOU CAN JUST--
CRIPES, I'M GOING.

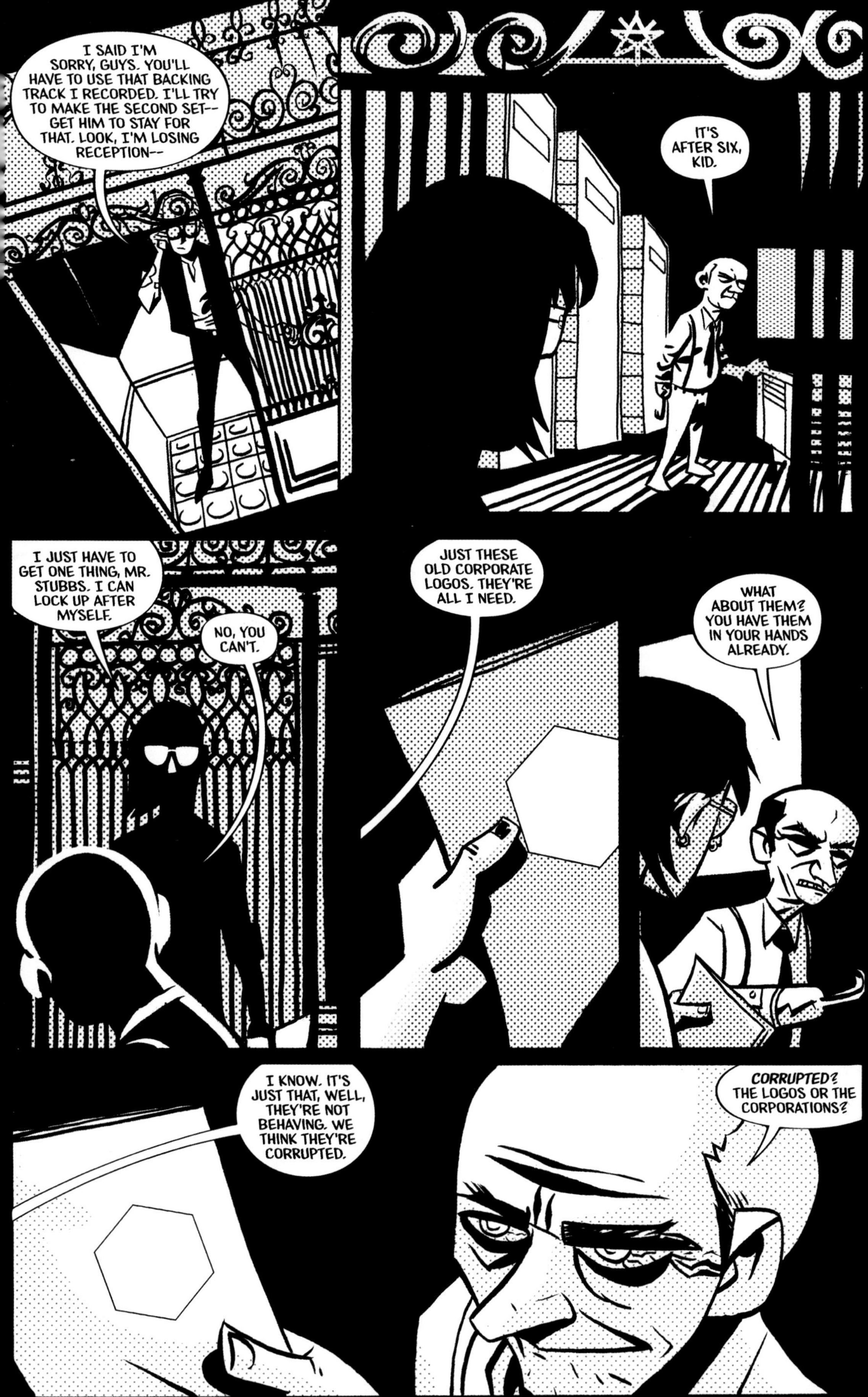
I SAID I'M SORRY, GUYS. YOU'LL HAVE TO USE THAT BACKING TRACK I RECORDED. I'LL TRY TO MAKE THE SECOND SET-- GET HIM TO STAY FOR THAT. LOOK, I'M LOSING RECEPTION--
IT'S AFTER SIX, KID.
I JUST HAVE TO GET ONE THING, MR. STUBBS. I CAN LOCK UP AFTER MYSELF.
NO, YOU CAN'T.
JUST THESE OLD CORPORATE LOGOS. THEY'RE ALL I NEED.
WHAT ABOUT THEM? YOU HAVE THEM IN YOUR HANDS ALREADY.
I KNOW. IT'S JUST THAT, WELL, THEY'RE NOT BEHAVING. WE THINK THEY'RE CORRUPTED.
*CORRUPTED?* THE LOGOS OR THE CORPORATIONS?

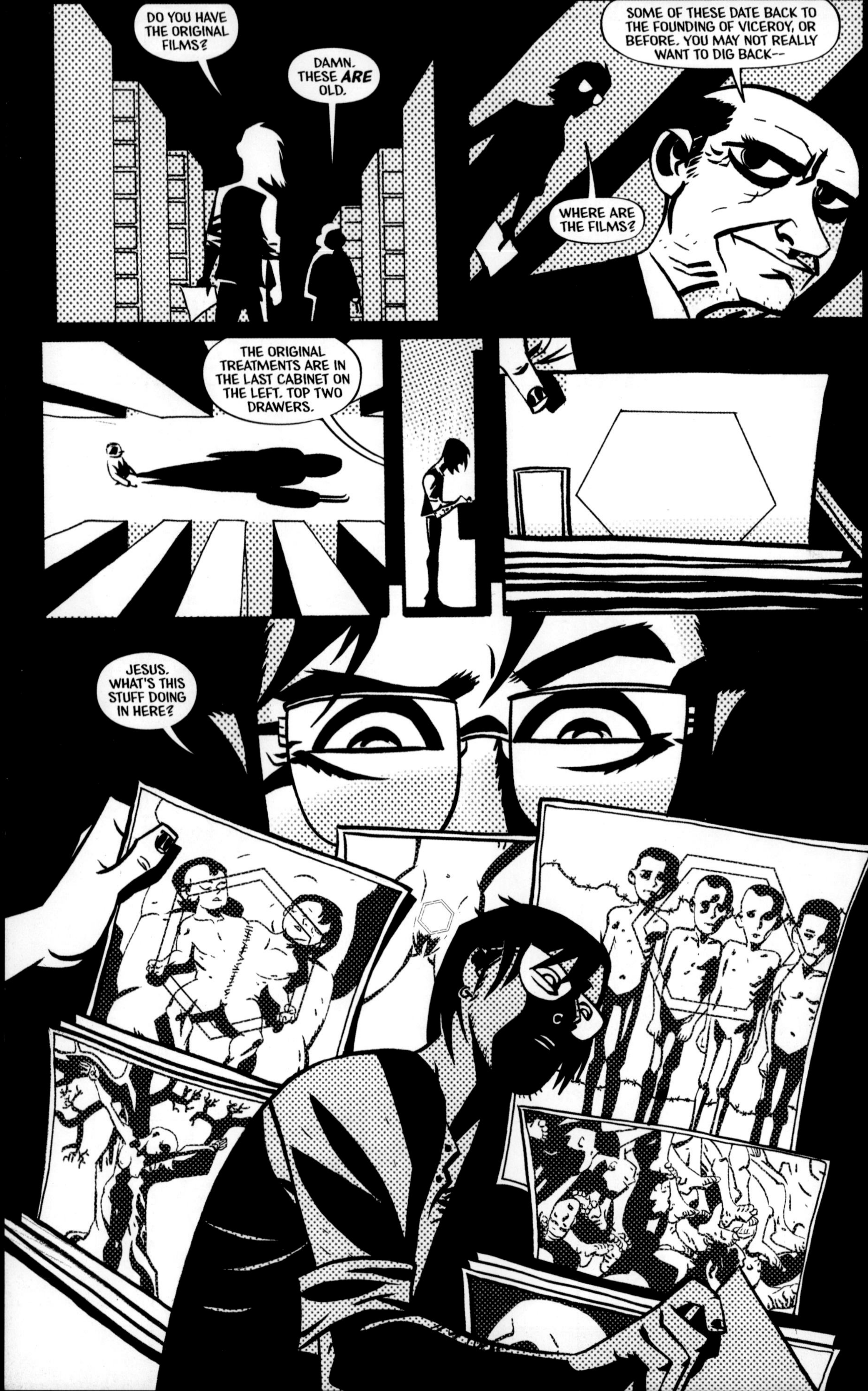
DO YOU HAVE THE ORIGINAL FILMS?
DAMN. THESE *ARE* OLD.
SOME OF THESE DATE BACK TO THE FOUNDING OF VICEROY, OR BEFORE. YOU MAY NOT REALLY WANT TO DIG BACK--
WHERE ARE THE FILMS?
THE ORIGINAL TREATMENTS ARE IN THE LAST CABINET ON THE LEFT. TOP TWO DRAWERS.
JESUS. WHAT'S THIS STUFF DOING IN HERE?

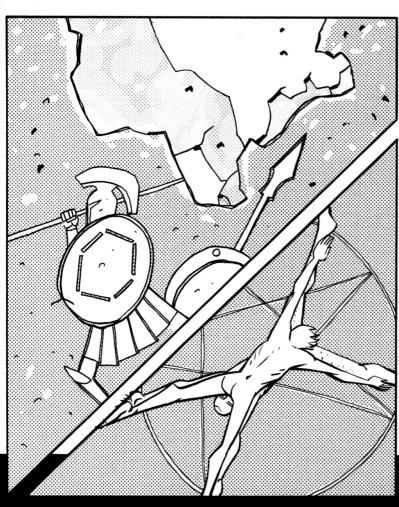

WHAT THE...?

SEE SOMETHING... *FAMILIAR?*

NO. NOTHING.

THEN WHY ARE YOU CLUTCHING THAT *FOLDER* LIKE THAT?

THOSE LOGOS... EVERYTHING...IS IT ALL REALLY BASED ON...?

ARTISTS FIND THEIR INSPIRATION IN STRANGE PLACES, SON. I GET THE SENSE *YOU* DO, TOO.

BUT WHO WOULD HAVE...?

THERE'S SOMEONE YOU SHOULD SEE. HE'S BEEN WAITING A *LONG TIME.*

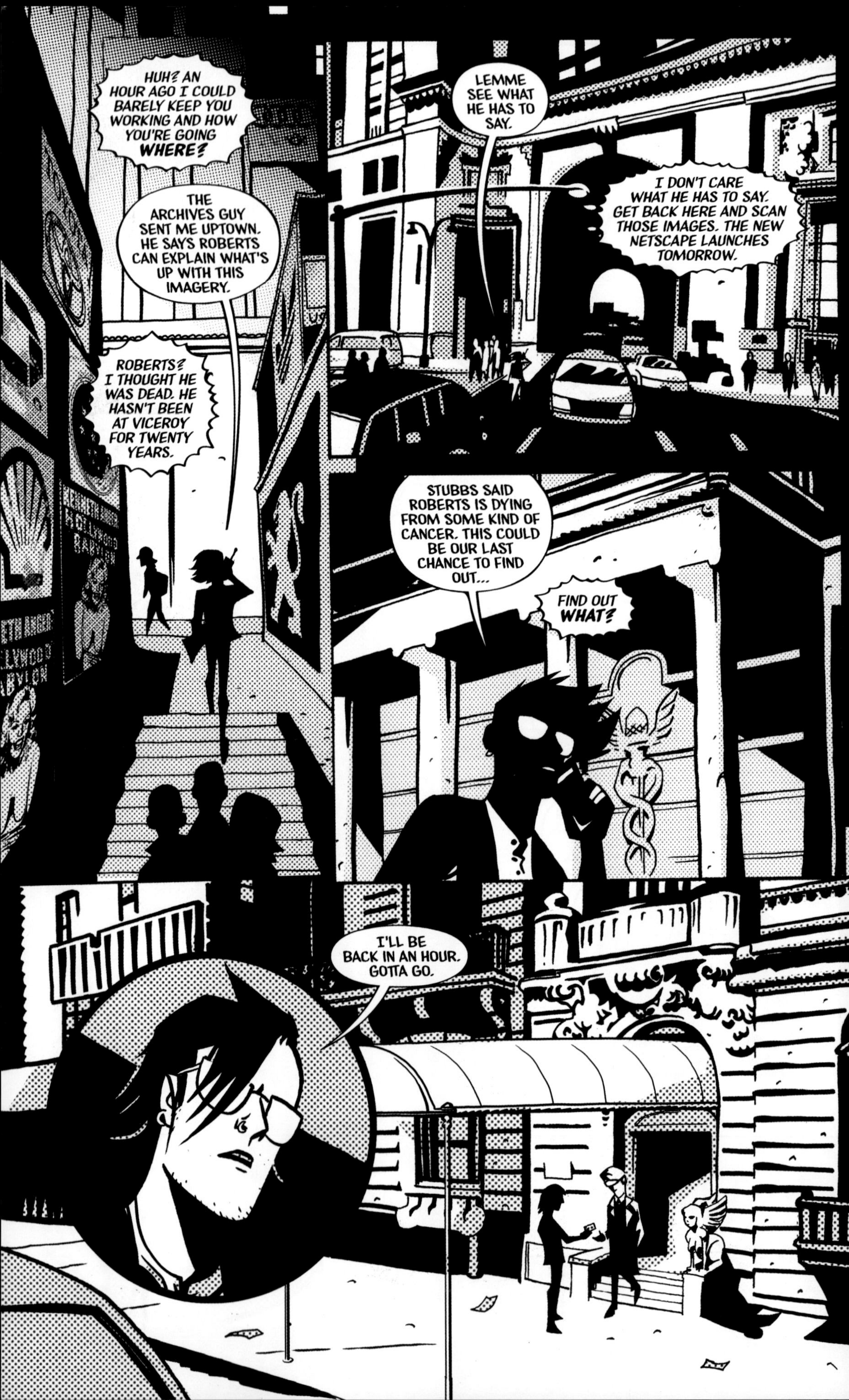
HUH? AN HOUR AGO I COULD BARELY KEEP YOU WORKING AND HOW YOU'RE GOING **WHERE?**
THE ARCHIVES GUY SENT ME UPTOWN. HE SAYS ROBERTS CAN EXPLAIN WHAT'S UP WITH THIS IMAGERY.
ROBERTS? I THOUGHT HE WAS DEAD. HE HASN'T BEEN AT VICEROY FOR TWENTY YEARS.
LEMME SEE WHAT HE HAS TO SAY.
I DON'T CARE WHAT HE HAS TO SAY. GET BACK HERE AND SCAN THOSE IMAGES. THE NEW NETSCAPE LAUNCHES TOMORROW.
STUBBS SAID ROBERTS IS DYING FROM SOME KIND OF CANCER. THIS COULD BE OUR LAST CHANCE TO FIND OUT...
FIND OUT **WHAT?**
I'LL BE BACK IN AN HOUR. GOTTA GO.

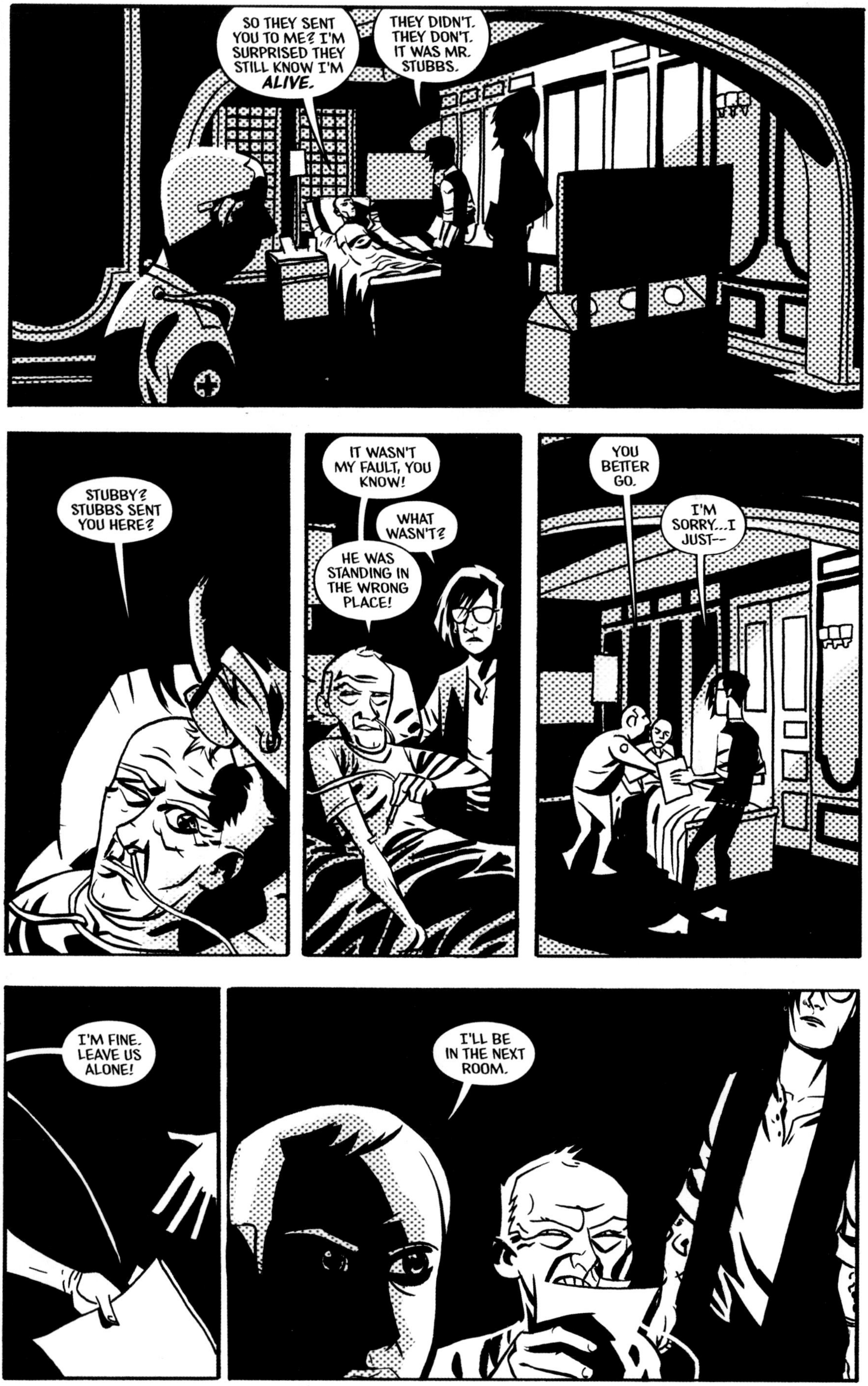

SO THEY SENT YOU TO ME? I'M SURPRISED THEY STILL KNOW I'M *ALIVE*.
THEY DIDN'T. THEY DON'T. IT WAS MR. STUBBS.
STUBBY? STUBBS SENT YOU HERE?
IT WASN'T MY FAULT, YOU KNOW!
WHAT WASN'T?
HE WAS STANDING IN THE WRONG PLACE!
YOU BETTER GO.
I'M SORRY...I JUST--
I'M FINE. LEAVE US ALONE!
I'LL BE IN THE NEXT ROOM.

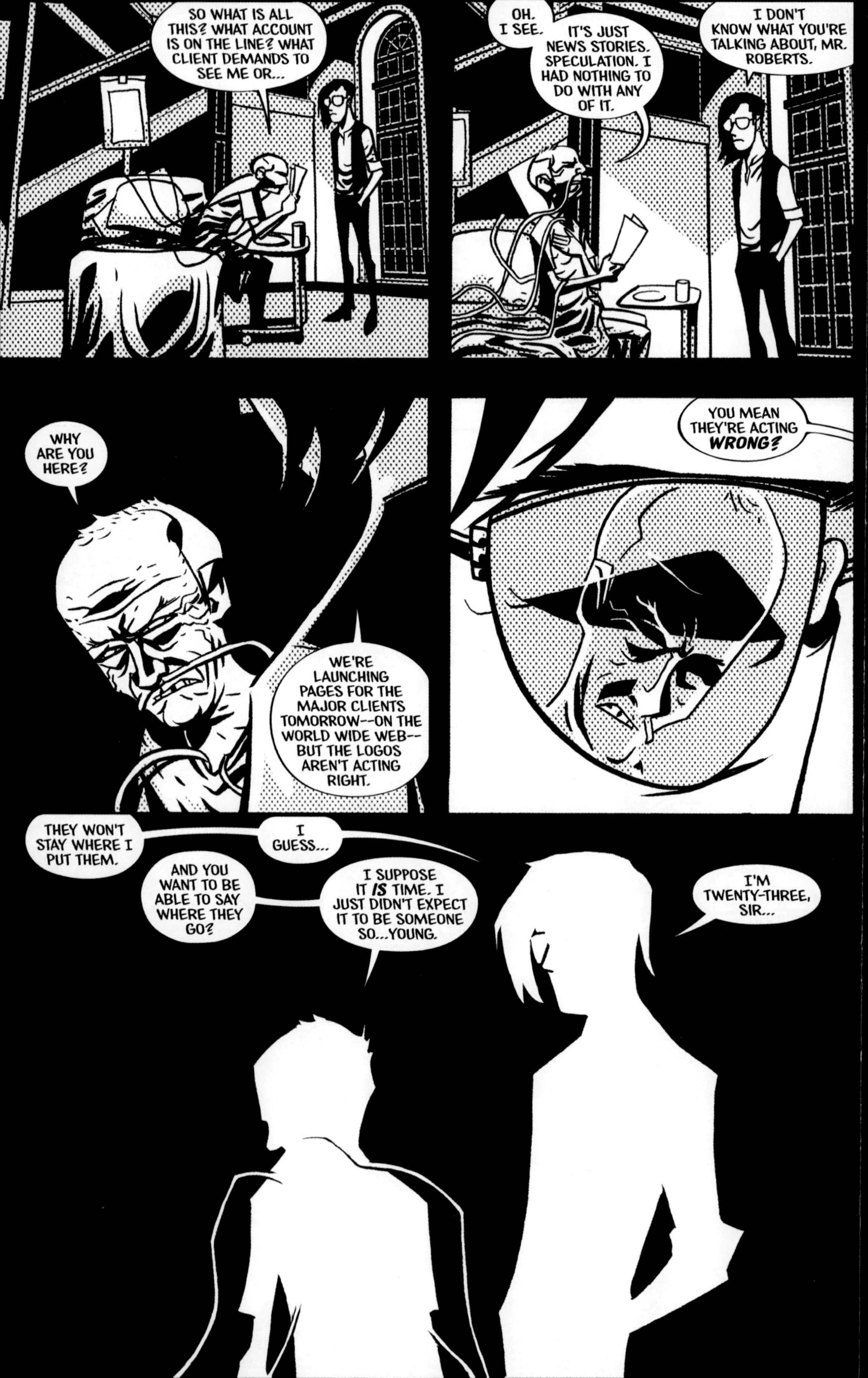

SO WHAT IS ALL THIS? WHAT ACCOUNT IS ON THE LINE? WHAT CLIENT DEMANDS TO SEE ME OR...
OH. I SEE.
IT'S JUST NEWS STORIES. SPECULATION. I HAD NOTHING TO DO WITH ANY OF IT.
I DON'T KNOW WHAT YOU'RE TALKING ABOUT, MR. ROBERTS.
WHY ARE YOU HERE?
WE'RE LAUNCHING PAGES FOR THE MAJOR CLIENTS TOMORROW--ON THE WORLD WIDE WEB--BUT THE LOGOS AREN'T ACTING RIGHT.
YOU MEAN THEY'RE ACTING *WRONG*?
THEY WON'T STAY WHERE I PUT THEM.
I GUESS...
AND YOU WANT TO BE ABLE TO SAY WHERE THEY GO?
I SUPPOSE IT *IS* TIME. I JUST DIDN'T EXPECT IT TO BE SOMEONE SO...YOUNG.
I'M TWENTY-THREE, SIR...

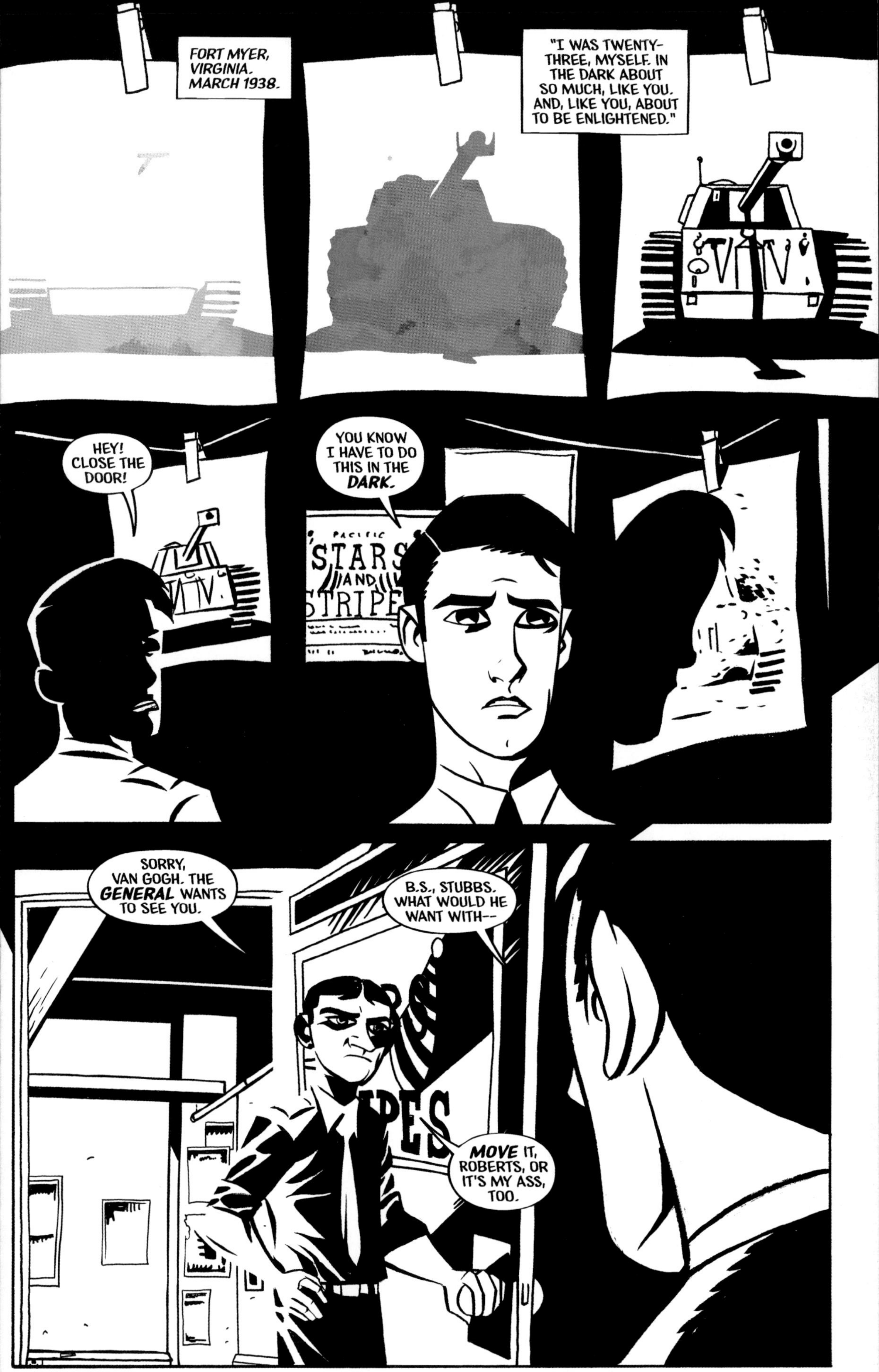
FORT MYER, VIRGINIA. MARCH 1938.
"I WAS TWENTY-THREE, MYSELF. IN THE DARK ABOUT SO MUCH, LIKE YOU. AND, LIKE YOU, ABOUT TO BE ENLIGHTENED."
HEY! CLOSE THE DOOR!
YOU KNOW I HAVE TO DO THIS IN THE DARK.
STARS AND STRIPES
SORRY, VAN GOGH. THE GENERAL WANTS TO SEE YOU.
B.S., STUBBS. WHAT WOULD HE WANT WITH--
MOVE IT, ROBERTS, OR IT'S MY ASS, TOO.

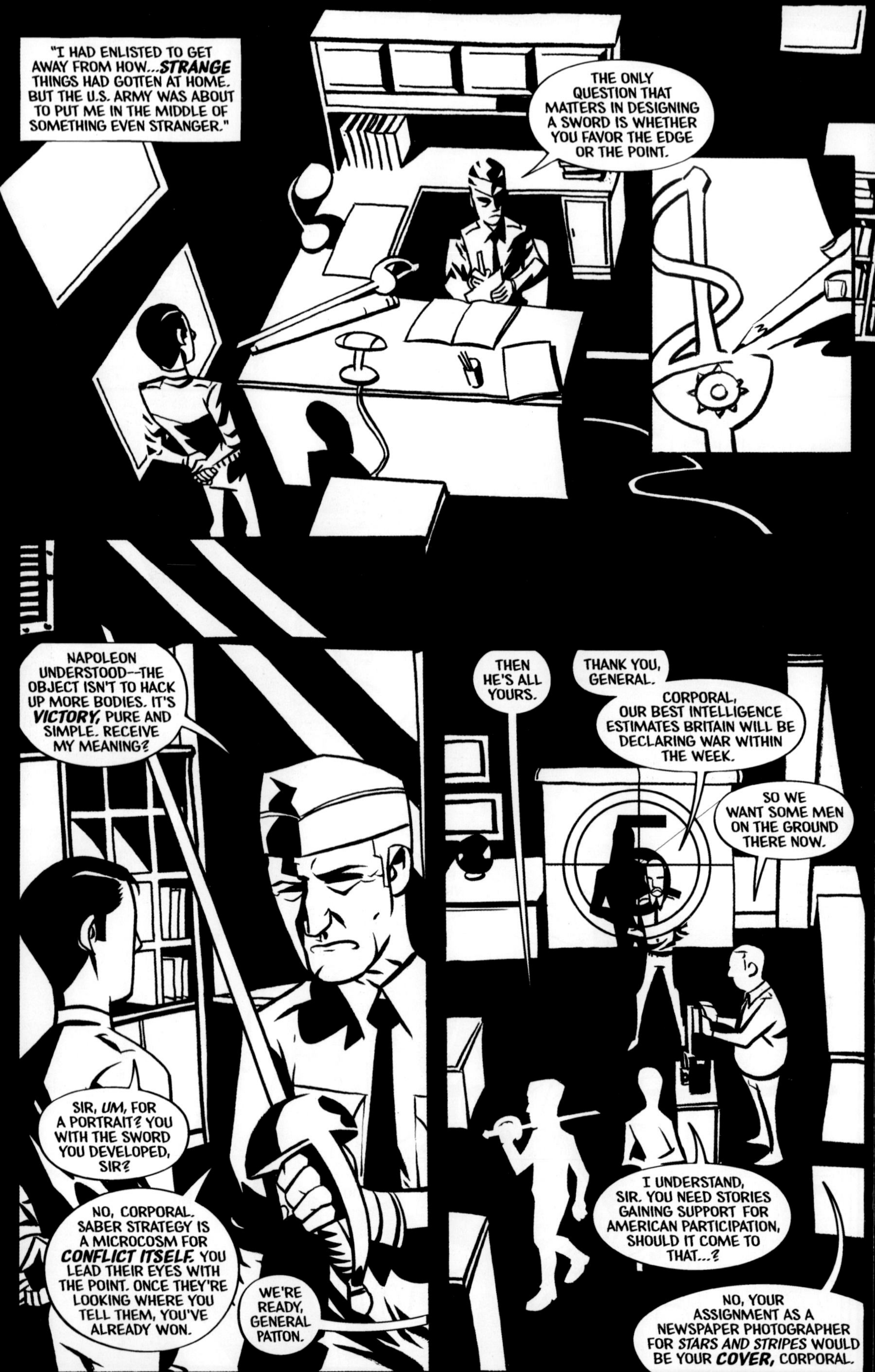
"I HAD ENLISTED TO GET AWAY FROM HOW... STRANGE THINGS HAD GOTTEN AT HOME. BUT THE U.S. ARMY WAS ABOUT TO PUT ME IN THE MIDDLE OF SOMETHING EVEN STRANGER."
THE ONLY QUESTION THAT MATTERS IN DESIGNING A SWORD IS WHETHER YOU FAVOR THE EDGE OR THE POINT.
NAPOLEON UNDERSTOOD--THE OBJECT ISN'T TO HACK UP MORE BODIES. IT'S VICTORY, PURE AND SIMPLE. RECEIVE MY MEANING?
SIR, UM, FOR A PORTRAIT? YOU WITH THE SWORD YOU DEVELOPED, SIR?
NO, CORPORAL. SABER STRATEGY IS A MICROCOSM FOR CONFLICT ITSELF. YOU LEAD THEIR EYES WITH THE POINT. ONCE THEY'RE LOOKING WHERE YOU TELL THEM, YOU'VE ALREADY WON.
WE'RE READY, GENERAL PATTON.
THEN HE'S ALL YOURS.
THANK YOU, GENERAL.
CORPORAL, OUR BEST INTELLIGENCE ESTIMATES BRITAIN WILL BE DECLARING WAR WITHIN THE WEEK.
SO WE WANT SOME MEN ON THE GROUND THERE NOW.
I UNDERSTAND, SIR. YOU NEED STORIES GAINING SUPPORT FOR AMERICAN PARTICIPATION, SHOULD IT COME TO THAT...?
NO, YOUR ASSIGNMENT AS A NEWSPAPER PHOTOGRAPHER FOR STARS AND STRIPES WOULD BE YOUR COVER, CORPORAL.

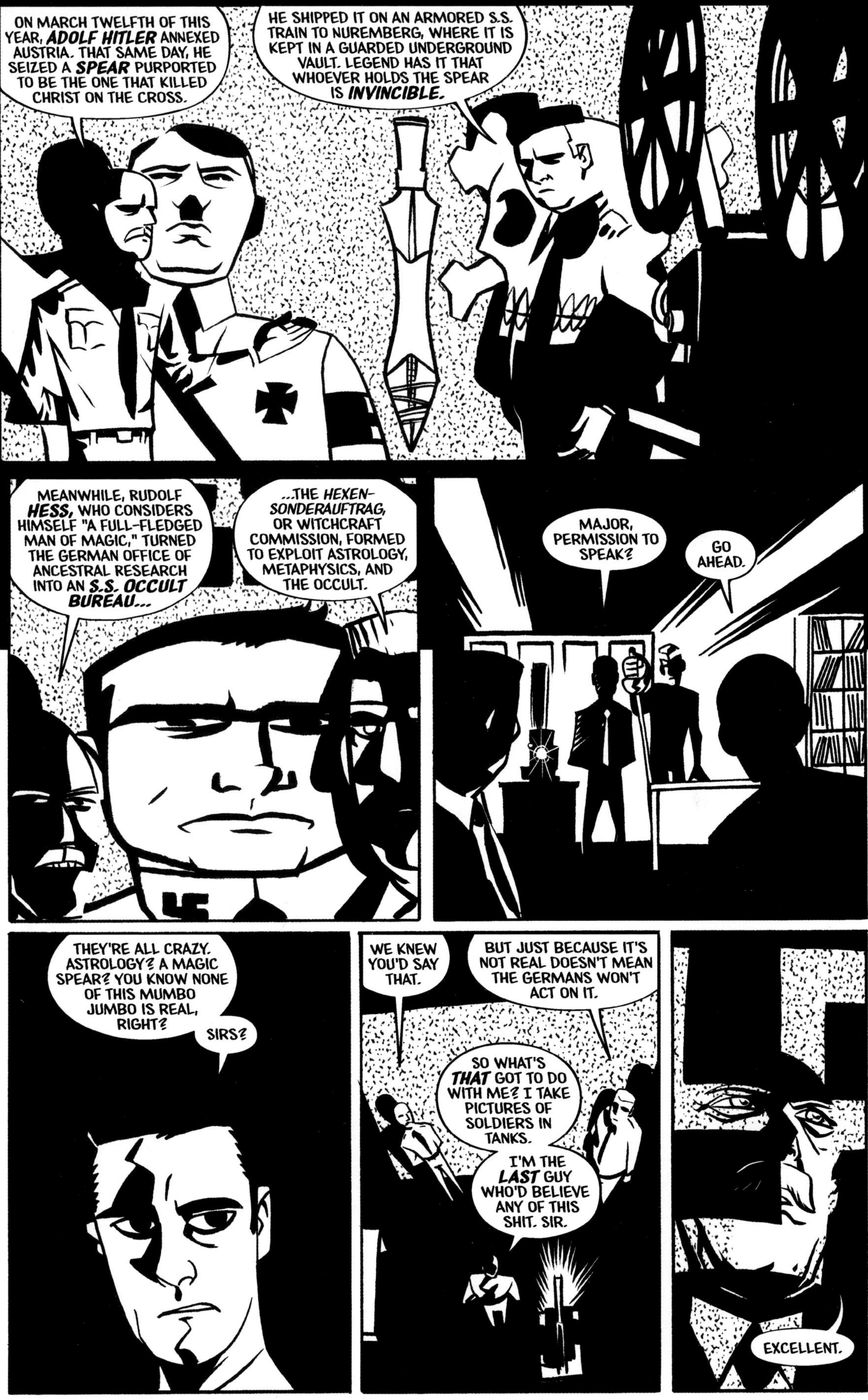
ON MARCH TWELFTH OF THIS YEAR, ADOLF HITLER ANNEXED AUSTRIA. THAT SAME DAY, HE SEIZED A SPEAR PURPORTED TO BE THE ONE THAT KILLED CHRIST ON THE CROSS.
HE SHIPPED IT ON AN ARMORED S.S. TRAIN TO NUREMBERG, WHERE IT IS KEPT IN A GUARDED UNDERGROUND VAULT. LEGEND HAS IT THAT WHOEVER HOLDS THE SPEAR IS INVINCIBLE.
MEANWHILE, RUDOLF HESS, WHO CONSIDERS HIMSELF "A FULL-FLEDGED MAN OF MAGIC," TURNED THE GERMAN OFFICE OF ANCESTRAL RESEARCH INTO AN S.S. OCCULT BUREAU...
...THE HEXEN-SONDERAUFTRAG, OR WITCHCRAFT COMMISSION, FORMED TO EXPLOIT ASTROLOGY, METAPHYSICS, AND THE OCCULT.
MAJOR, PERMISSION TO SPEAK?
GO AHEAD.
THEY'RE ALL CRAZY. ASTROLOGY? A MAGIC SPEAR? YOU KNOW NONE OF THIS MUMBO JUMBO IS REAL, RIGHT?
SIRS?
WE KNEW YOU'D SAY THAT.
BUT JUST BECAUSE IT'S NOT REAL DOESN'T MEAN THE GERMANS WON'T ACT ON IT.
SO WHAT'S THAT GOT TO DO WITH ME? I TAKE PICTURES OF SOLDIERS IN TANKS.
I'M THE LAST GUY WHO'D BELIEVE ANY OF THIS SHIT, SIR.
EXCELLENT.

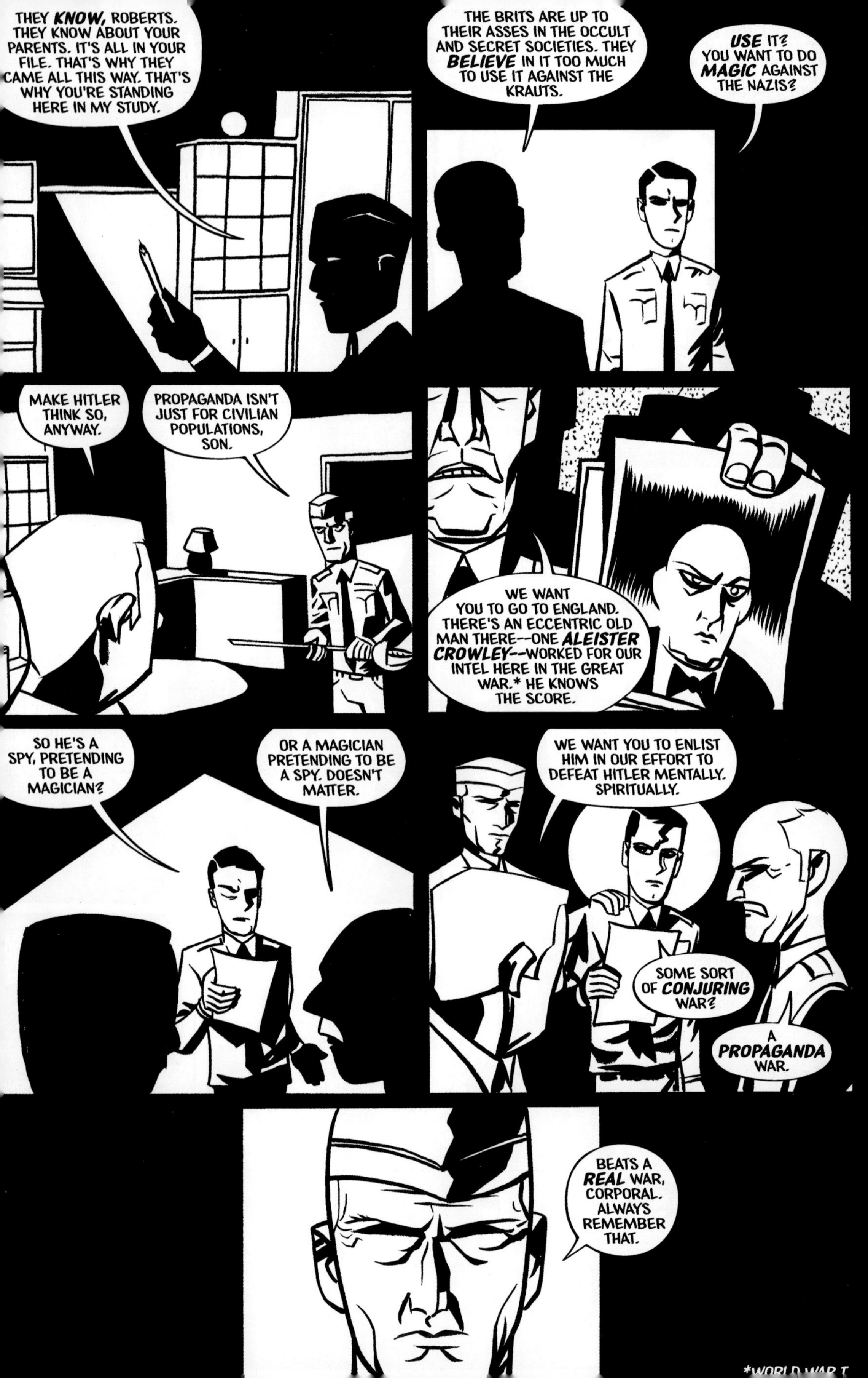
THEY KNOW, ROBERTS. THEY KNOW ABOUT YOUR PARENTS. IT'S ALL IN YOUR FILE. THAT'S WHY THEY CAME ALL THIS WAY. THAT'S WHY YOU'RE STANDING HERE IN MY STUDY.
THE BRITS ARE UP TO THEIR ASSES IN THE OCCULT AND SECRET SOCIETIES. THEY BELIEVE IN IT TOO MUCH TO USE IT AGAINST THE KRAUTS.
USE IT? YOU WANT TO DO MAGIC AGAINST THE NAZIS?
MAKE HITLER THINK SO, ANYWAY.
PROPAGANDA ISN'T JUST FOR CIVILIAN POPULATIONS, SON.
WE WANT YOU TO GO TO ENGLAND. THERE'S AN ECCENTRIC OLD MAN THERE--ONE ALEISTER CROWLEY--WORKED FOR OUR INTEL HERE IN THE GREAT WAR.* HE KNOWS THE SCORE.
SO HE'S A SPY, PRETENDING TO BE A MAGICIAN?
OR A MAGICIAN PRETENDING TO BE A SPY. DOESN'T MATTER.
WE WANT YOU TO ENLIST HIM IN OUR EFFORT TO DEFEAT HITLER MENTALLY. SPIRITUALLY.
SOME SORT OF CONJURING WAR?
A PROPAGANDA WAR.
BEATS A REAL WAR, CORPORAL. ALWAYS REMEMBER THAT.
*WORLD WAR I

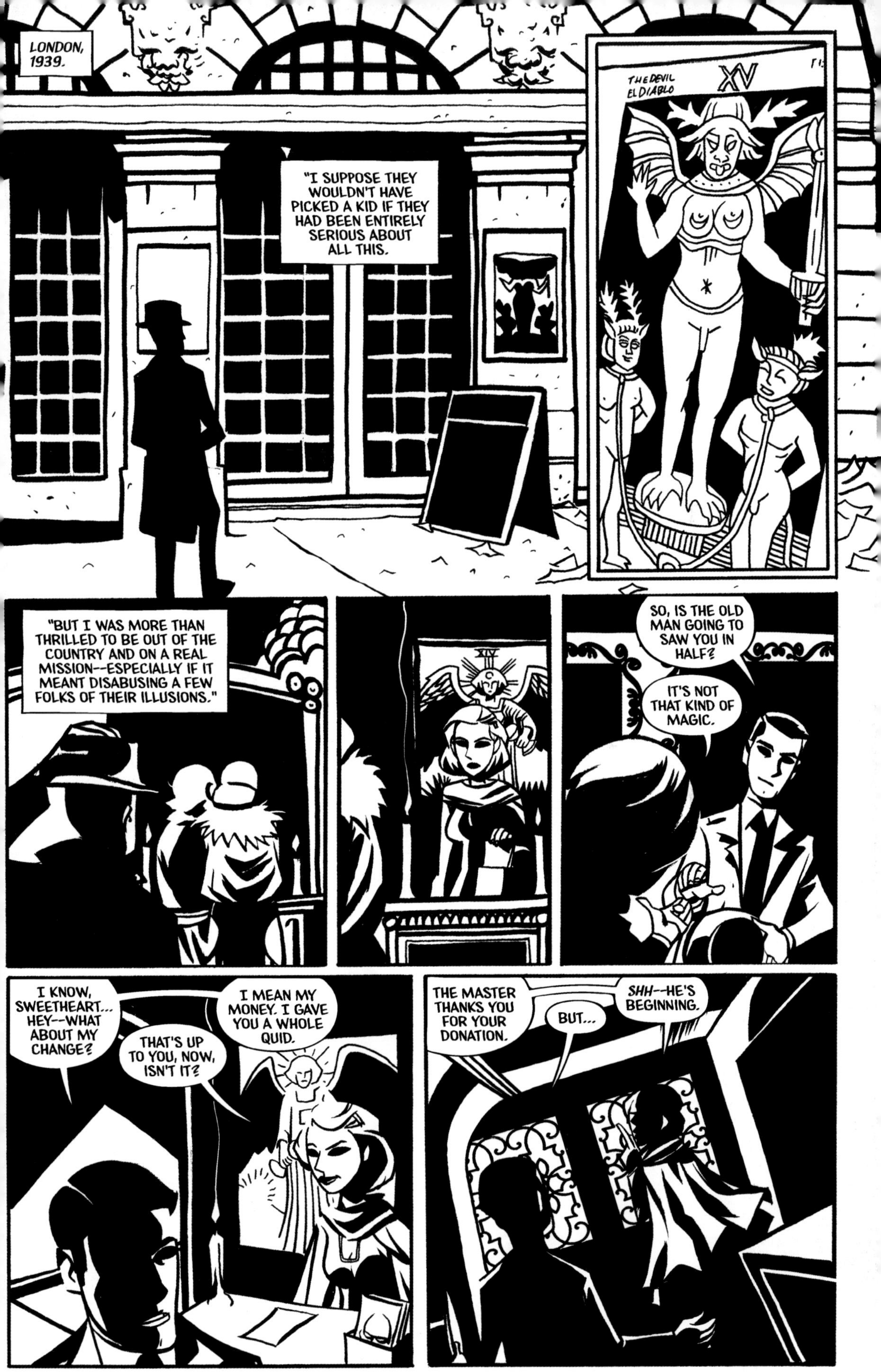
LONDON, 1939.
THE DEVIL
EL DIABLO
XV
"I SUPPOSE THEY WOULDN'T HAVE PICKED A KID IF THEY HAD BEEN ENTIRELY SERIOUS ABOUT ALL THIS.
"BUT I WAS MORE THAN THRILLED TO BE OUT OF THE COUNTRY AND ON A REAL MISSION--ESPECIALLY IF IT MEANT DISABUSING A FEW FOLKS OF THEIR ILLUSIONS."
XIV
SO, IS THE OLD MAN GOING TO SAW YOU IN HALF?
IT'S NOT THAT KIND OF MAGIC.
I KNOW, SWEETHEART... HEY--WHAT ABOUT MY CHANGE?
THAT'S UP TO YOU, NOW, ISN'T IT?
I MEAN MY MONEY. I GAVE YOU A WHOLE QUID.
THE MASTER THANKS YOU FOR YOUR DONATION.
BUT...
SHH--HE'S BEGINNING.

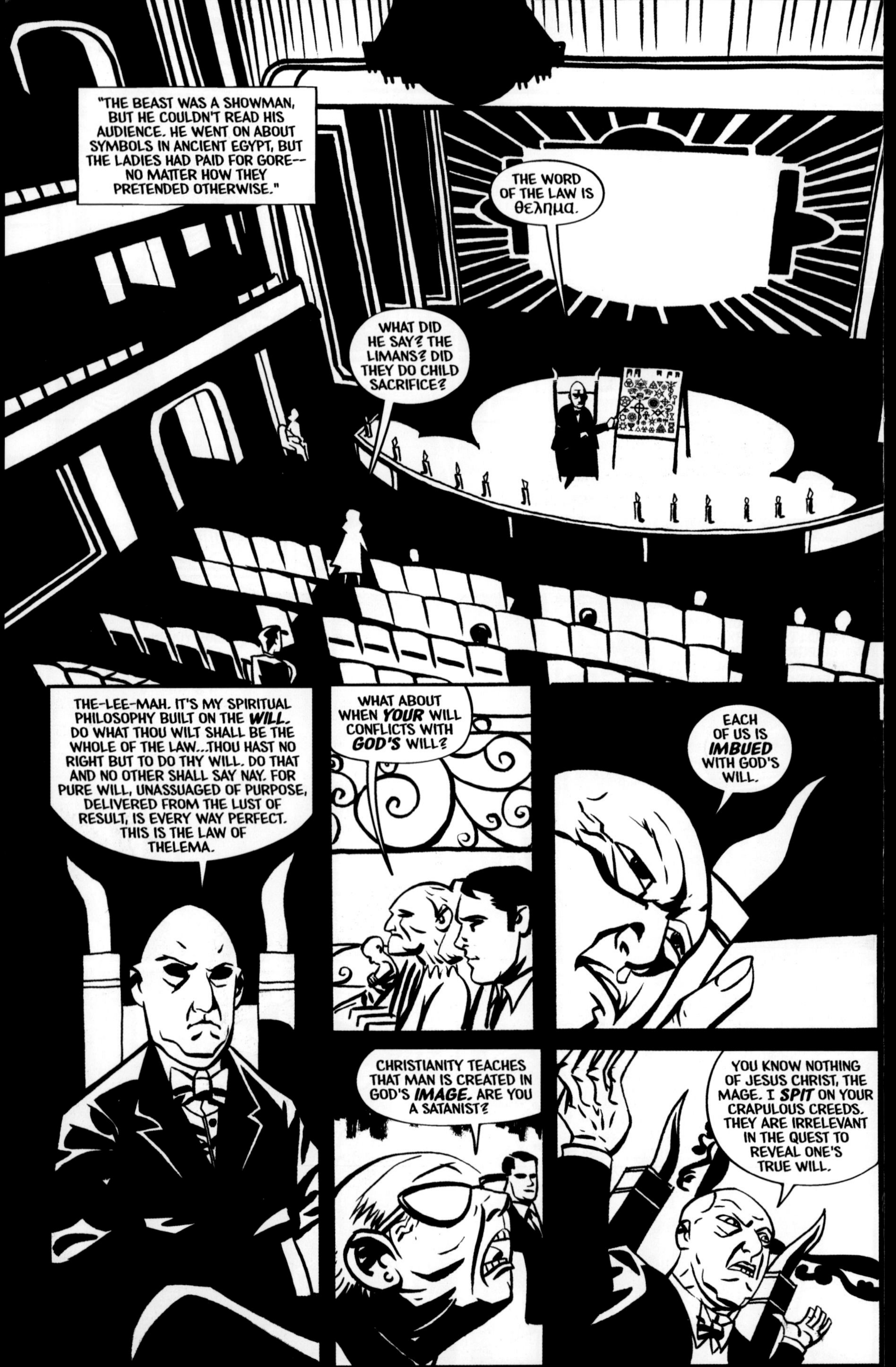
"THE BEAST WAS A SHOWMAN, BUT HE COULDN'T READ HIS AUDIENCE. HE WENT ON ABOUT SYMBOLS IN ANCIENT EGYPT, BUT THE LADIES HAD PAID FOR GORE-- NO MATTER HOW THEY PRETENDED OTHERWISE."
THE WORD OF THE LAW IS θελημα.
WHAT DID HE SAY? THE LIMANS? DID THEY DO CHILD SACRIFICE?
THE-LEE-MAH. IT'S MY SPIRITUAL PHILOSOPHY BUILT ON THE WILL. DO WHAT THOU WILT SHALL BE THE WHOLE OF THE LAW...THOU HAST NO RIGHT BUT TO DO THY WILL. DO THAT AND NO OTHER SHALL SAY NAY. FOR PURE WILL, UNASSUAGED OF PURPOSE, DELIVERED FROM THE LUST OF RESULT, IS EVERY WAY PERFECT. THIS IS THE LAW OF THELEMA.
WHAT ABOUT WHEN YOUR WILL CONFLICTS WITH GOD'S WILL?
EACH OF US IS IMBUED WITH GOD'S WILL.
CHRISTIANITY TEACHES THAT MAN IS CREATED IN GOD'S IMAGE. ARE YOU A SATANIST?
YOU KNOW NOTHING OF JESUS CHRIST, THE MAGE. I SPIT ON YOUR CRAPULOUS CREEDS. THEY ARE IRRELEVANT IN THE QUEST TO REVEAL ONE'S TRUE WILL.

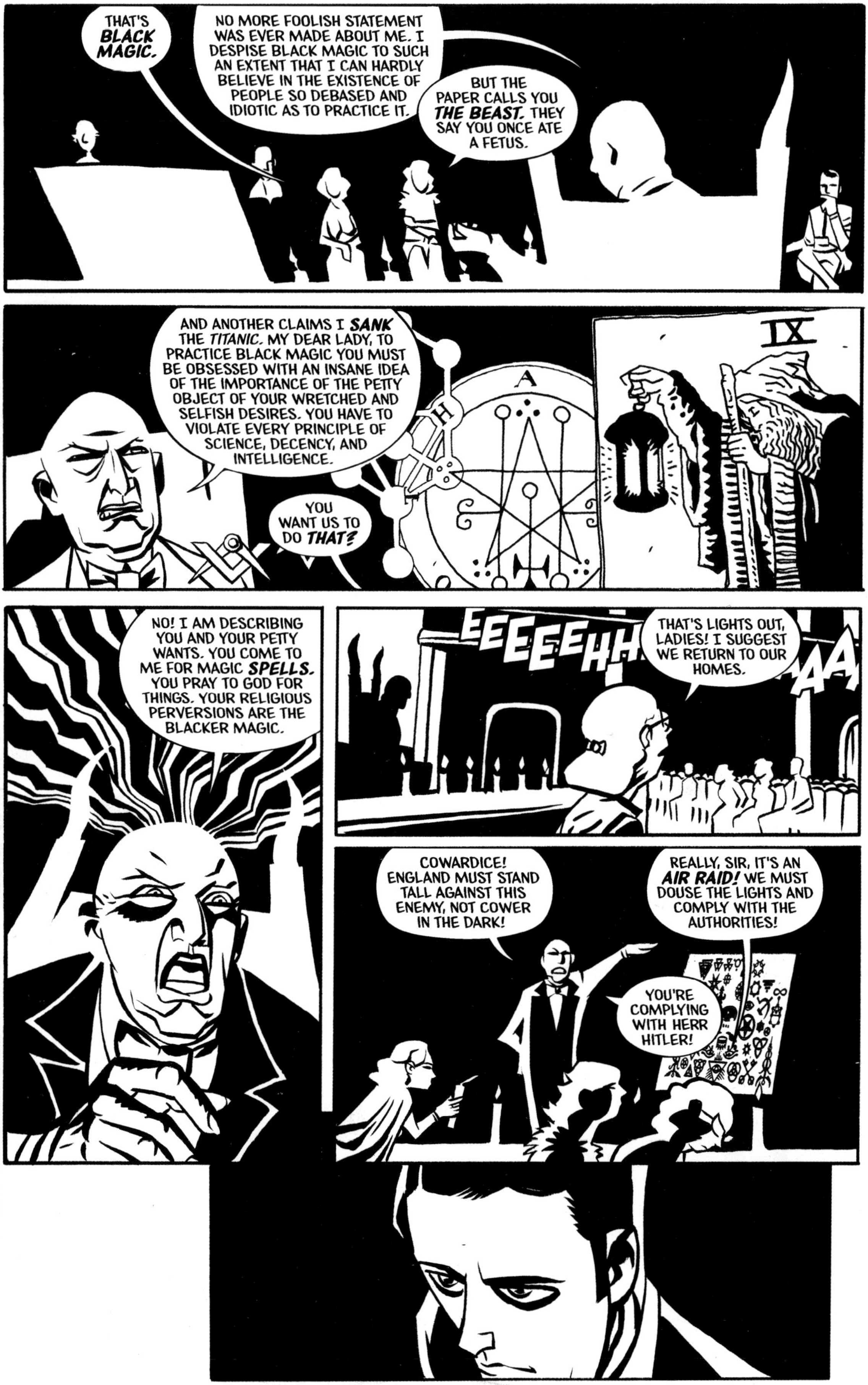
THAT'S BLACK MAGIC.
NO MORE FOOLISH STATEMENT WAS EVER MADE ABOUT ME. I DESPISE BLACK MAGIC TO SUCH AN EXTENT THAT I CAN HARDLY BELIEVE IN THE EXISTENCE OF PEOPLE SO DEBASED AND IDIOTIC AS TO PRACTICE IT.
BUT THE PAPER CALLS YOU THE BEAST. THEY SAY YOU ONCE ATE A FETUS.
AND ANOTHER CLAIMS I SANK THE TITANIC. MY DEAR LADY, TO PRACTICE BLACK MAGIC YOU MUST BE OBSESSED WITH AN INSANE IDEA OF THE IMPORTANCE OF THE PETTY OBJECT OF YOUR WRETCHED AND SELFISH DESIRES. YOU HAVE TO VIOLATE EVERY PRINCIPLE OF SCIENCE, DECENCY, AND INTELLIGENCE.
YOU WANT US TO DO THAT?
A
H
IX
NO! I AM DESCRIBING YOU AND YOUR PETTY WANTS. YOU COME TO ME FOR MAGIC SPELLS. YOU PRAY TO GOD FOR THINGS. YOUR RELIGIOUS PERVERSIONS ARE THE BLACKER MAGIC.
EEEEEEHH
THAT'S LIGHTS OUT, LADIES! I SUGGEST WE RETURN TO OUR HOMES.
AA
COWARDICE! ENGLAND MUST STAND TALL AGAINST THIS ENEMY, NOT COWER IN THE DARK!
REALLY, SIR, IT'S AN AIR RAID! WE MUST DOUSE THE LIGHTS AND COMPLY WITH THE AUTHORITIES!
YOU'RE COMPLYING WITH HERR HITLER!

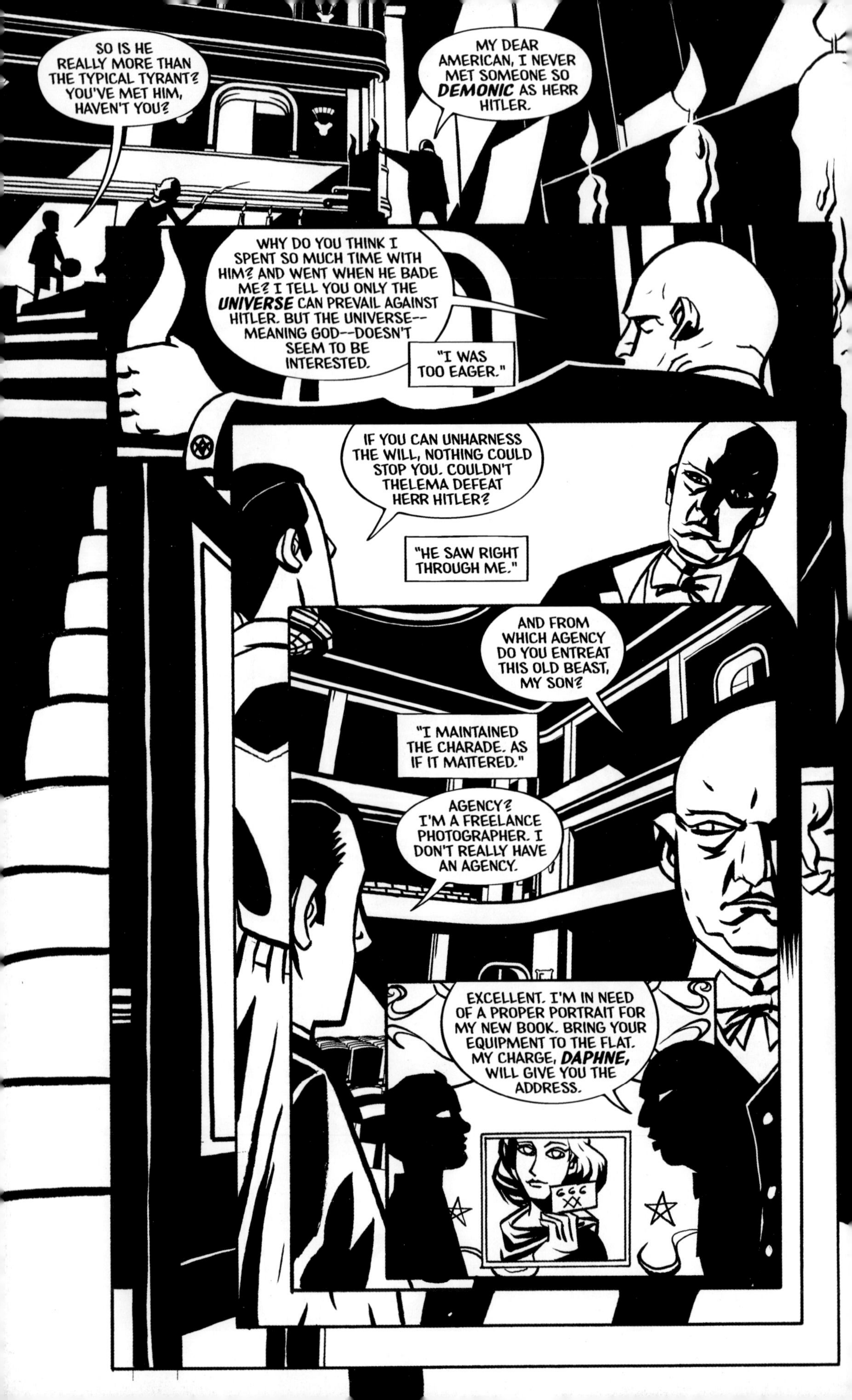
SO IS HE REALLY MORE THAN THE TYPICAL TYRANT? YOU'VE MET HIM, HAVEN'T YOU?
MY DEAR AMERICAN, I NEVER MET SOMEONE SO DEMONIC AS HERR HITLER.
WHY DO YOU THINK I SPENT SO MUCH TIME WITH HIM? AND WENT WHEN HE BADE ME? I TELL YOU ONLY THE UNIVERSE CAN PREVAIL AGAINST HITLER. BUT THE UNIVERSE--MEANING GOD--DOESN'T SEEM TO BE INTERESTED.
"I WAS TOO EAGER."
IF YOU CAN UNHARNESS THE WILL, NOTHING COULD STOP YOU. COULDN'T THELEMA DEFEAT HERR HITLER?
"HE SAW RIGHT THROUGH ME."
AND FROM WHICH AGENCY DO YOU ENTREAT THIS OLD BEAST, MY SON?
"I MAINTAINED THE CHARADE. AS IF IT MATTERED."
AGENCY? I'M A FREELANCE PHOTOGRAPHER. I DON'T REALLY HAVE AN AGENCY.
EXCELLENT. I'M IN NEED OF A PROPER PORTRAIT FOR MY NEW BOOK. BRING YOUR EQUIPMENT TO THE FLAT. MY CHARGE, DAPHNE, WILL GIVE YOU THE ADDRESS.
666

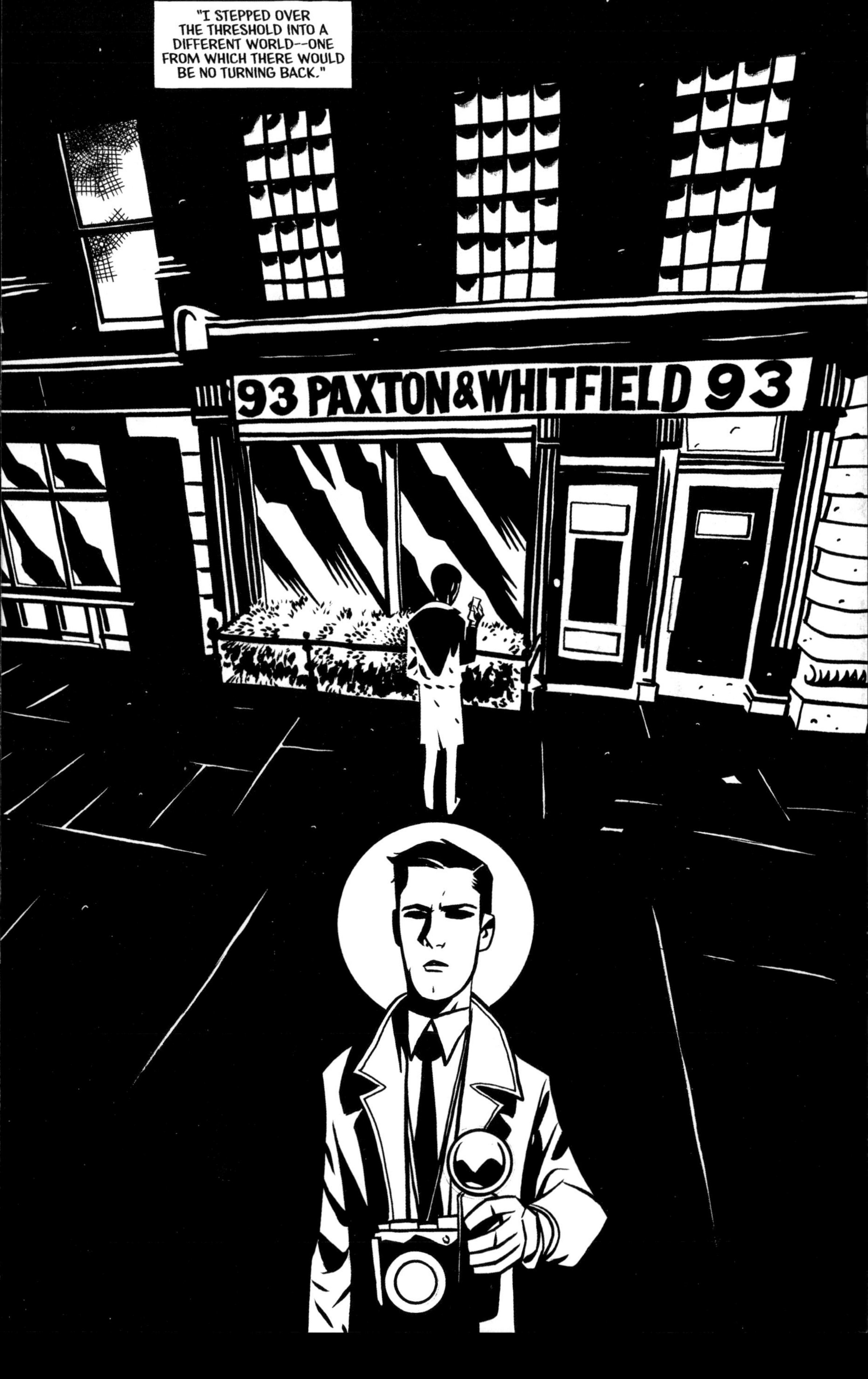
"I STEPPED OVER THE THRESHOLD INTO A DIFFERENT WORLD--ONE FROM WHICH THERE WOULD BE NO TURNING BACK."
93 PAXTON&WHITFIELD 93

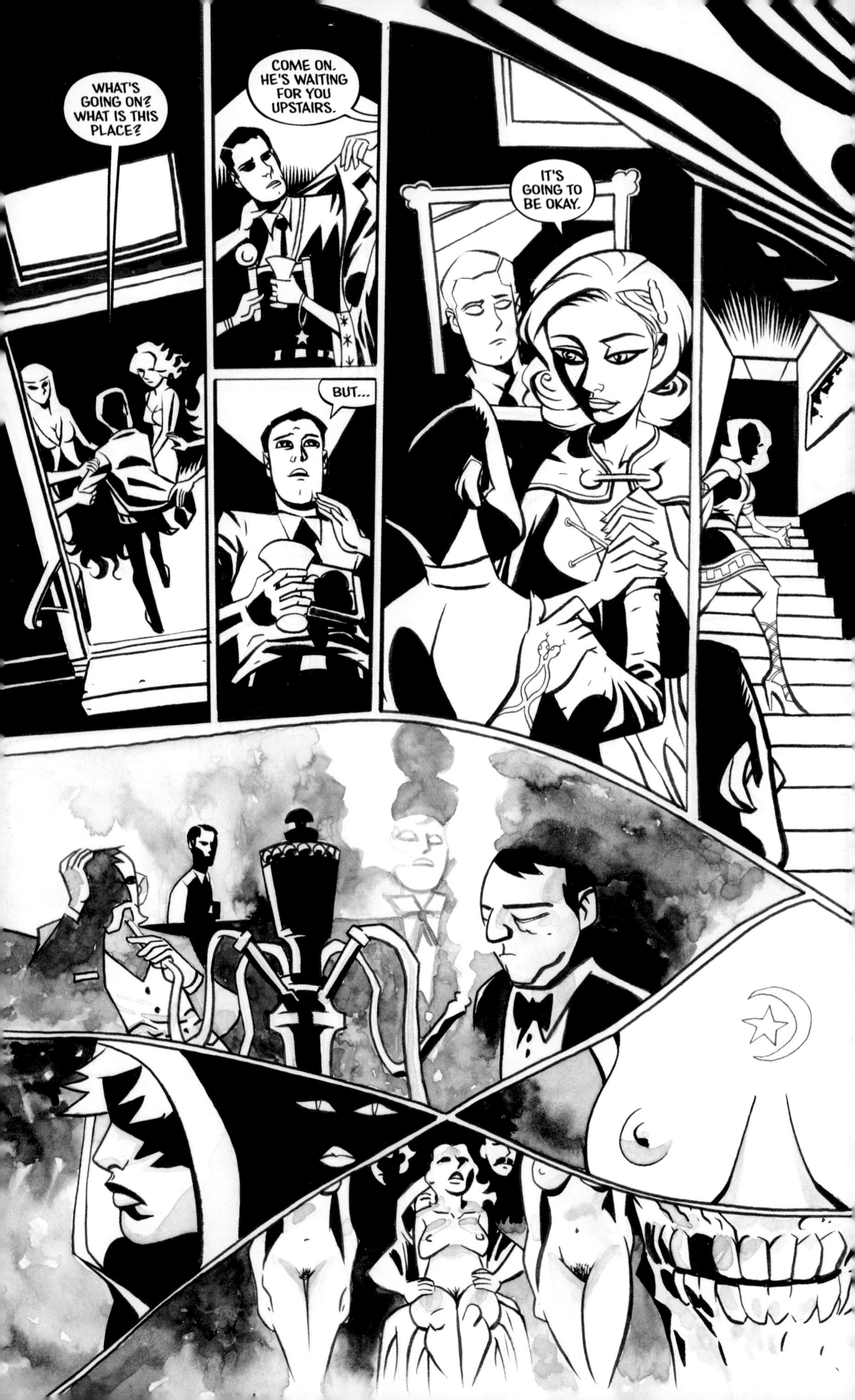
WHAT'S GOING ON? WHAT IS THIS PLACE?
COME ON. HE'S WAITING FOR YOU UPSTAIRS.
BUT...
IT'S GOING TO BE OKAY.

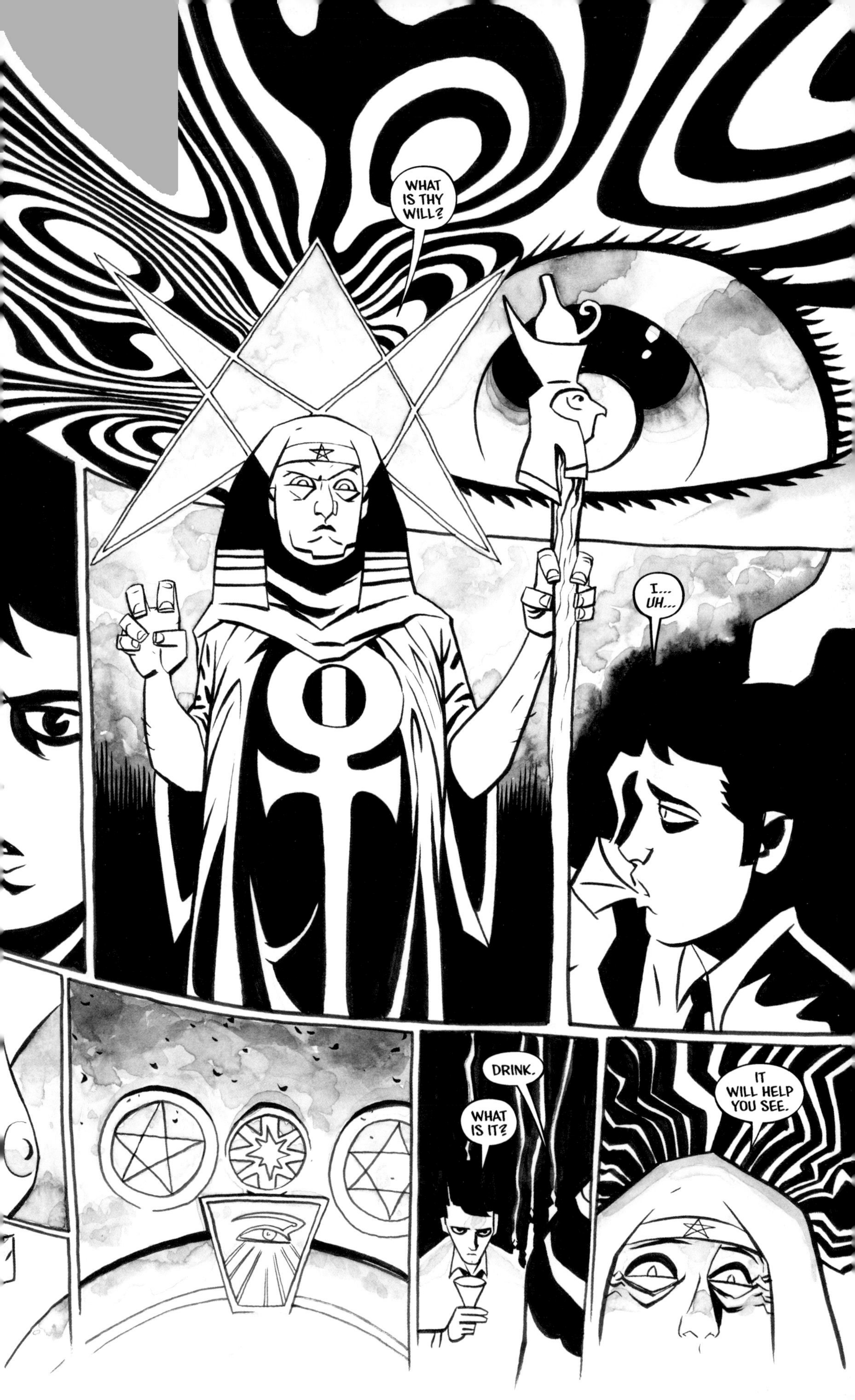
WHAT IS THY WILL?
I... UH...
DRINK.
WHAT IS IT?
IT WILL HELP YOU SEE.

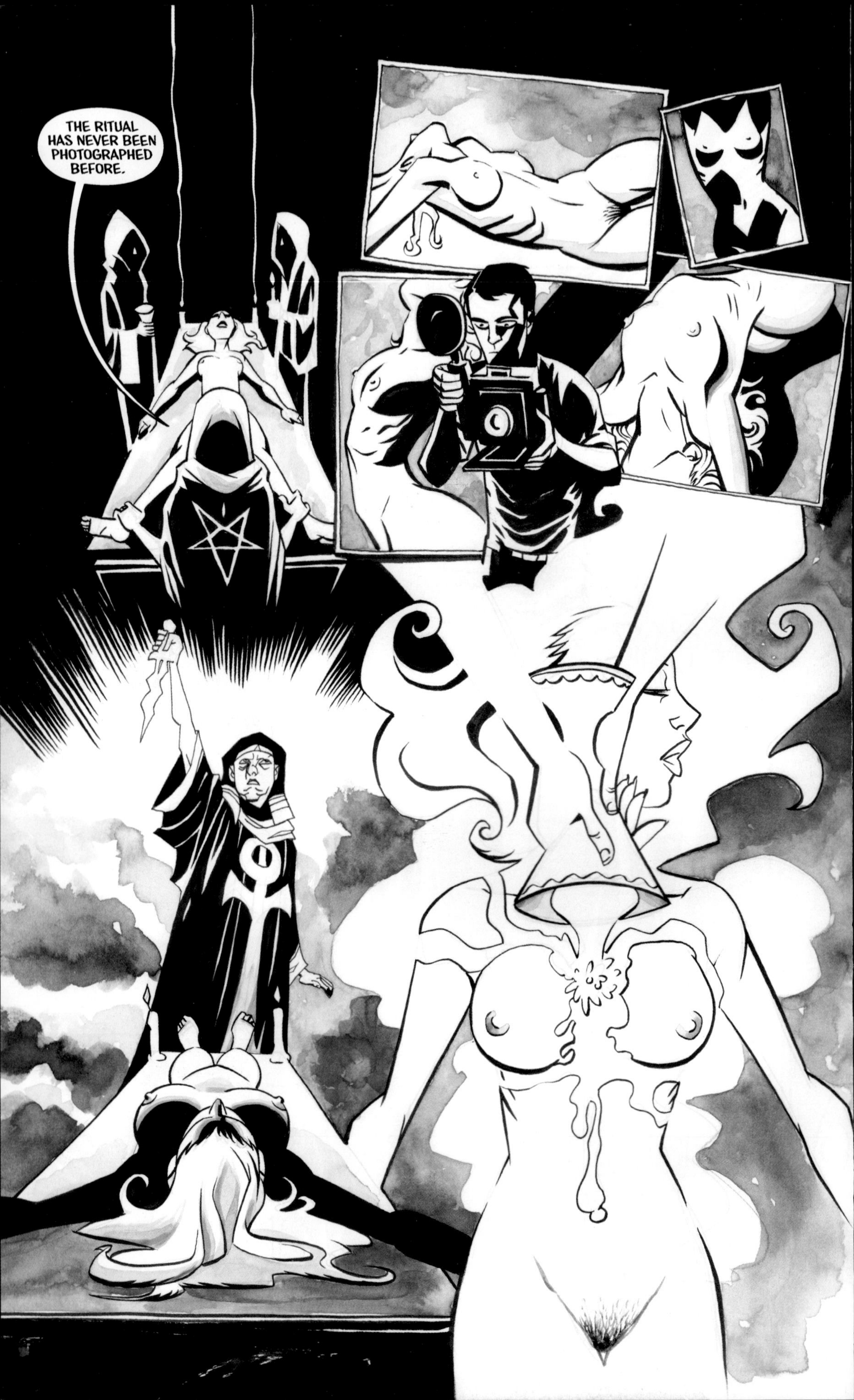
THE RITUAL HAS NEVER BEEN PHOTOGRAPHED BEFORE.

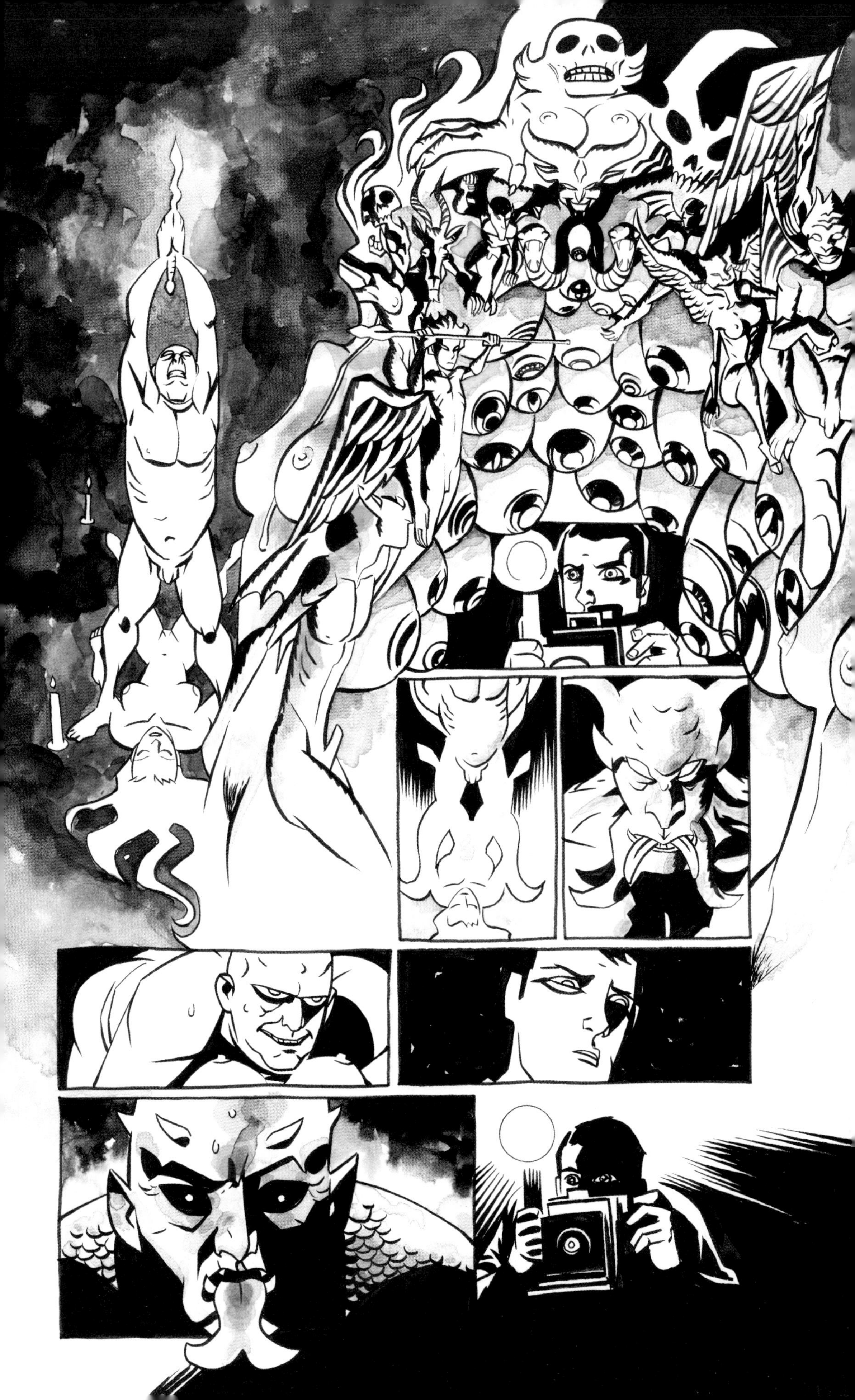

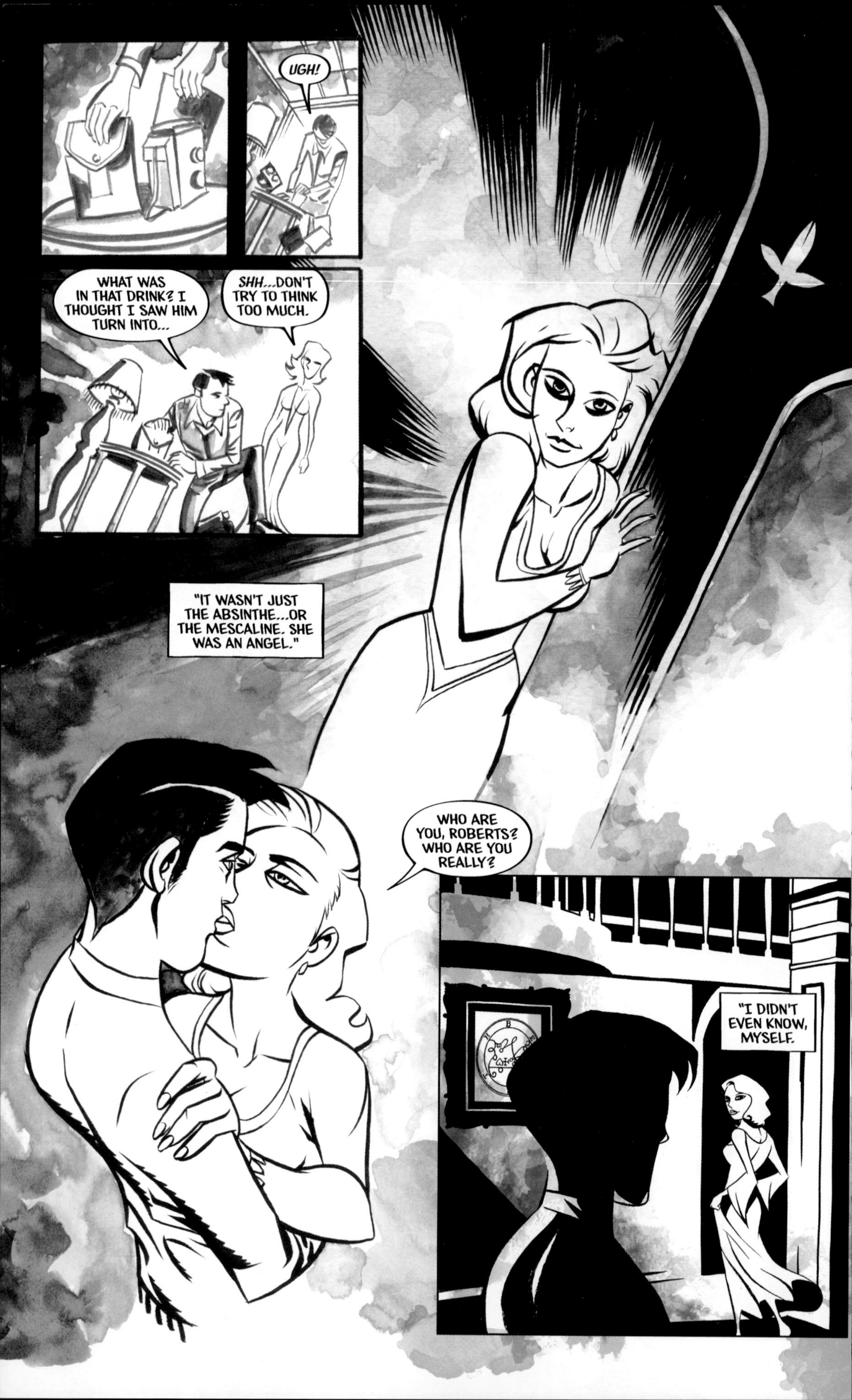
UGH!
WHAT WAS IN THAT DRINK? I THOUGHT I SAW HIM TURN INTO...
SHH...DON'T TRY TO THINK TOO MUCH.
"IT WASN'T JUST THE ABSINTHE...OR THE MESCALINE. SHE WAS AN ANGEL."
WHO ARE YOU, ROBERTS? WHO ARE YOU REALLY?
"I DIDN'T EVEN KNOW, MYSELF.

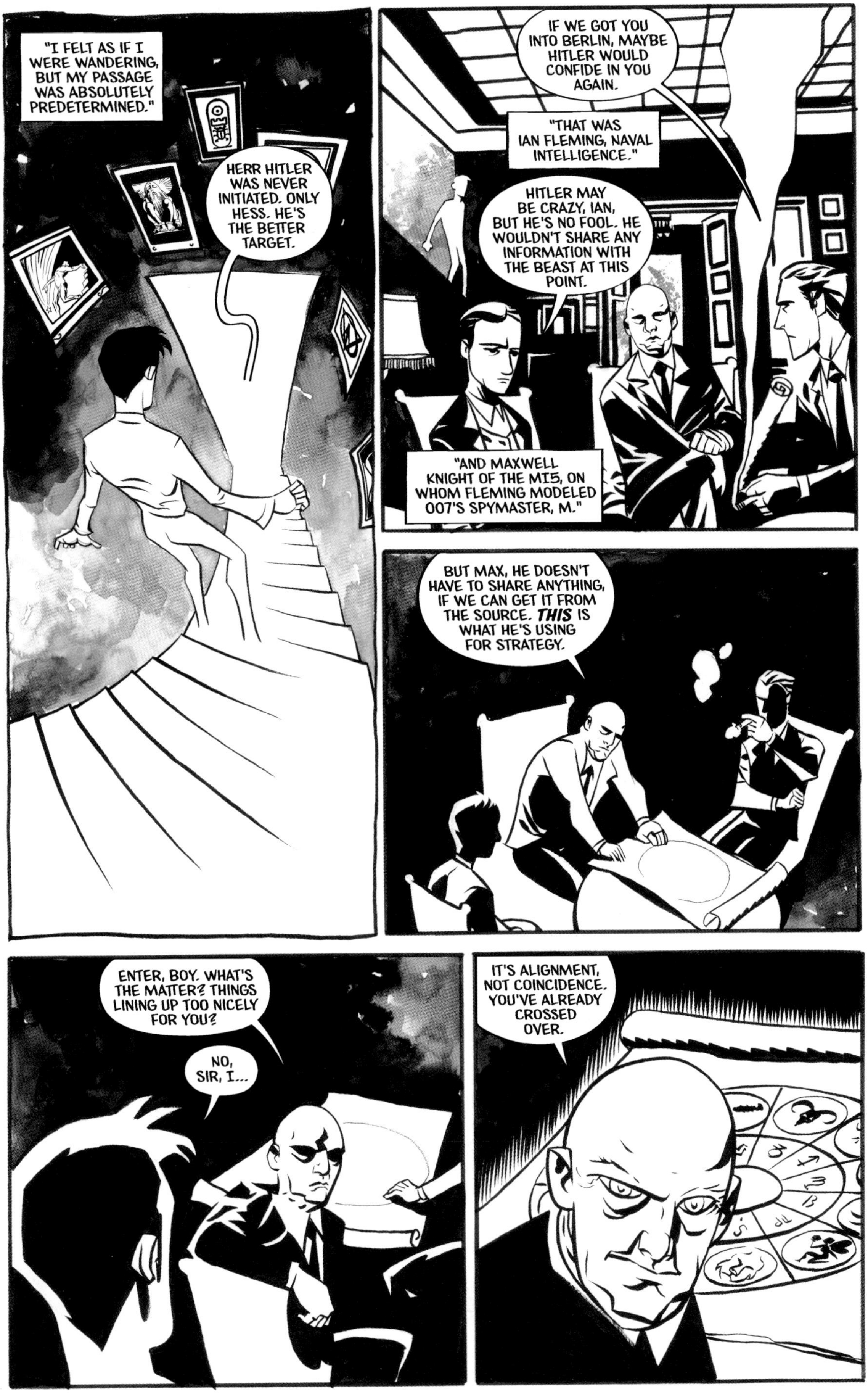

"I FELT AS IF I WERE WANDERING, BUT MY PASSAGE WAS ABSOLUTELY PREDETERMINED."
HERR HITLER WAS NEVER INITIATED. ONLY HESS. HE'S THE BETTER TARGET.
IF WE GOT YOU INTO BERLIN, MAYBE HITLER WOULD CONFIDE IN YOU AGAIN.
"THAT WAS IAN FLEMING, NAVAL INTELLIGENCE."
HITLER MAY BE CRAZY, IAN, BUT HE'S NO FOOL. HE WOULDN'T SHARE ANY INFORMATION WITH THE BEAST AT THIS POINT.
"AND MAXWELL KNIGHT OF THE MI5, ON WHOM FLEMING MODELED 007'S SPYMASTER, M."
BUT MAX, HE DOESN'T HAVE TO SHARE ANYTHING, IF WE CAN GET IT FROM THE SOURCE. *THIS* IS WHAT HE'S USING FOR STRATEGY.
ENTER, BOY. WHAT'S THE MATTER? THINGS LINING UP TOO NICELY FOR YOU?
NO, SIR, I...
IT'S ALIGNMENT, NOT COINCIDENCE. YOU'VE ALREADY CROSSED OVER.

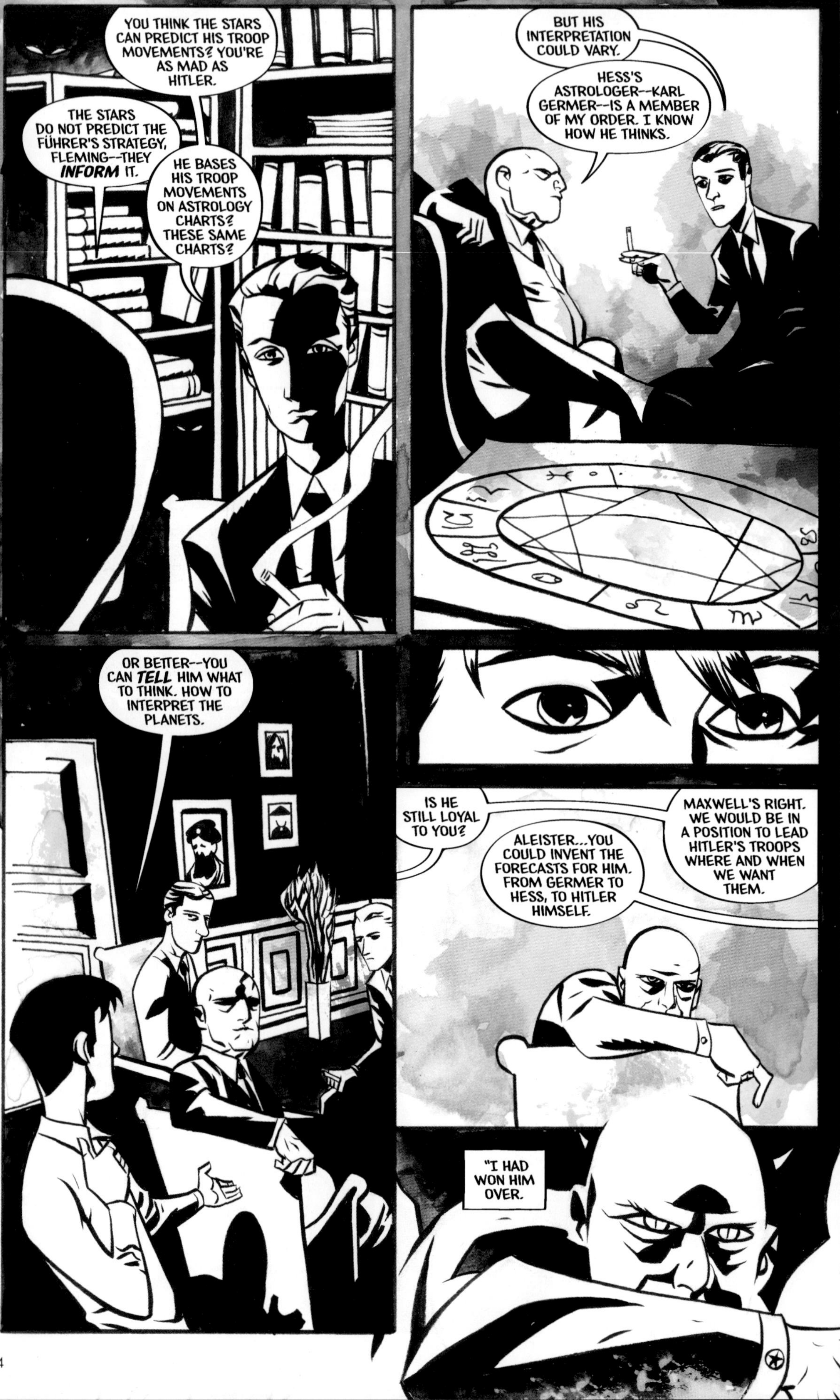
THE STARS DO NOT PREDICT THE FÜHRER'S STRATEGY, FLEMING--THEY INFORM IT.
YOU THINK THE STARS CAN PREDICT HIS TROOP MOVEMENTS? YOU'RE AS MAD AS HITLER.
HE BASES HIS TROOP MOVEMENTS ON ASTROLOGY CHARTS? THESE SAME CHARTS?
BUT HIS INTERPRETATION COULD VARY.
HESS'S ASTROLOGER--KARL GERMER--IS A MEMBER OF MY ORDER. I KNOW HOW HE THINKS.
OR BETTER--YOU CAN TELL HIM WHAT TO THINK. HOW TO INTERPRET THE PLANETS.
IS HE STILL LOYAL TO YOU?
ALEISTER...YOU COULD INVENT THE FORECASTS FOR HIM. FROM GERMER TO HESS, TO HITLER HIMSELF.
MAXWELL'S RIGHT. WE WOULD BE IN A POSITION TO LEAD HITLER'S TROOPS WHERE AND WHEN WE WANT THEM.
"I HAD WON HIM OVER.

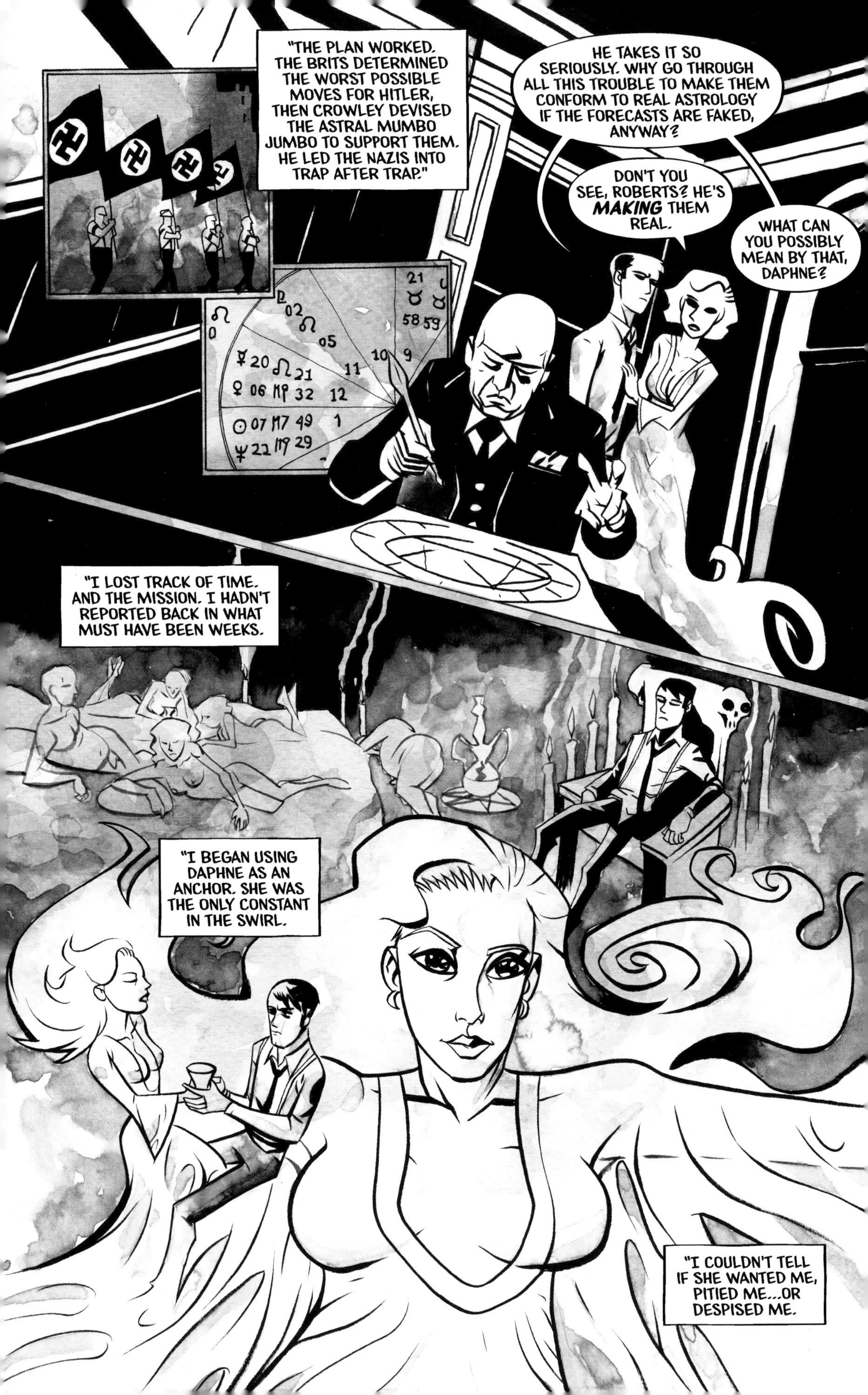
"THE PLAN WORKED. THE BRITS DETERMINED THE WORST POSSIBLE MOVES FOR HITLER, THEN CROWLEY DEVISED THE ASTRAL MUMBO JUMBO TO SUPPORT THEM. HE LED THE NAZIS INTO TRAP AFTER TRAP."
HE TAKES IT SO SERIOUSLY. WHY GO THROUGH ALL THIS TROUBLE TO MAKE THEM CONFORM TO REAL ASTROLOGY IF THE FORECASTS ARE FAKED, ANYWAY?
DON'T YOU SEE, ROBERTS? HE'S *MAKING* THEM REAL.
WHAT CAN YOU POSSIBLY MEAN BY THAT, DAPHNE?
"I LOST TRACK OF TIME. AND THE MISSION. I HADN'T REPORTED BACK IN WHAT MUST HAVE BEEN WEEKS.
"I BEGAN USING DAPHNE AS AN ANCHOR. SHE WAS THE ONLY CONSTANT IN THE SWIRL.
"I COULDN'T TELL IF SHE WANTED ME, PITIED ME...OR DESPISED ME.

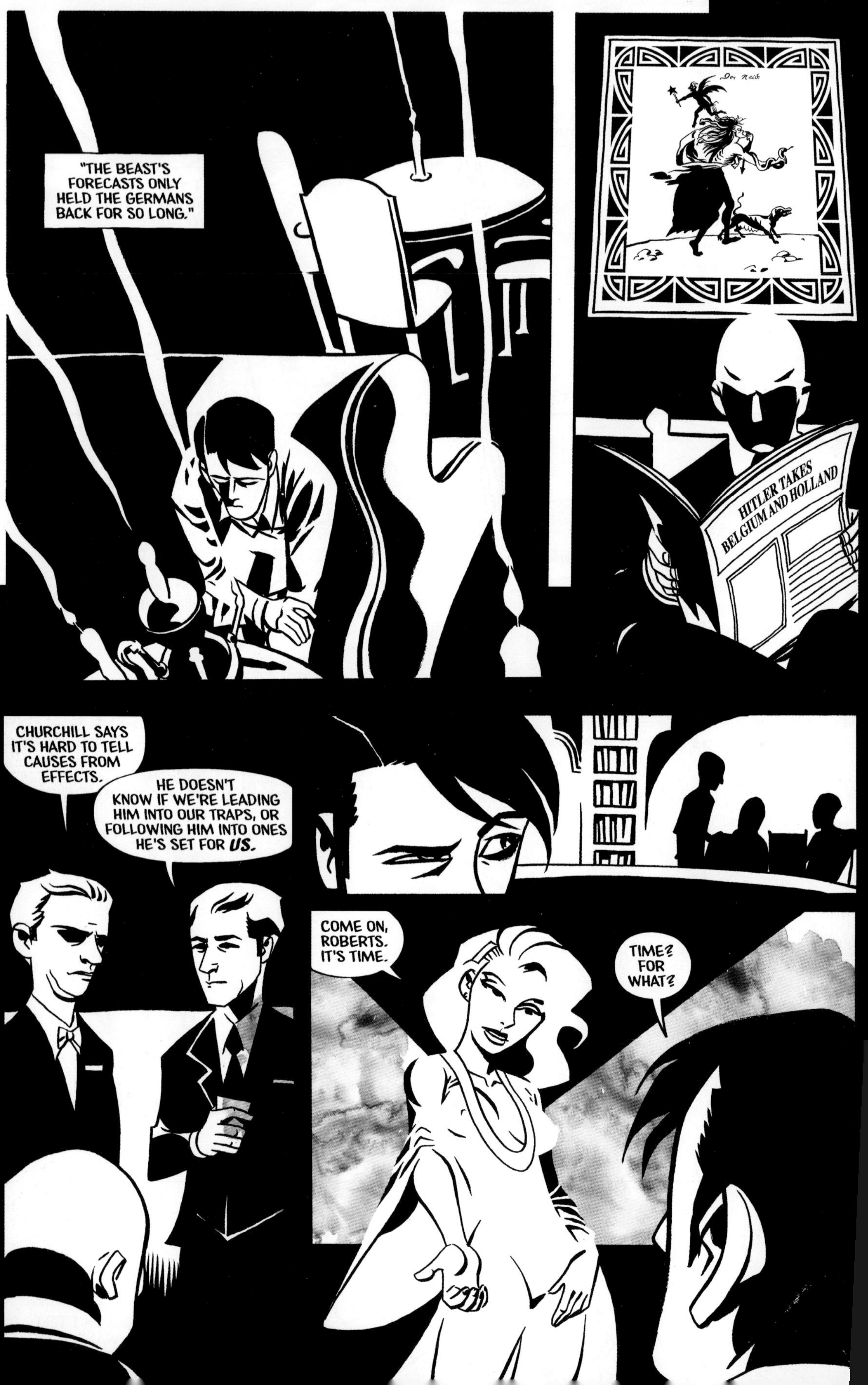
"THE BEAST'S FORECASTS ONLY HELD THE GERMANS BACK FOR SO LONG."
HITLER TAKES BELGIUM AND HOLLAND
CHURCHILL SAYS IT'S HARD TO TELL CAUSES FROM EFFECTS.
HE DOESN'T KNOW IF WE'RE LEADING HIM INTO OUR TRAPS, OR FOLLOWING HIM INTO ONES HE'S SET FOR *US*.
COME ON, ROBERTS. IT'S TIME.
TIME? FOR WHAT?

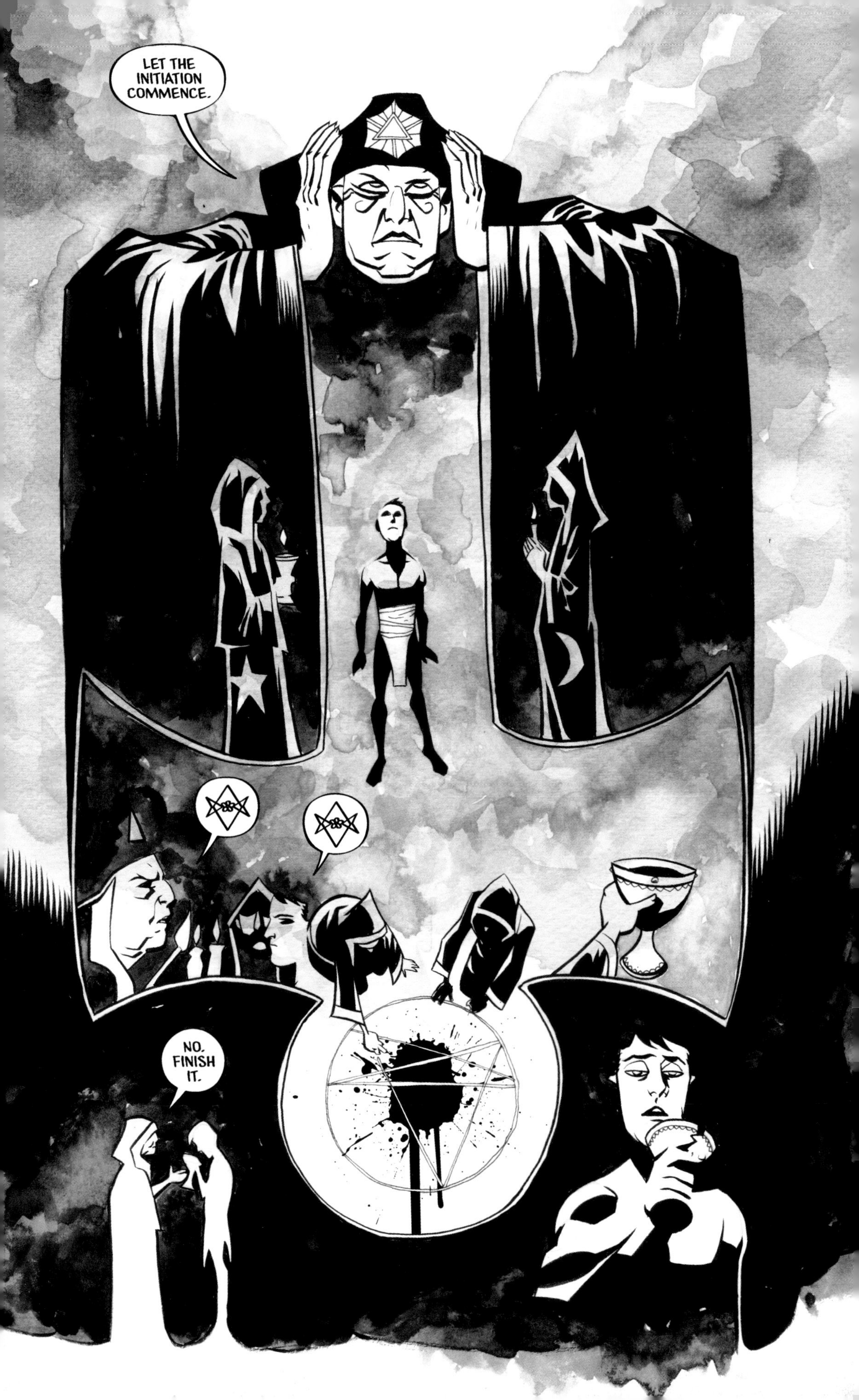
LET THE INITIATION COMMENCE.
NO, FINISH IT.

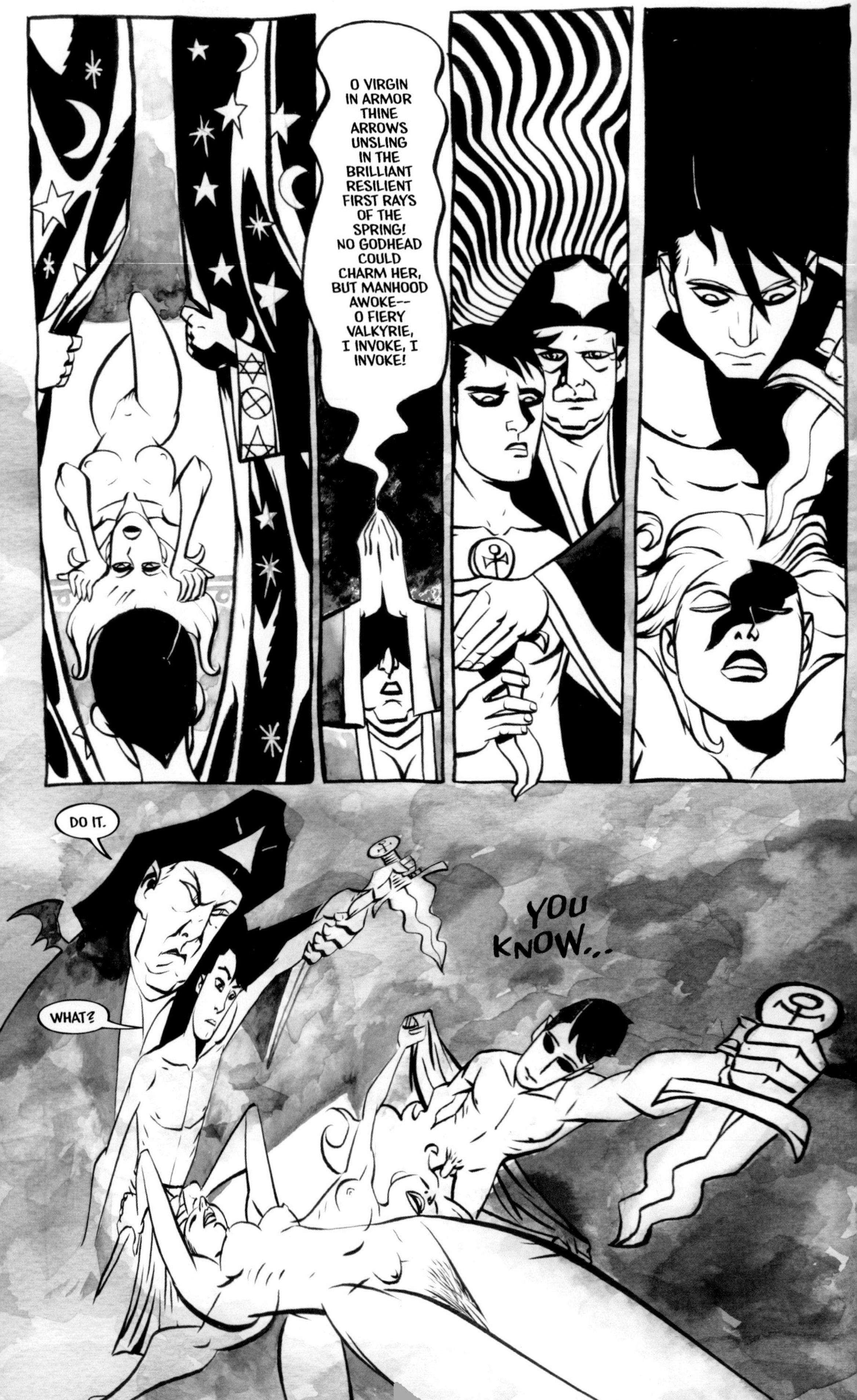
O VIRGIN IN ARMOR THINE ARROWS UNSLING IN THE BRILLIANT RESILIENT FIRST RAYS OF THE SPRING! NO GODHEAD COULD CHARM HER, BUT MANHOOD AWOKE-- O FIERY VALKYRIE, I INVOKE, I INVOKE!
DO IT.
WHAT?
YOU KNOW...

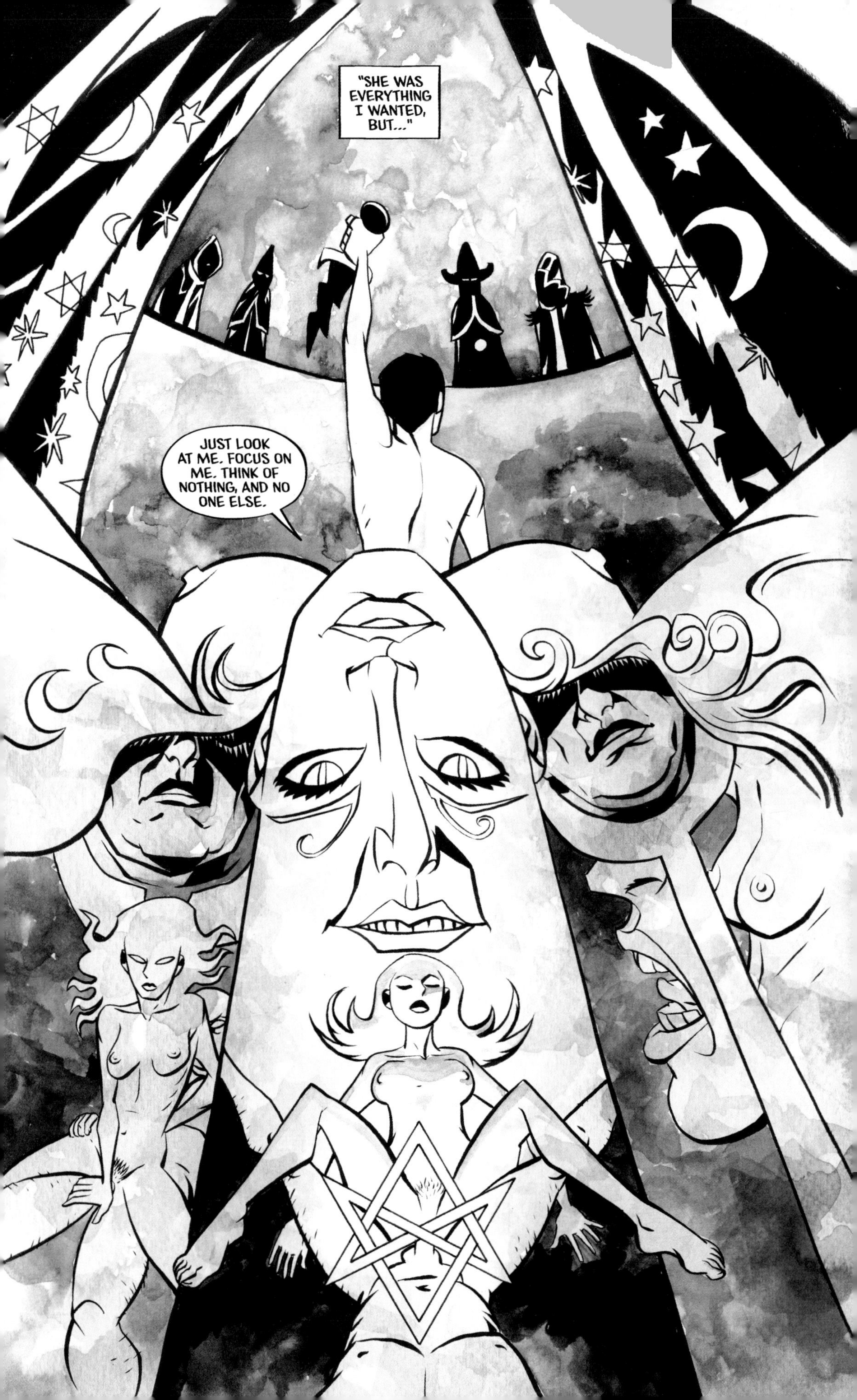
"SHE WAS EVERYTHING I WANTED, BUT..."
JUST LOOK AT ME. FOCUS ON ME. THINK OF NOTHING, AND NO ONE ELSE.

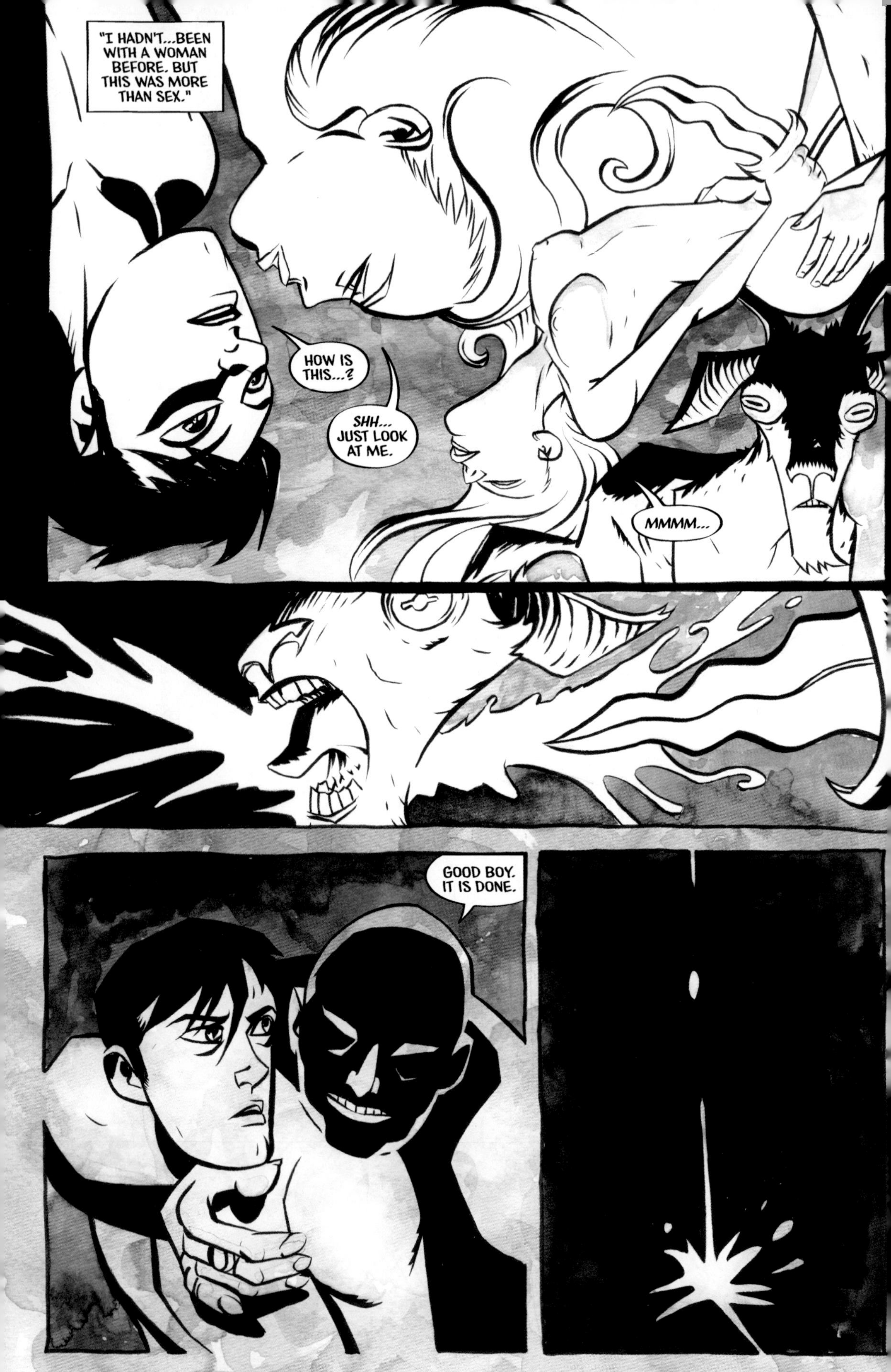
"I HADN'T...BEEN WITH A WOMAN BEFORE. BUT THIS WAS MORE THAN SEX."
HOW IS THIS...?
SHH... JUST LOOK AT ME.
MMMM...
GOOD BOY. IT IS DONE.

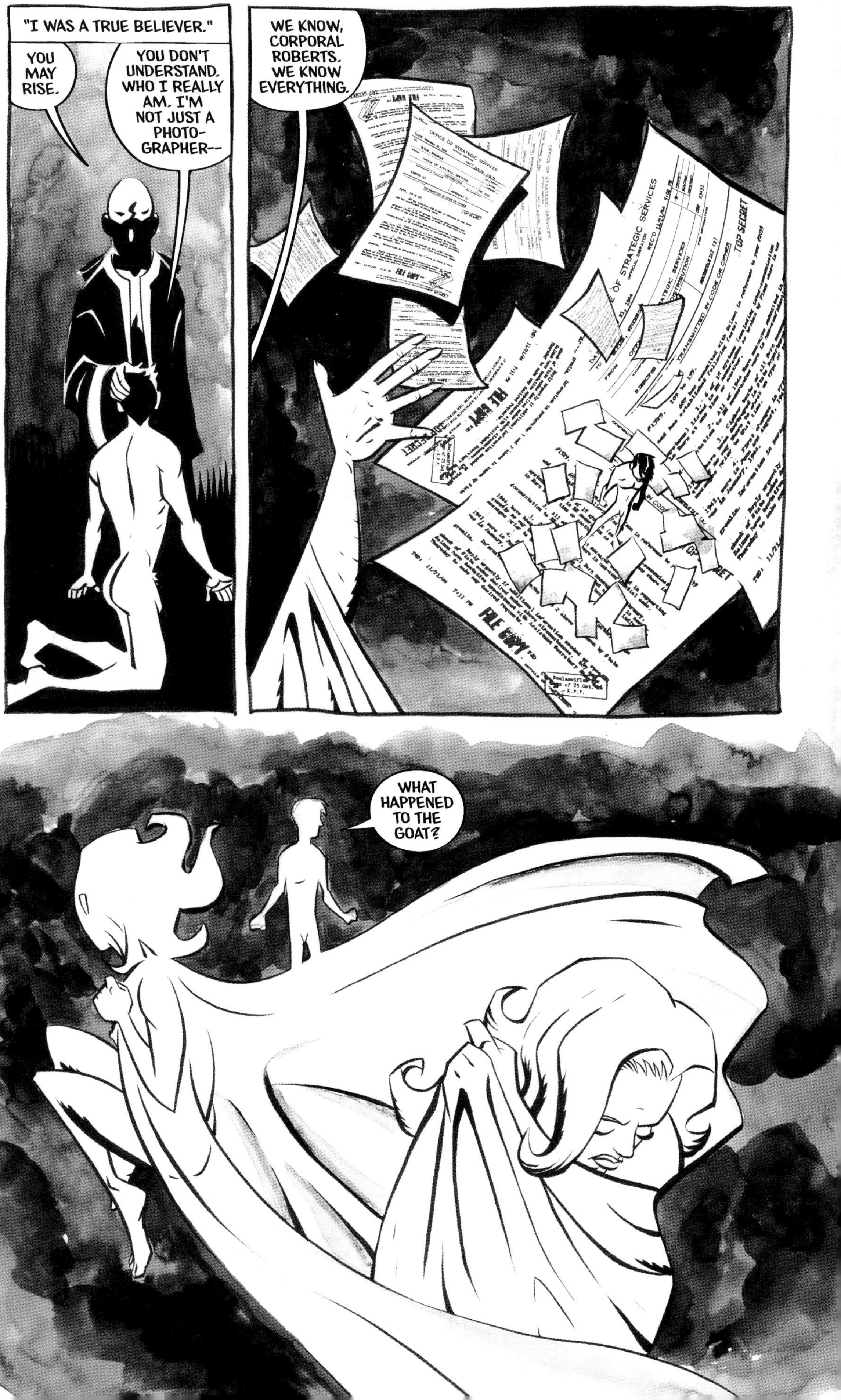
"I WAS A TRUE BELIEVER."
YOU MAY RISE.
YOU DON'T UNDERSTAND. WHO I REALLY AM. I'M NOT JUST A PHOTO-GRAPHER--
WE KNOW, CORPORAL ROBERTS. WE KNOW EVERYTHING.
OFFICE OF STRATEGIC SERVICES
TOP SECRET
FILE COPY
WHAT HAPPENED TO THE GOAT?

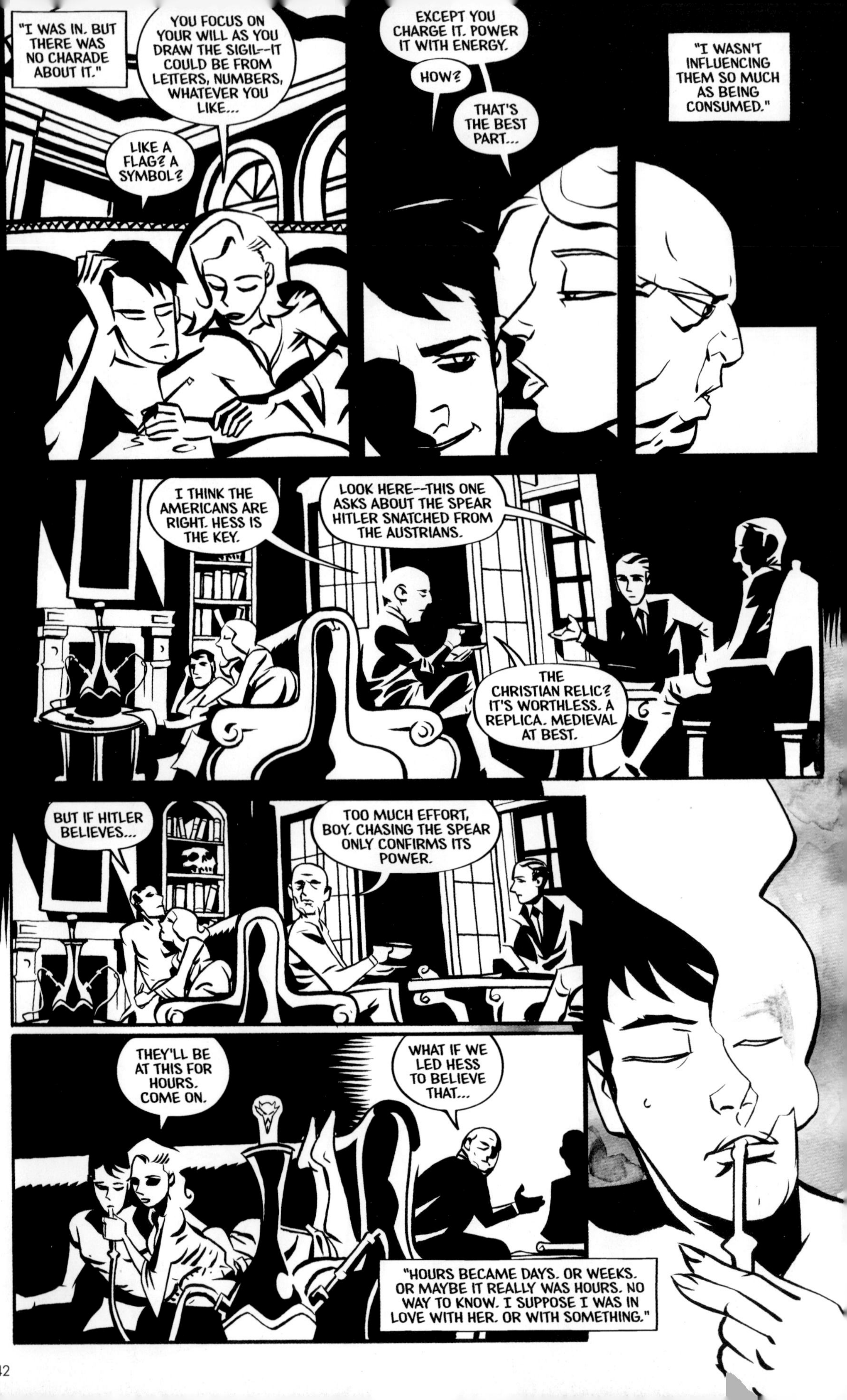
"I WAS IN. BUT THERE WAS NO CHARADE ABOUT IT."
YOU FOCUS ON YOUR WILL AS YOU DRAW THE SIGIL--IT COULD BE FROM LETTERS, NUMBERS, WHATEVER YOU LIKE...
LIKE A FLAG? A SYMBOL?
EXCEPT YOU CHARGE IT. POWER IT WITH ENERGY.
HOW?
THAT'S THE BEST PART...
"I WASN'T INFLUENCING THEM SO MUCH AS BEING CONSUMED."
I THINK THE AMERICANS ARE RIGHT. HESS IS THE KEY.
LOOK HERE--THIS ONE ASKS ABOUT THE SPEAR HITLER SNATCHED FROM THE AUSTRIANS.
THE CHRISTIAN RELIC? IT'S WORTHLESS. A REPLICA. MEDIEVAL AT BEST.
BUT IF HITLER BELIEVES...
TOO MUCH EFFORT, BOY. CHASING THE SPEAR ONLY CONFIRMS ITS POWER.
THEY'LL BE AT THIS FOR HOURS. COME ON.
WHAT IF WE LED HESS TO BELIEVE THAT...
"HOURS BECAME DAYS. OR WEEKS. OR MAYBE IT REALLY WAS HOURS. NO WAY TO KNOW. I SUPPOSE I WAS IN LOVE WITH HER. OR WITH SOMETHING."

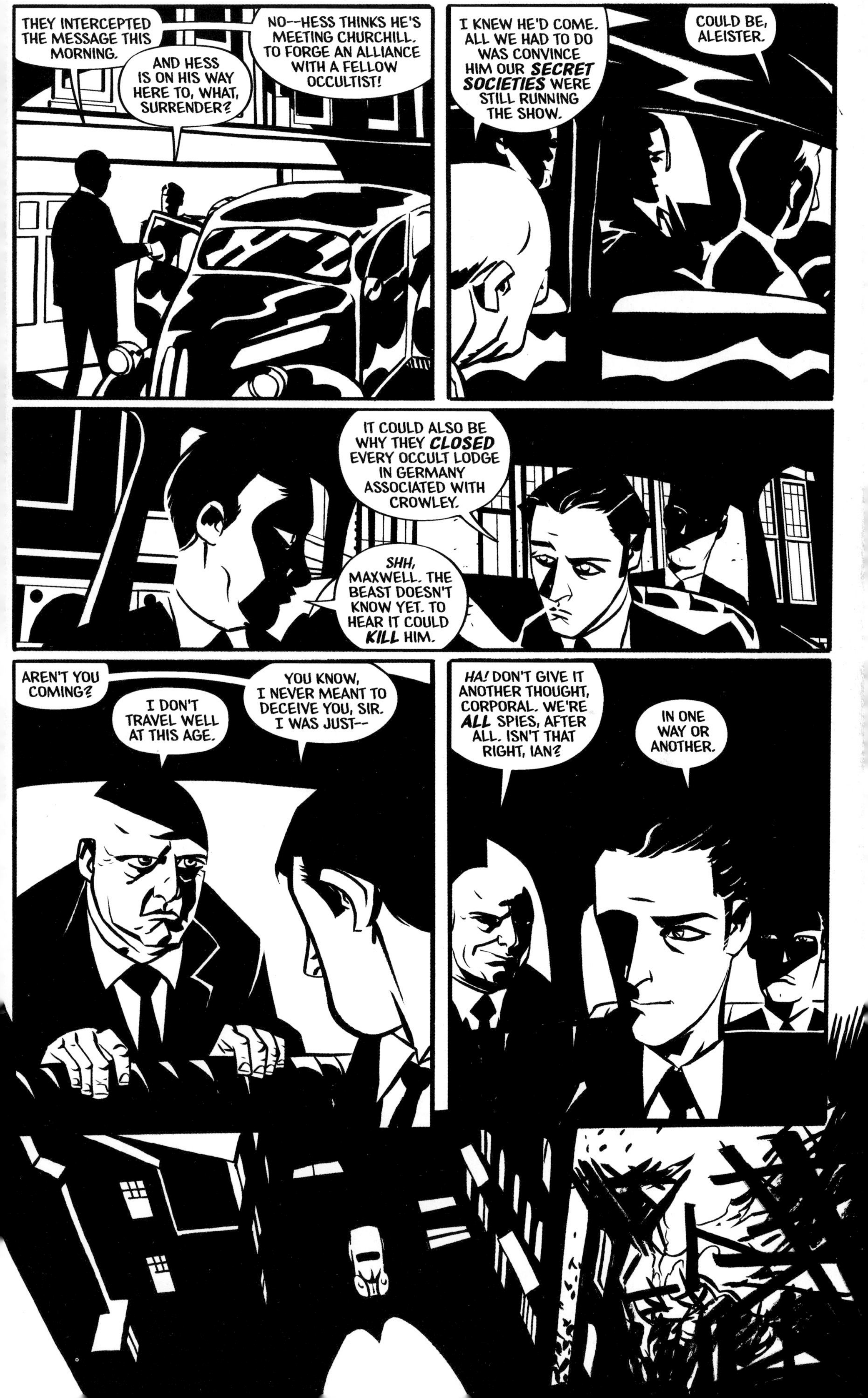
THEY INTERCEPTED THE MESSAGE THIS MORNING.
AND HESS IS ON HIS WAY HERE TO, WHAT, SURRENDER?
NO--HESS THINKS HE'S MEETING CHURCHILL. TO FORGE AN ALLIANCE WITH A FELLOW OCCULTIST!
I KNEW HE'D COME. ALL WE HAD TO DO WAS CONVINCE HIM OUR SECRET SOCIETIES WERE STILL RUNNING THE SHOW.
COULD BE, ALEISTER.
IT COULD ALSO BE WHY THEY CLOSED EVERY OCCULT LODGE IN GERMANY ASSOCIATED WITH CROWLEY.
SHH, MAXWELL. THE BEAST DOESN'T KNOW YET. TO HEAR IT COULD KILL HIM.
AREN'T YOU COMING?
I DON'T TRAVEL WELL AT THIS AGE.
YOU KNOW, I NEVER MEANT TO DECEIVE YOU, SIR. I WAS JUST--
HA! DON'T GIVE IT ANOTHER THOUGHT, CORPORAL. WE'RE ALL SPIES, AFTER ALL. ISN'T THAT RIGHT, IAN?
IN ONE WAY OR ANOTHER.

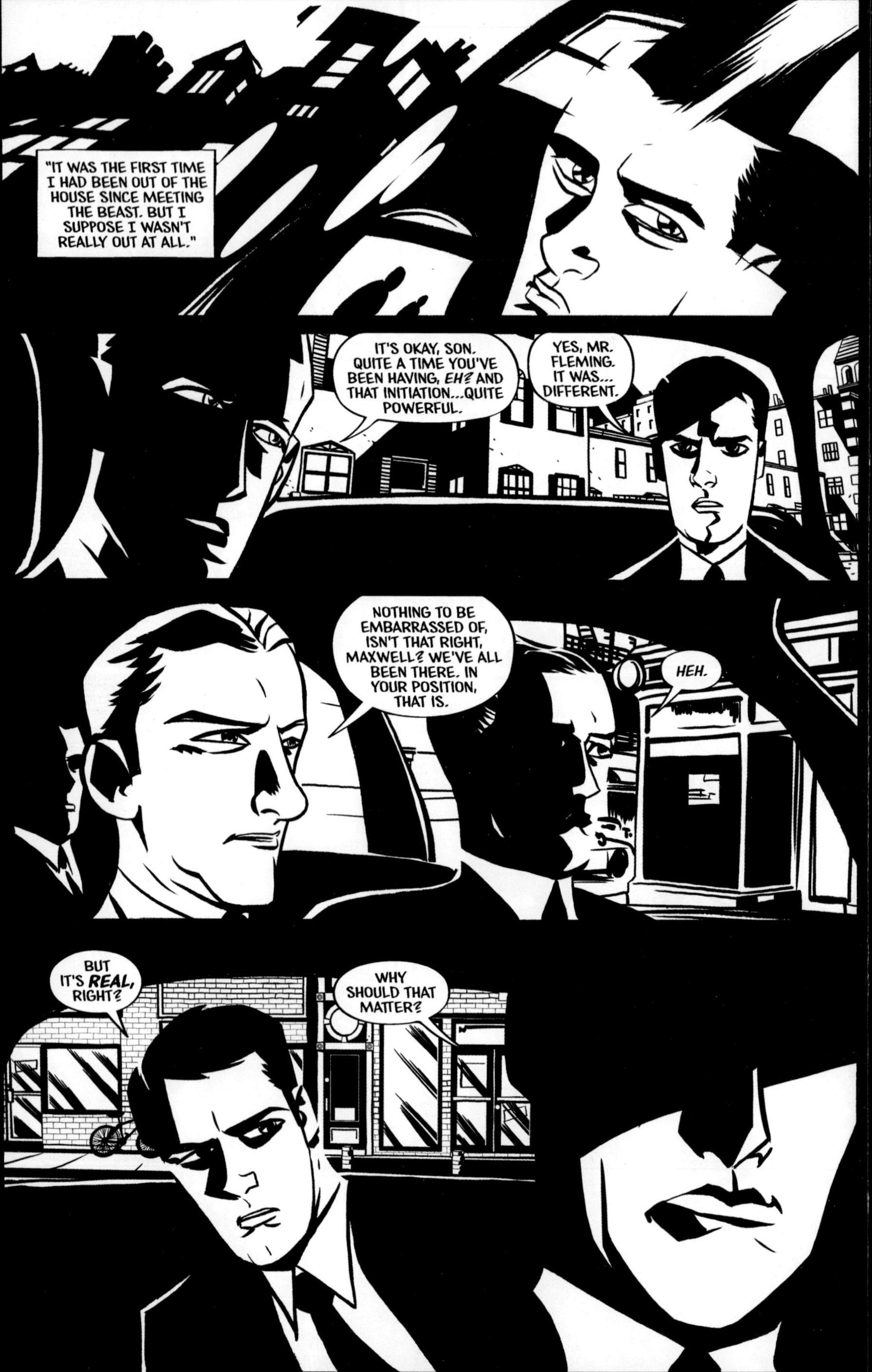
"IT WAS THE FIRST TIME I HAD BEEN OUT OF THE HOUSE SINCE MEETING THE BEAST. BUT I SUPPOSE I WASN'T REALLY OUT AT ALL."
IT'S OKAY, SON. QUITE A TIME YOU'VE BEEN HAVING, *EH?* AND THAT INITIATION... QUITE POWERFUL.
YES, MR. FLEMING. IT WAS... DIFFERENT.
NOTHING TO BE EMBARRASSED OF, ISN'T THAT RIGHT, MAXWELL? WE'VE ALL BEEN THERE. IN YOUR POSITION, THAT IS.
*HEH.*
BUT IT'S ***REAL***, RIGHT?
WHY SHOULD THAT MATTER?

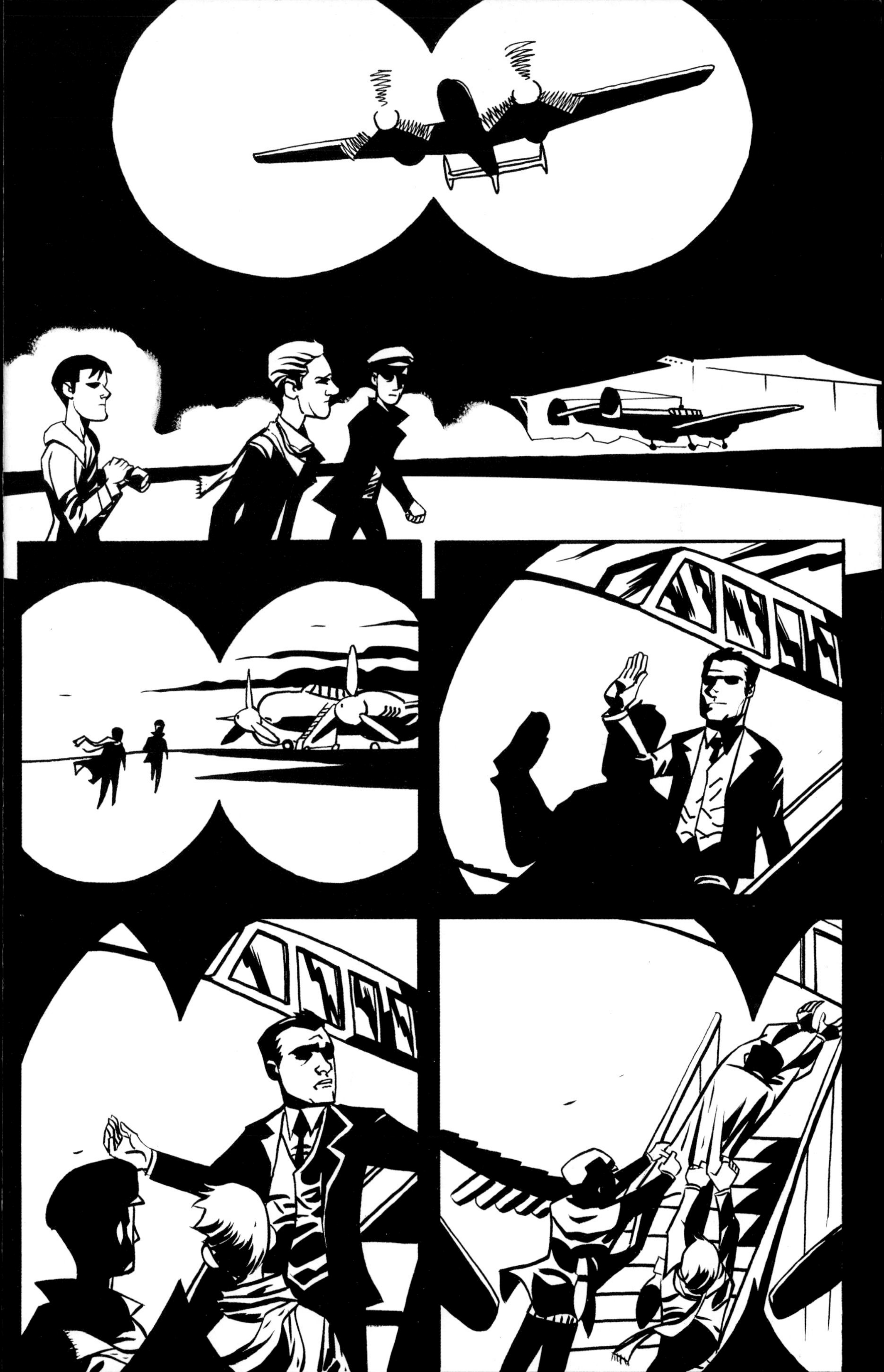

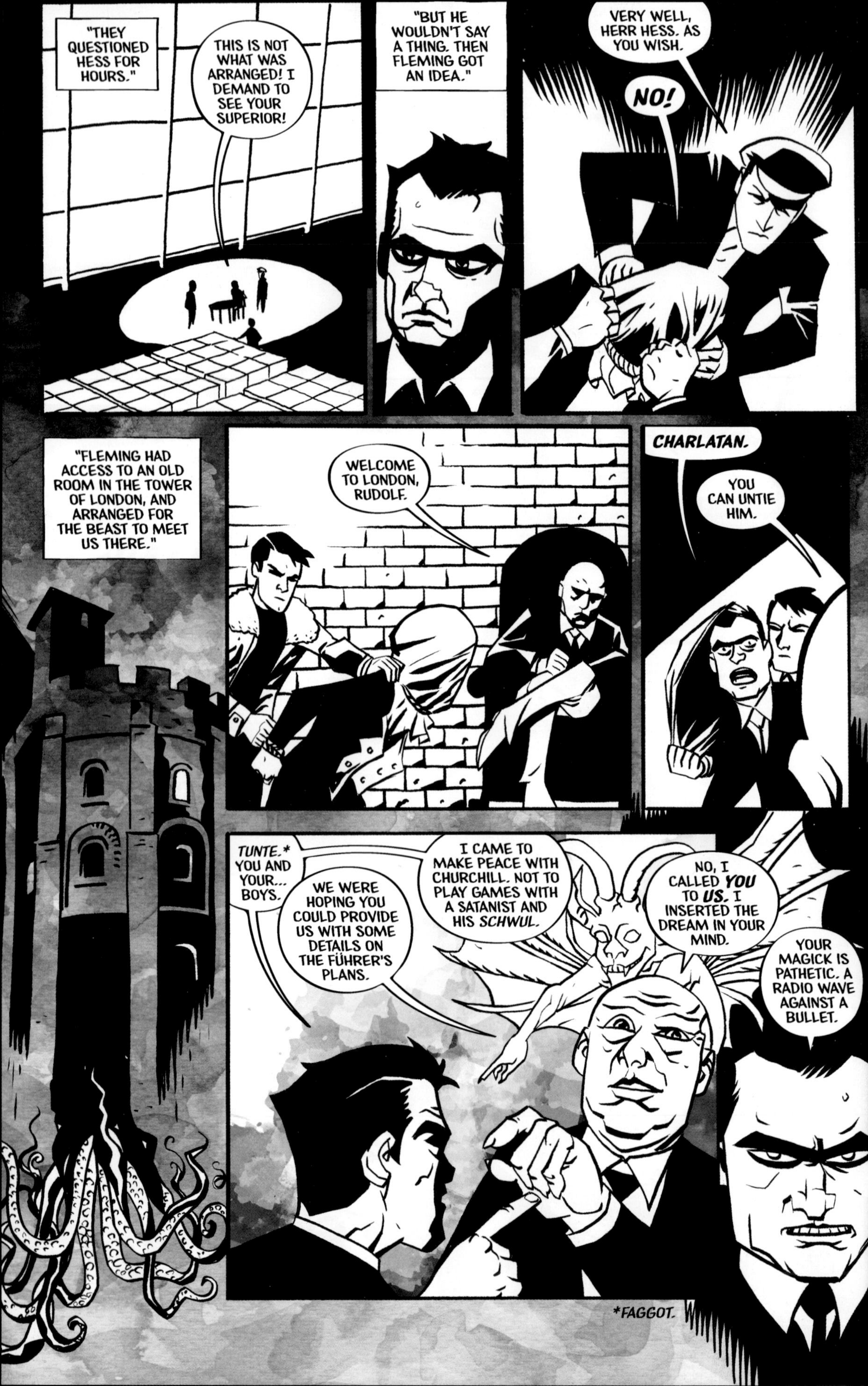
"THEY QUESTIONED HESS FOR HOURS."
THIS IS NOT WHAT WAS ARRANGED! I DEMAND TO SEE YOUR SUPERIOR!
"BUT HE WOULDN'T SAY A THING. THEN FLEMING GOT AN IDEA."
VERY WELL, HERR HESS. AS YOU WISH.
NO!
"FLEMING HAD ACCESS TO AN OLD ROOM IN THE TOWER OF LONDON, AND ARRANGED FOR THE BEAST TO MEET US THERE."
WELCOME TO LONDON, RUDOLF.
CHARLATAN.
YOU CAN UNTIE HIM.
TUNTE.* YOU AND YOUR... BOYS.
WE WERE HOPING YOU COULD PROVIDE US WITH SOME DETAILS ON THE FÜHRER'S PLANS.
I CAME TO MAKE PEACE WITH CHURCHILL. NOT TO PLAY GAMES WITH A SATANIST AND HIS SCHWUL.
NO, I CALLED YOU TO US. I INSERTED THE DREAM IN YOUR MIND.
YOUR MAGICK IS PATHETIC. A RADIO WAVE AGAINST A BULLET.
*FAGGOT.

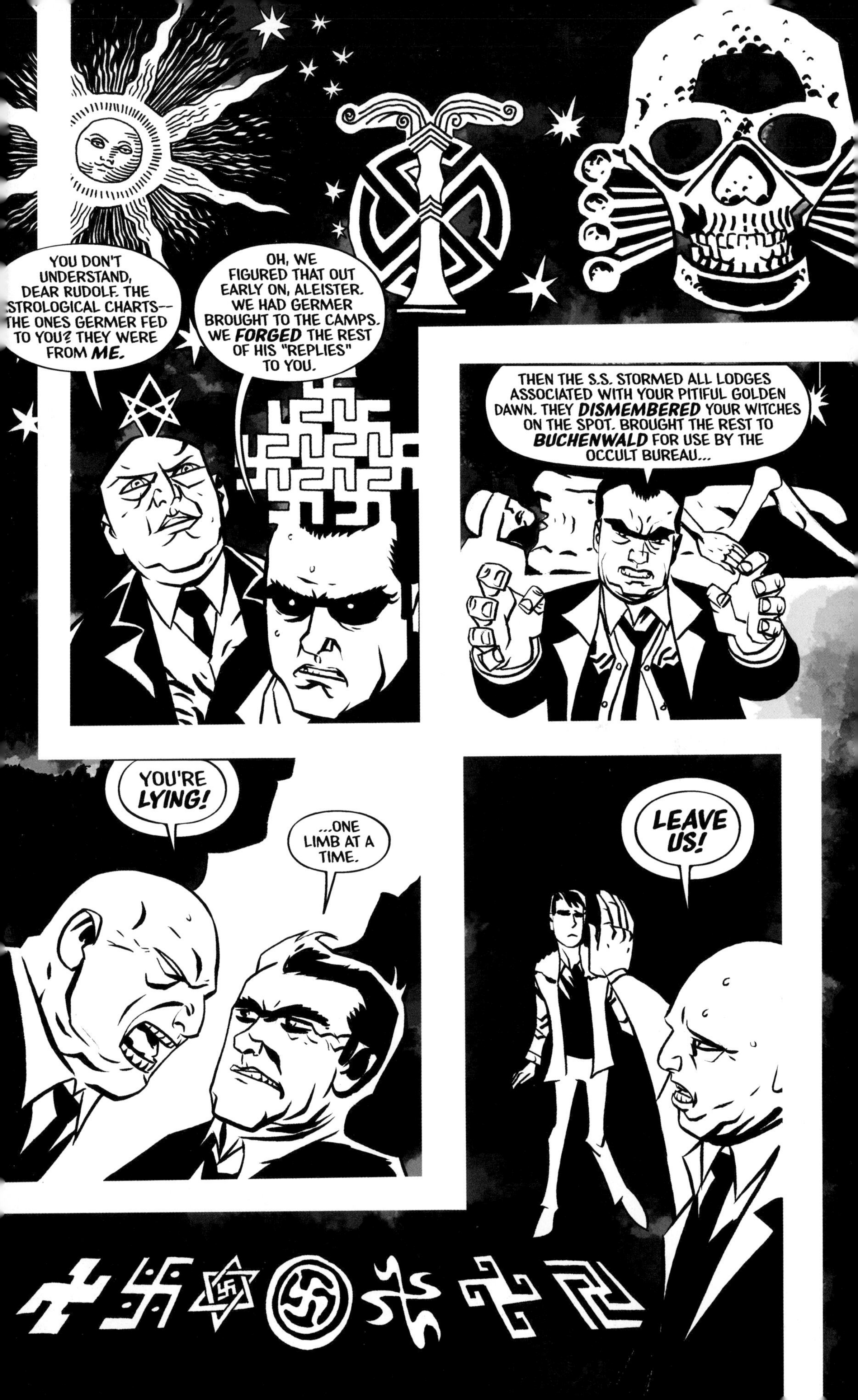
YOU DON'T UNDERSTAND, DEAR RUDOLF. THE STROLOGICAL CHARTS-- THE ONES GERMER FED TO YOU? THEY WERE FROM ME.
OH, WE FIGURED THAT OUT EARLY ON, ALEISTER. WE HAD GERMER BROUGHT TO THE CAMPS. WE FORGED THE REST OF HIS "REPLIES" TO YOU.
THEN THE S.S. STORMED ALL LODGES ASSOCIATED WITH YOUR PITIFUL GOLDEN DAWN. THEY DISMEMBERED YOUR WITCHES ON THE SPOT. BROUGHT THE REST TO BUCHENWALD FOR USE BY THE OCCULT BUREAU...
YOU'RE LYING!
...ONE LIMB AT A TIME.
LEAVE US!

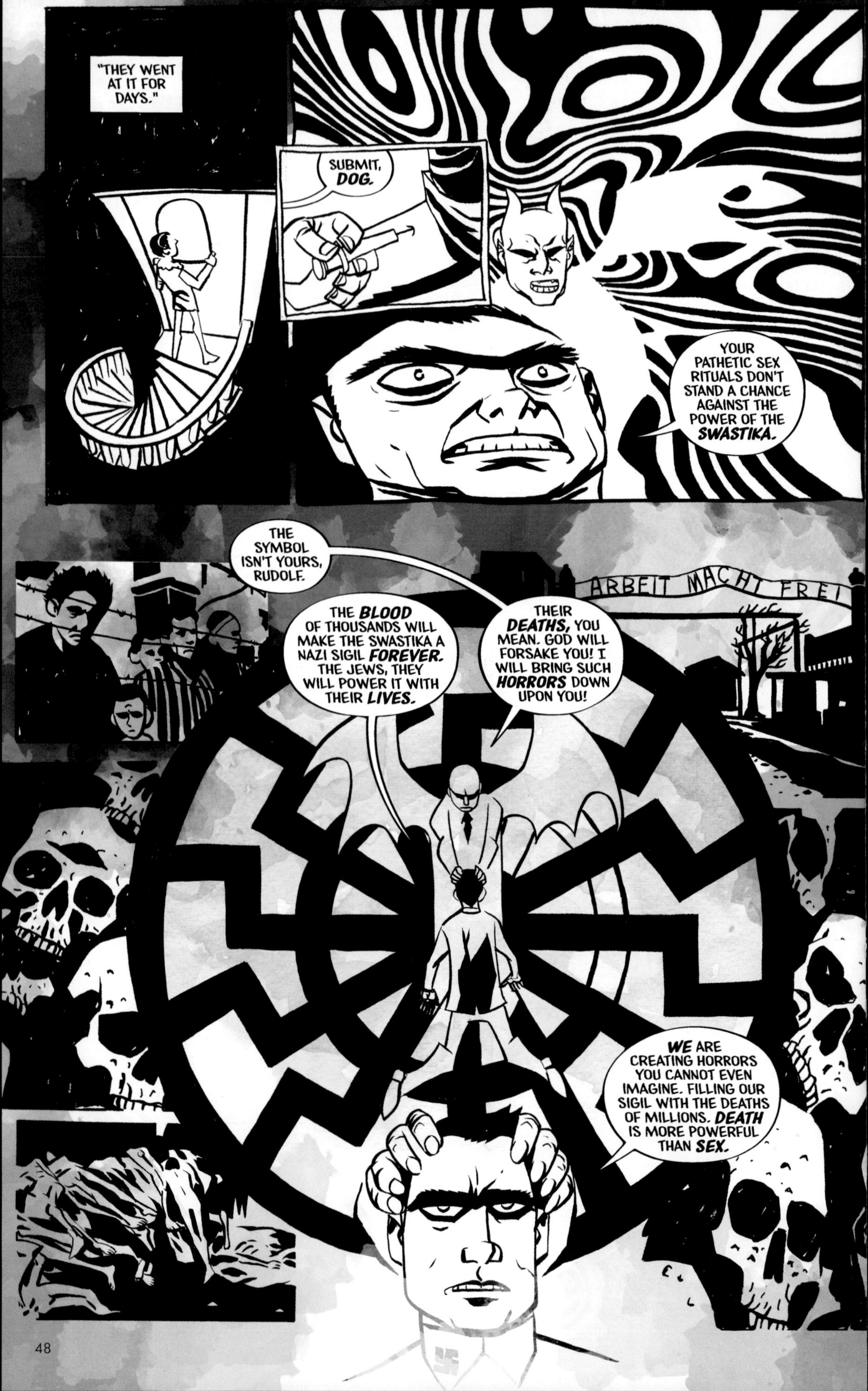
"THEY WENT AT IT FOR DAYS."
SUBMIT, DOG.
YOUR PATHETIC SEX RITUALS DON'T STAND A CHANCE AGAINST THE POWER OF THE SWASTIKA.
THE SYMBOL ISN'T YOURS, RUDOLF.
ARBEIT MACHT FREI
THE BLOOD OF THOUSANDS WILL MAKE THE SWASTIKA A NAZI SIGIL FOREVER. THE JEWS, THEY WILL POWER IT WITH THEIR LIVES.
THEIR DEATHS, YOU MEAN. GOD WILL FORSAKE YOU! I WILL BRING SUCH HORRORS DOWN UPON YOU!
WE ARE CREATING HORRORS YOU CANNOT EVEN IMAGINE. FILLING OUR SIGIL WITH THE DEATHS OF MILLIONS. DEATH IS MORE POWERFUL THAN SEX.

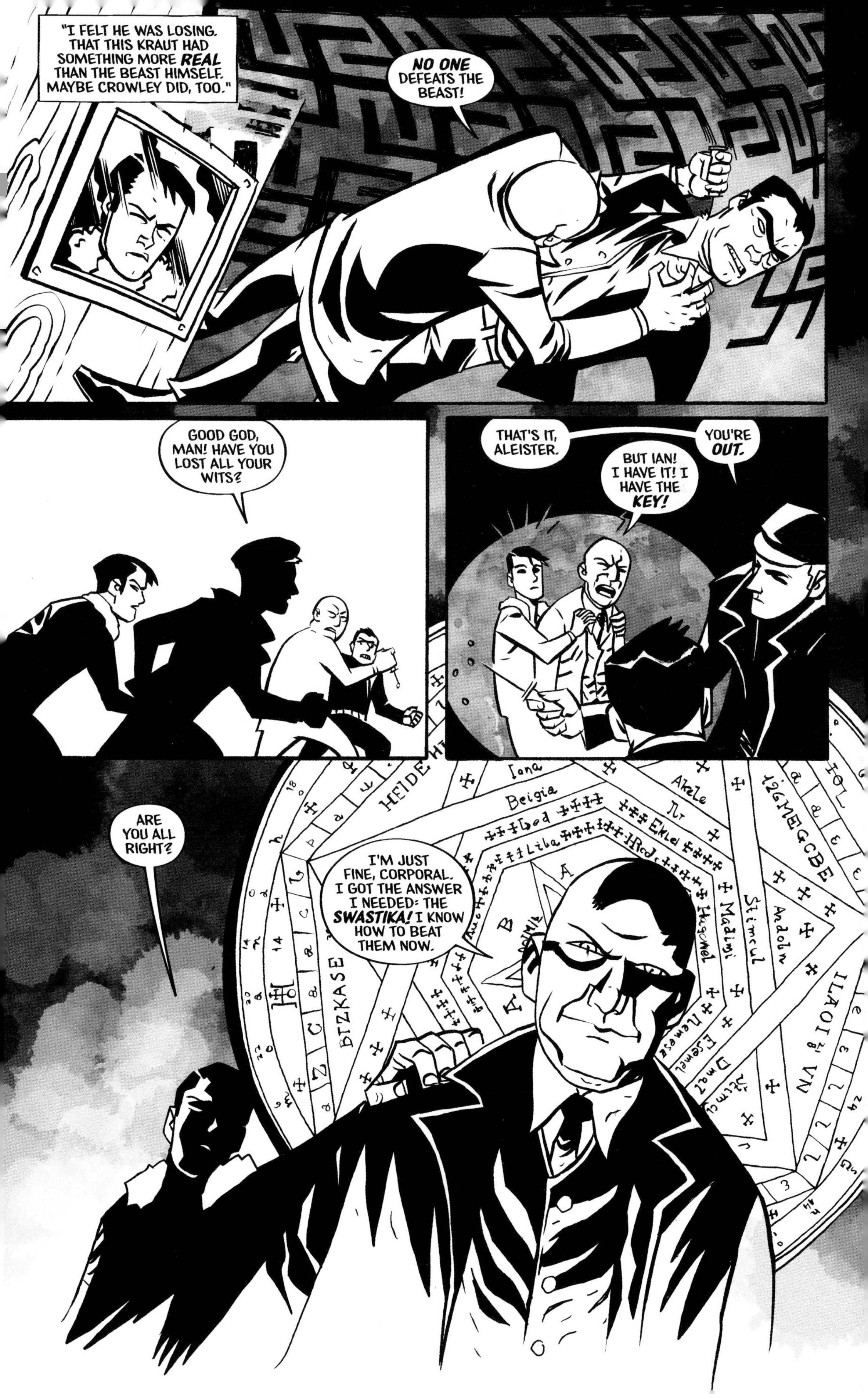
"I FELT HE WAS LOSING. THAT THIS KRAUT HAD SOMETHING MORE REAL THAN THE BEAST HIMSELF. MAYBE CROWLEY DID, TOO."
NO ONE DEFEATS THE BEAST!
GOOD GOD, MAN! HAVE YOU LOST ALL YOUR WITS?
THAT'S IT, ALEISTER.
YOU'RE OUT.
BUT IAN! I HAVE IT! I HAVE THE KEY!
ARE YOU ALL RIGHT?
I'M JUST FINE, CORPORAL. I GOT THE ANSWER I NEEDED: THE SWASTIKA! I KNOW HOW TO BEAT THEM NOW.

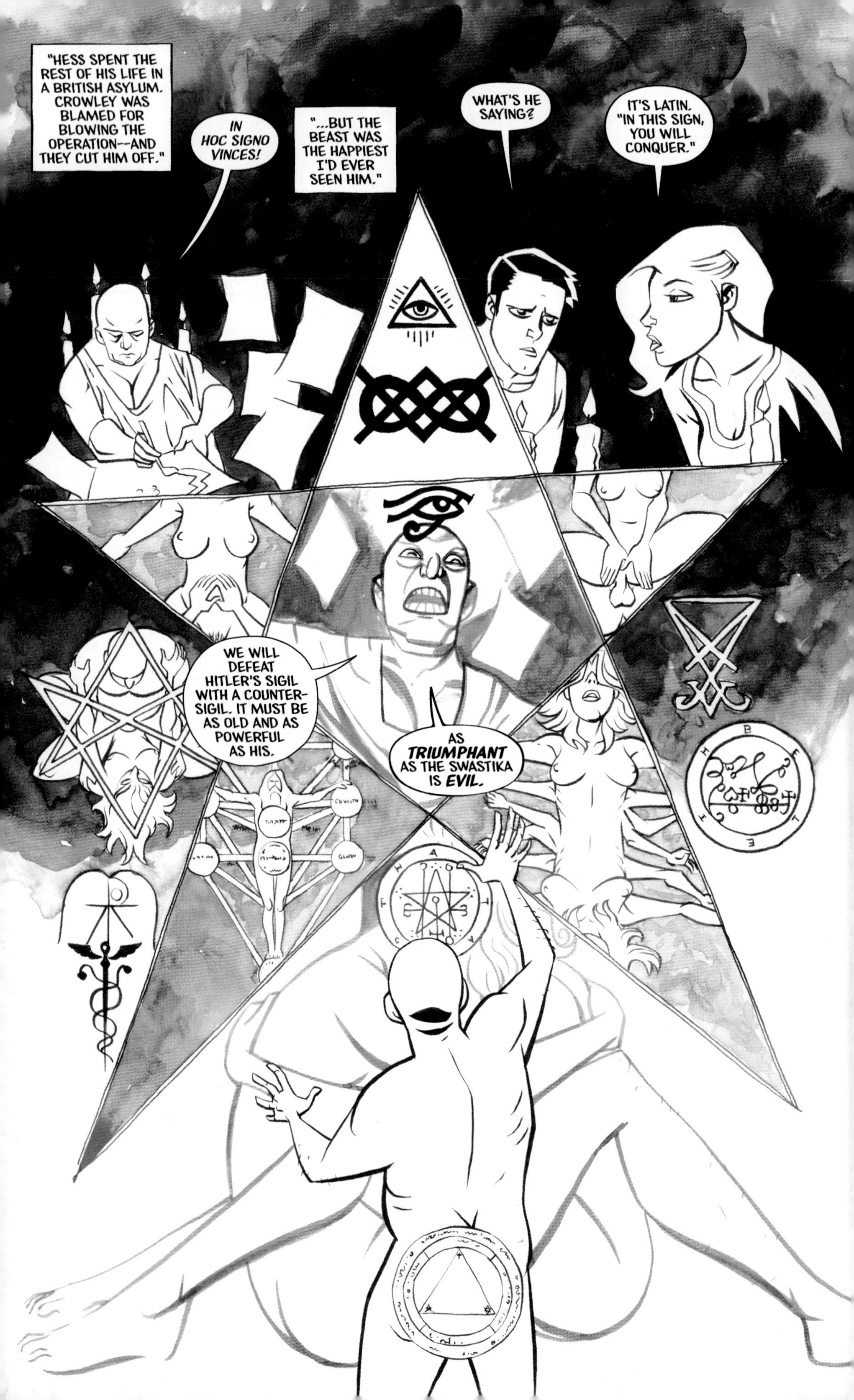
"HESS SPENT THE REST OF HIS LIFE IN A BRITISH ASYLUM. CROWLEY WAS BLAMED FOR BLOWING THE OPERATION--AND THEY CUT HIM OFF."
IN HOC SIGNO VINCES!
"...BUT THE BEAST WAS THE HAPPIEST I'D EVER SEEN HIM."
WHAT'S HE SAYING?
IT'S LATIN. "IN THIS SIGN, YOU WILL CONQUER."
WE WILL DEFEAT HITLER'S SIGIL WITH A COUNTER-SIGIL. IT MUST BE AS OLD AND AS POWERFUL AS HIS.
AS TRIUMPHANT AS THE SWASTIKA IS EVIL.

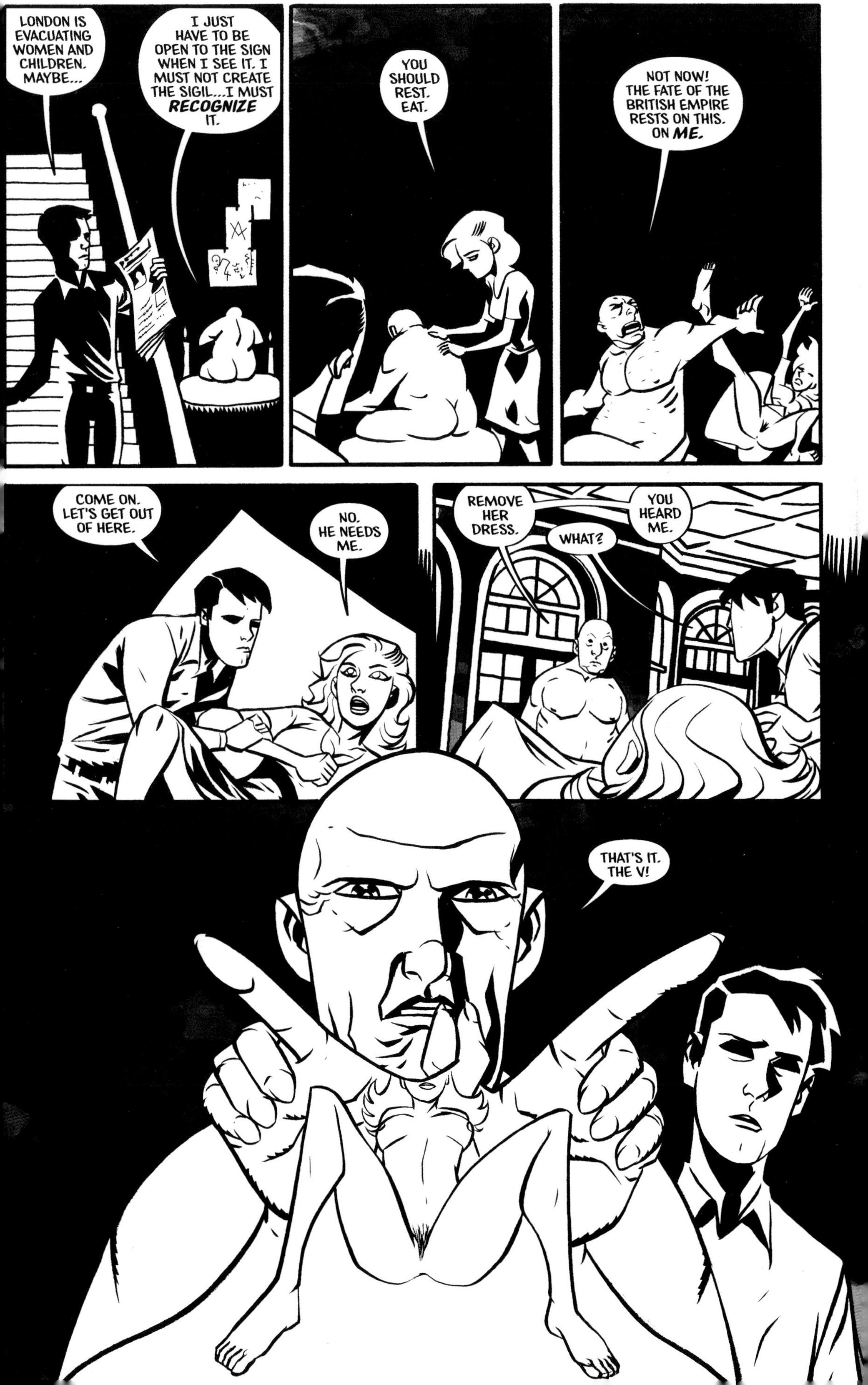
LONDON IS EVACUATING WOMEN AND CHILDREN. MAYBE...
I JUST HAVE TO BE OPEN TO THE SIGN WHEN I SEE IT. I MUST NOT CREATE THE SIGIL...I MUST RECOGNIZE IT.
YOU SHOULD REST. EAT.
NOT NOW! THE FATE OF THE BRITISH EMPIRE RESTS ON THIS. ON ME.
COME ON. LET'S GET OUT OF HERE.
NO. HE NEEDS ME.
REMOVE HER DRESS.
WHAT?
YOU HEARD ME.
THAT'S IT. THE V!

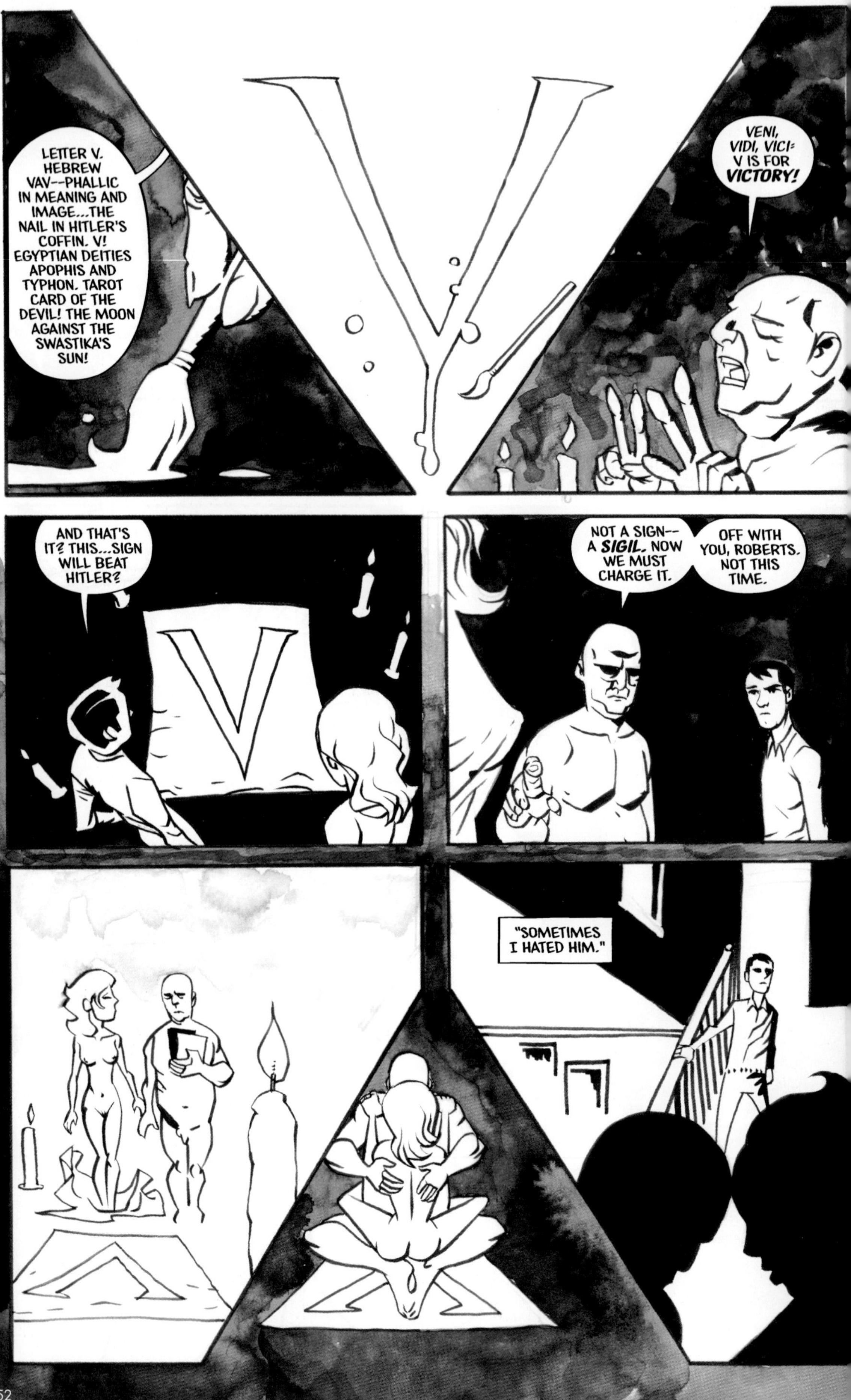
LETTER V. HEBREW VAV--PHALLIC IN MEANING AND IMAGE...THE NAIL IN HITLER'S COFFIN. V! EGYPTIAN DEITIES APOPHIS AND TYPHON. TAROT CARD OF THE DEVIL! THE MOON AGAINST THE SWASTIKA'S SUN!
VENI, VIDI, VICI: V IS FOR VICTORY!
AND THAT'S IT? THIS...SIGN WILL BEAT HITLER?
NOT A SIGN--A SIGIL. NOW WE MUST CHARGE IT.
OFF WITH YOU, ROBERTS. NOT THIS TIME.
"SOMETIMES I HATED HIM."

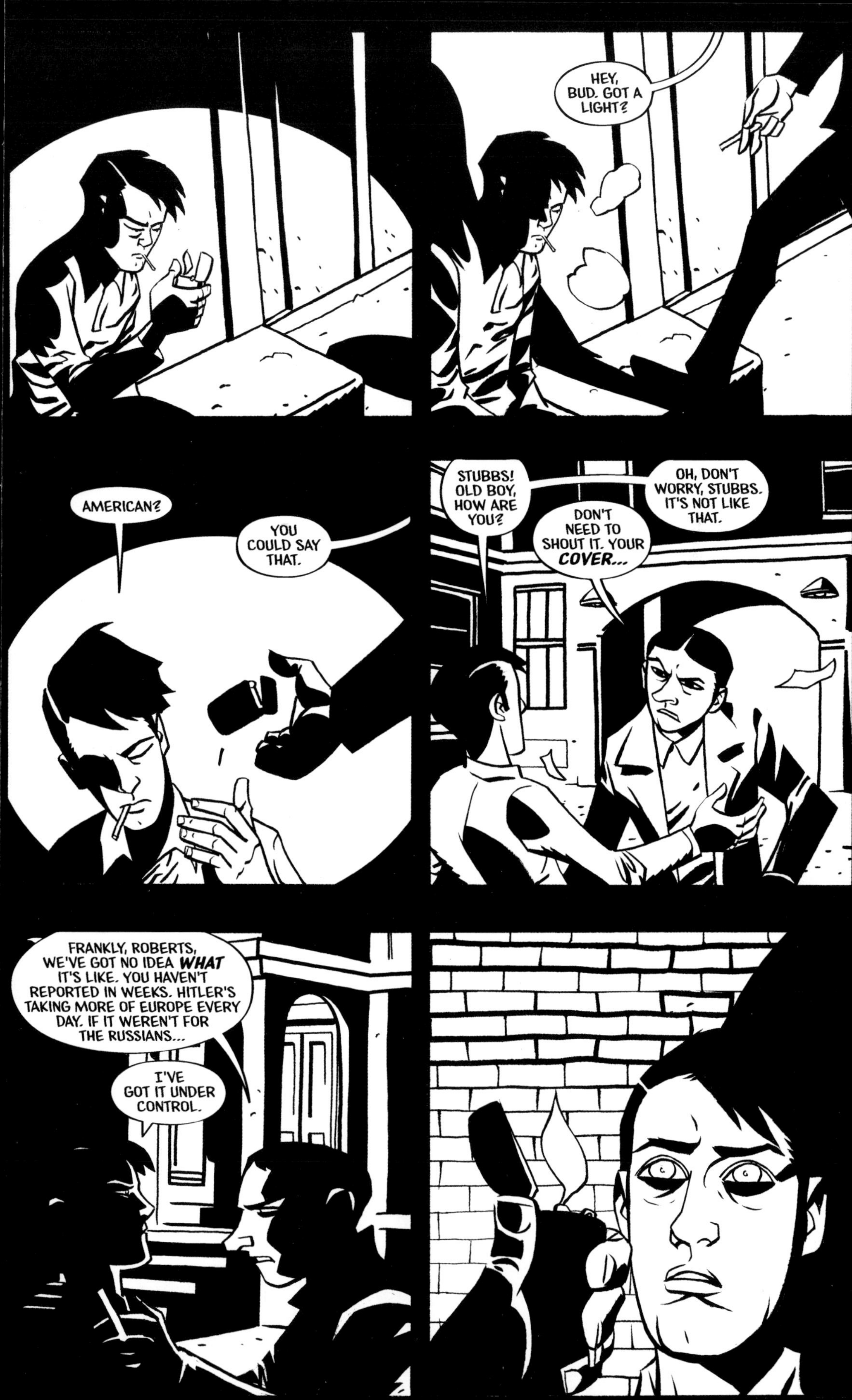
HEY, BUD. GOT A LIGHT?
AMERICAN?
YOU COULD SAY THAT.
STUBBS! OLD BOY, HOW ARE YOU?
DON'T NEED TO SHOUT IT. YOUR *COVER...*
OH, DON'T WORRY, STUBBS. IT'S NOT LIKE THAT.
FRANKLY, ROBERTS, WE'VE GOT NO IDEA *WHAT* IT'S LIKE. YOU HAVEN'T REPORTED IN WEEKS. HITLER'S TAKING MORE OF EUROPE EVERY DAY. IF IT WEREN'T FOR THE RUSSIANS...
I'VE GOT IT UNDER CONTROL.

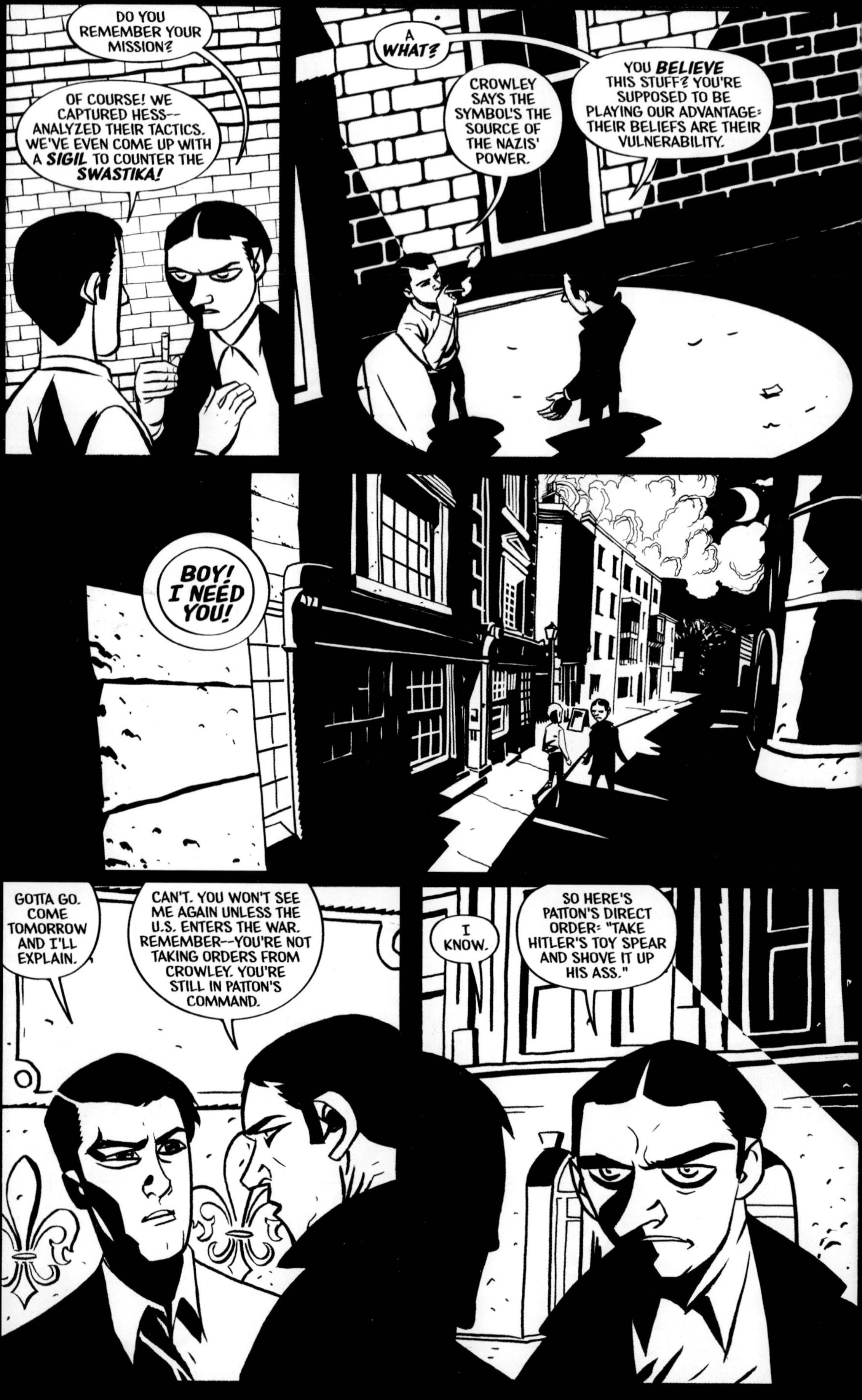
DO YOU REMEMBER YOUR MISSION?
OF COURSE! WE CAPTURED HESS--ANALYZED THEIR TACTICS. WE'VE EVEN COME UP WITH A **SIGIL** TO COUNTER THE **SWASTIKA!**
A **WHAT?**
CROWLEY SAYS THE SYMBOL'S THE SOURCE OF THE NAZIS' POWER.
YOU **BELIEVE** THIS STUFF? YOU'RE SUPPOSED TO BE PLAYING OUR ADVANTAGE: THEIR BELIEFS ARE THEIR VULNERABILITY.
BOY! I NEED YOU!
GOTTA GO. COME TOMORROW AND I'LL EXPLAIN.
CAN'T. YOU WON'T SEE ME AGAIN UNLESS THE U.S. ENTERS THE WAR. REMEMBER--YOU'RE NOT TAKING ORDERS FROM CROWLEY. YOU'RE STILL IN PATTON'S COMMAND.
I KNOW.
SO HERE'S PATTON'S DIRECT ORDER: "TAKE HITLER'S TOY SPEAR AND SHOVE IT UP HIS ASS."

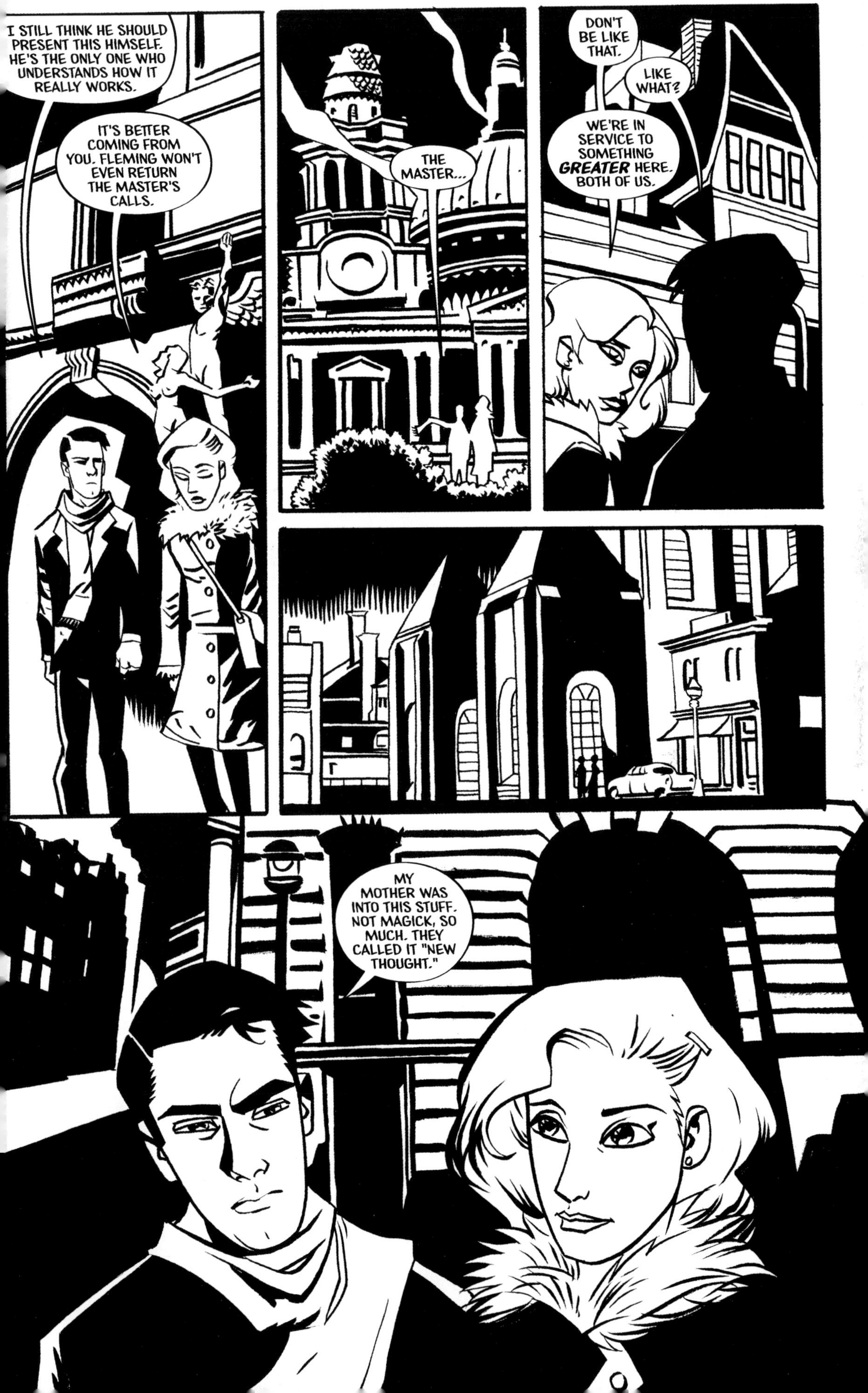
I STILL THINK HE SHOULD PRESENT THIS HIMSELF. HE'S THE ONLY ONE WHO UNDERSTANDS HOW IT REALLY WORKS.
IT'S BETTER COMING FROM YOU. FLEMING WON'T EVEN RETURN THE MASTER'S CALLS.
THE MASTER...
DON'T BE LIKE THAT.
LIKE WHAT?
WE'RE IN SERVICE TO SOMETHING GREATER HERE. BOTH OF US.
MY MOTHER WAS INTO THIS STUFF. NOT MAGICK, SO MUCH. THEY CALLED IT "NEW THOUGHT."

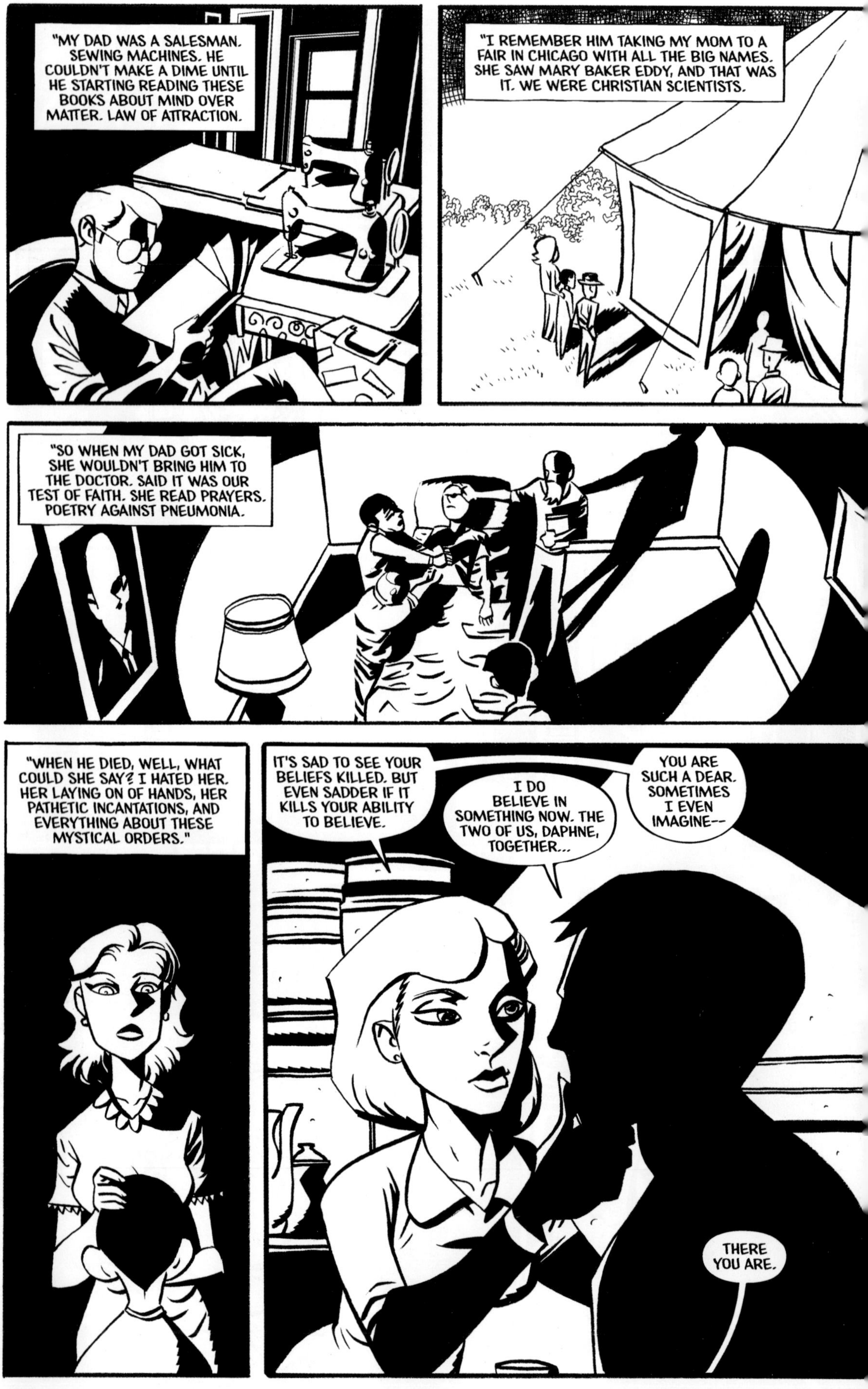
"MY DAD WAS A SALESMAN. SEWING MACHINES. HE COULDN'T MAKE A DIME UNTIL HE STARTING READING THESE BOOKS ABOUT MIND OVER MATTER. LAW OF ATTRACTION.
"I REMEMBER HIM TAKING MY MOM TO A FAIR IN CHICAGO WITH ALL THE BIG NAMES. SHE SAW MARY BAKER EDDY, AND THAT WAS IT. WE WERE CHRISTIAN SCIENTISTS.
"SO WHEN MY DAD GOT SICK, SHE WOULDN'T BRING HIM TO THE DOCTOR. SAID IT WAS OUR TEST OF FAITH. SHE READ PRAYERS. POETRY AGAINST PNEUMONIA.
"WHEN HE DIED, WELL, WHAT COULD SHE SAY? I HATED HER. HER LAYING ON OF HANDS, HER PATHETIC INCANTATIONS, AND EVERYTHING ABOUT THESE MYSTICAL ORDERS."
IT'S SAD TO SEE YOUR BELIEFS KILLED. BUT EVEN SADDER IF IT KILLS YOUR ABILITY TO BELIEVE.
I DO BELIEVE IN SOMETHING NOW. THE TWO OF US, DAPHNE, TOGETHER...
YOU ARE SUCH A DEAR. SOMETIMES I EVEN IMAGINE--
THERE YOU ARE.

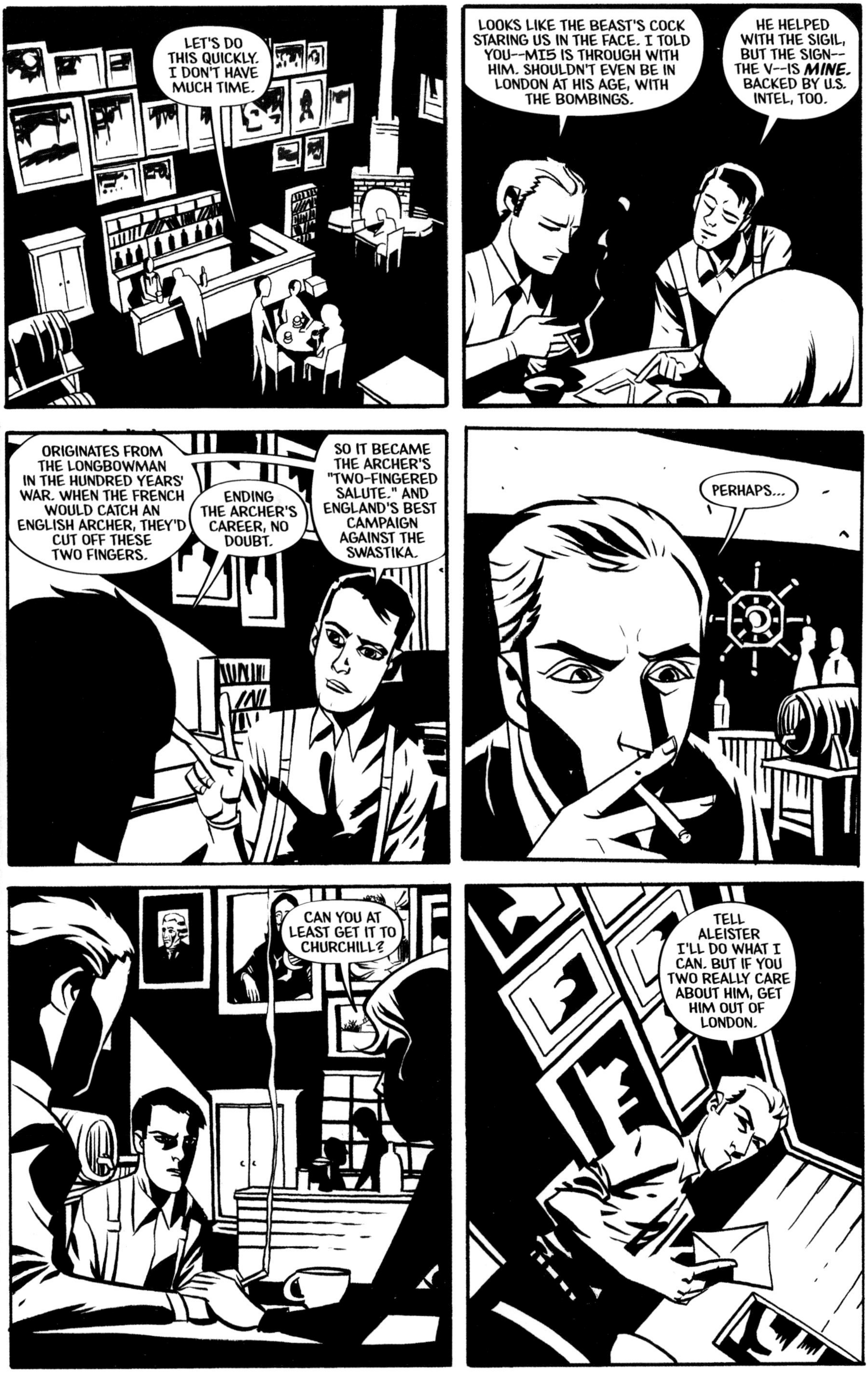
LET'S DO THIS QUICKLY. I DON'T HAVE MUCH TIME.
LOOKS LIKE THE BEAST'S COCK STARING US IN THE FACE. I TOLD YOU--MI5 IS THROUGH WITH HIM. SHOULDN'T EVEN BE IN LONDON AT HIS AGE, WITH THE BOMBINGS.
HE HELPED WITH THE SIGIL, BUT THE SIGN--THE V--IS MINE. BACKED BY U.S. INTEL, TOO.
ORIGINATES FROM THE LONGBOWMAN IN THE HUNDRED YEARS' WAR. WHEN THE FRENCH WOULD CATCH AN ENGLISH ARCHER, THEY'D CUT OFF THESE TWO FINGERS.
ENDING THE ARCHER'S CAREER, NO DOUBT.
SO IT BECAME THE ARCHER'S "TWO-FINGERED SALUTE." AND ENGLAND'S BEST CAMPAIGN AGAINST THE SWASTIKA.
PERHAPS...
CAN YOU AT LEAST GET IT TO CHURCHILL?
TELL ALEISTER I'LL DO WHAT I CAN. BUT IF YOU TWO REALLY CARE ABOUT HIM, GET HIM OUT OF LONDON.

# V IS FOR VICTORY!

The Prime Minister announces effort to promote "V Is for Victory" throughout Europe, urging people to use the V symbol whenever possible, paint it on walls and on streets, to undermine German morale while solidifying anti-Nazi

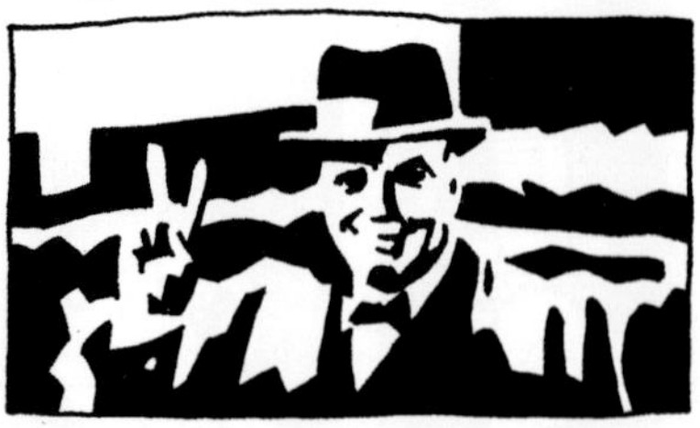

**CHURCHILL LAUNCHES "V" CAMPAIGN**

"The V sign is the symbol of the unconquerable will of the occupied territories and a portent of the fate awaiting Nazi tyranny. So long as the peoples continue to refuse all collaboration with the invader it is sure that his cause will perish and that Europe will be liberated."

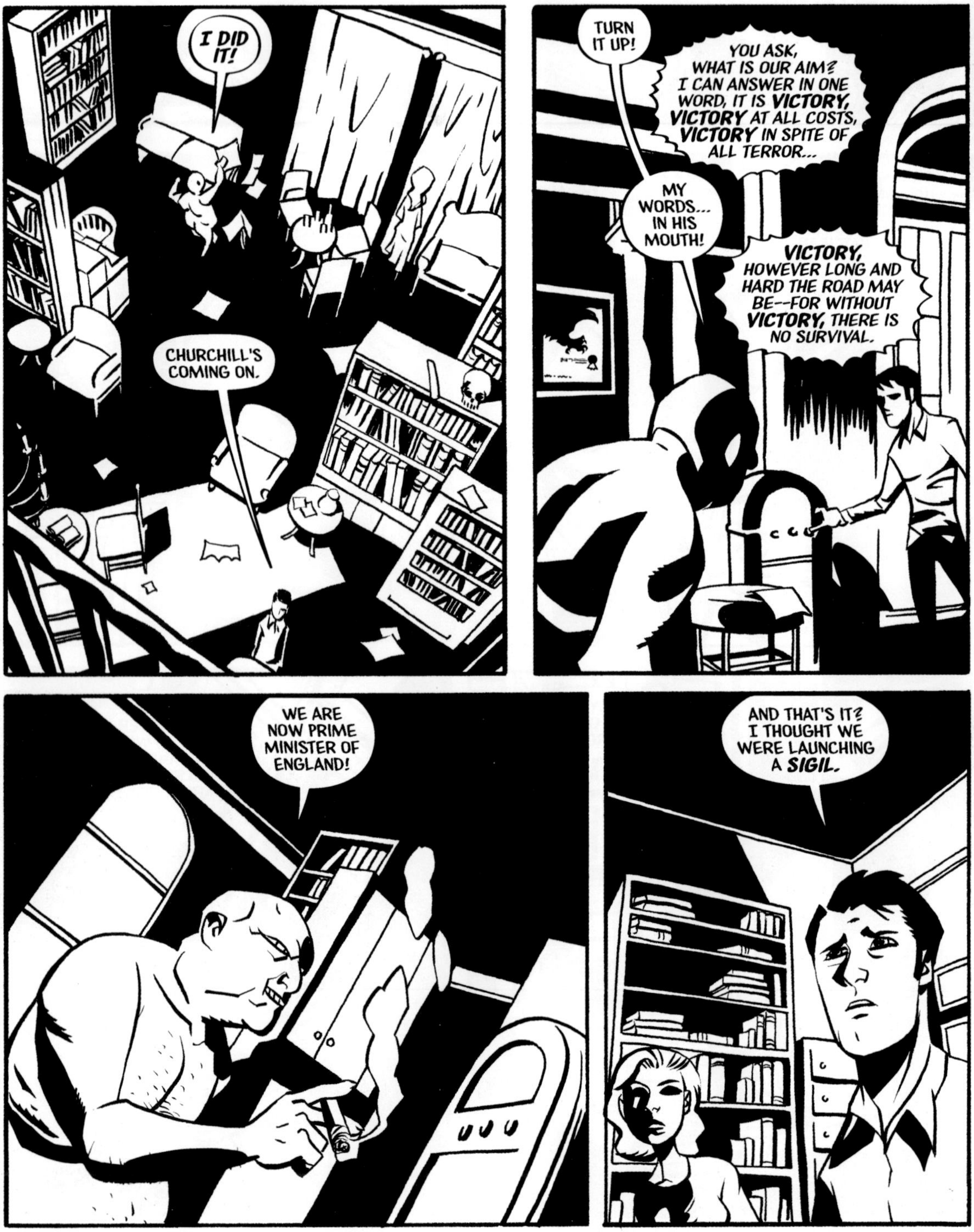

I DID IT!
CHURCHILL'S COMING ON.
TURN IT UP!
YOU ASK, WHAT IS OUR AIM? I CAN ANSWER IN ONE WORD, IT IS VICTORY, VICTORY AT ALL COSTS, VICTORY IN SPITE OF ALL TERROR...
MY WORDS... IN HIS MOUTH!
VICTORY, HOWEVER LONG AND HARD THE ROAD MAY BE--FOR WITHOUT VICTORY, THERE IS NO SURVIVAL.
WE ARE NOW PRIME MINISTER OF ENGLAND!
AND THAT'S IT? I THOUGHT WE WERE LAUNCHING A SIGIL.

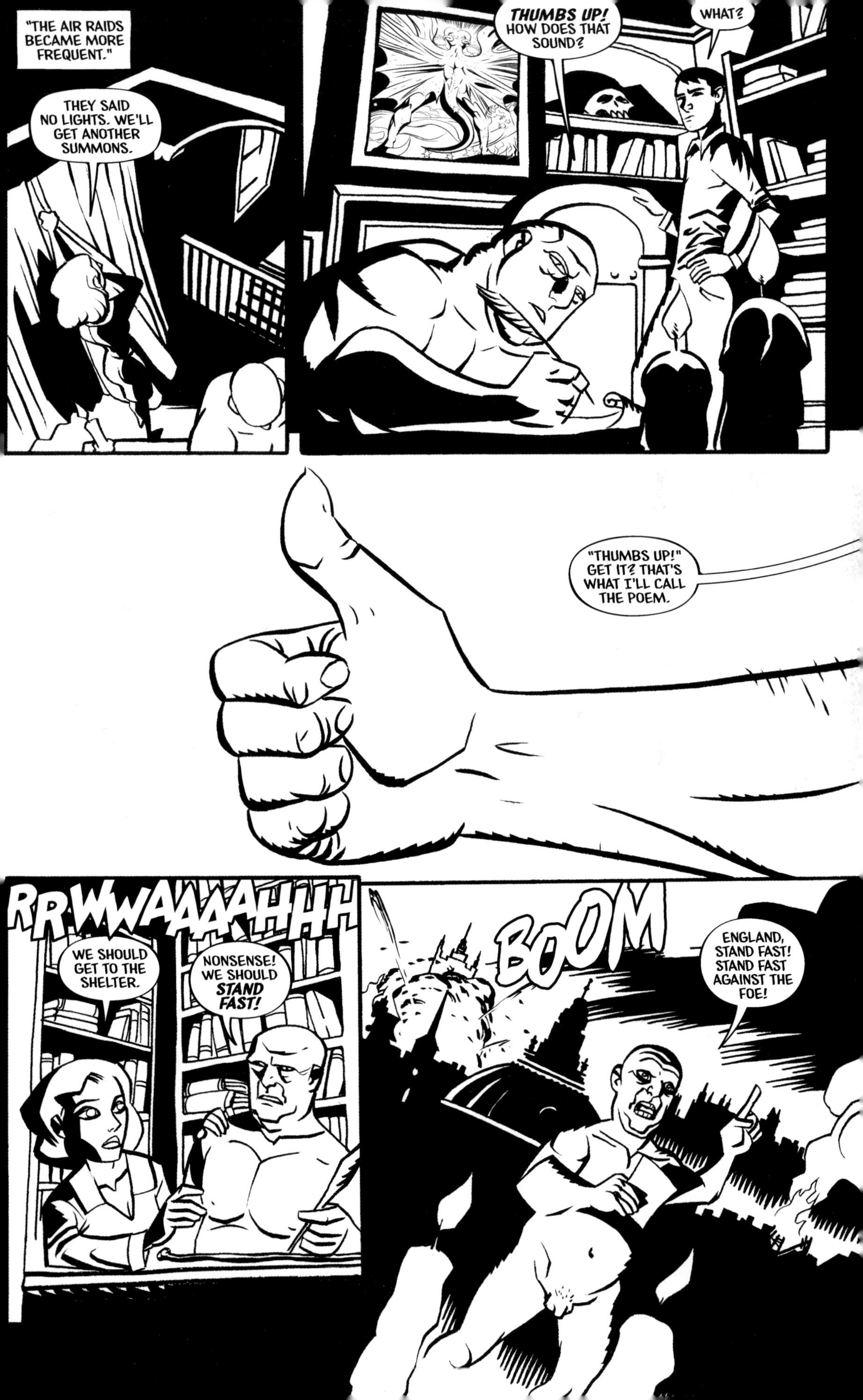
"THE AIR RAIDS BECAME MORE FREQUENT."
THEY SAID NO LIGHTS. WE'LL GET ANOTHER SUMMONS.
THUMBS UP! HOW DOES THAT SOUND?
WHAT?
"THUMBS UP!" GET IT? THAT'S WHAT I'LL CALL THE POEM.
RRWWAAAAHHH
WE SHOULD GET TO THE SHELTER.
NONSENSE! WE SHOULD STAND FAST!
BOOM
ENGLAND, STAND FAST! STAND FAST AGAINST THE FOE!

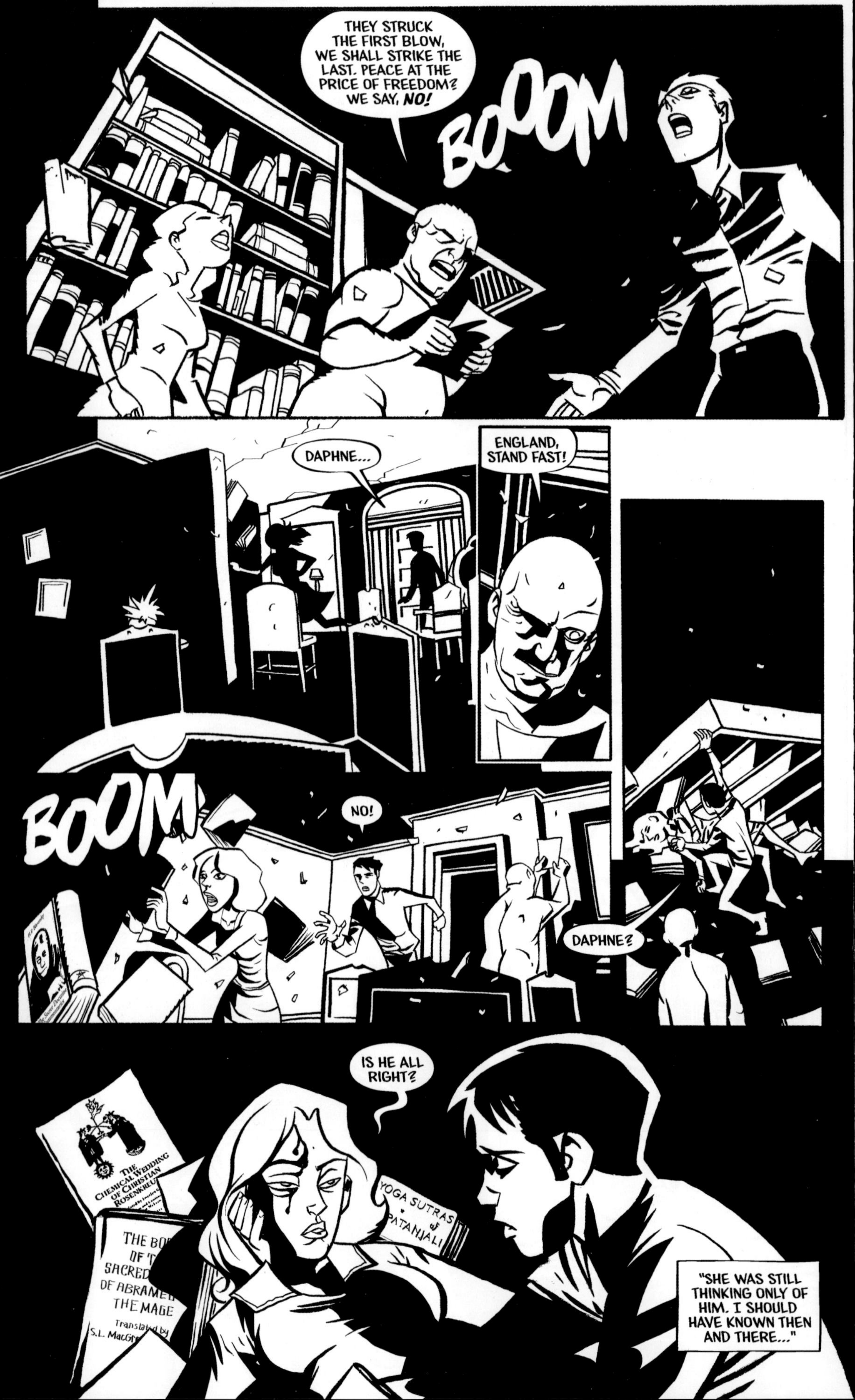
THEY STRUCK THE FIRST BLOW, WE SHALL STRIKE THE LAST. PEACE AT THE PRICE OF FREEDOM? WE SAY, NO!
BOOOM
DAPHNE...
ENGLAND, STAND FAST!
BOOM
NO!
DAPHNE?
IS HE ALL RIGHT?
THE CHEMICAL WEDDING OF CHRISTIAN
YOGA SUTRAS of PATANJALI
THE MAGE
"SHE WAS STILL THINKING ONLY OF HIM. I SHOULD HAVE KNOWN THEN AND THERE..."

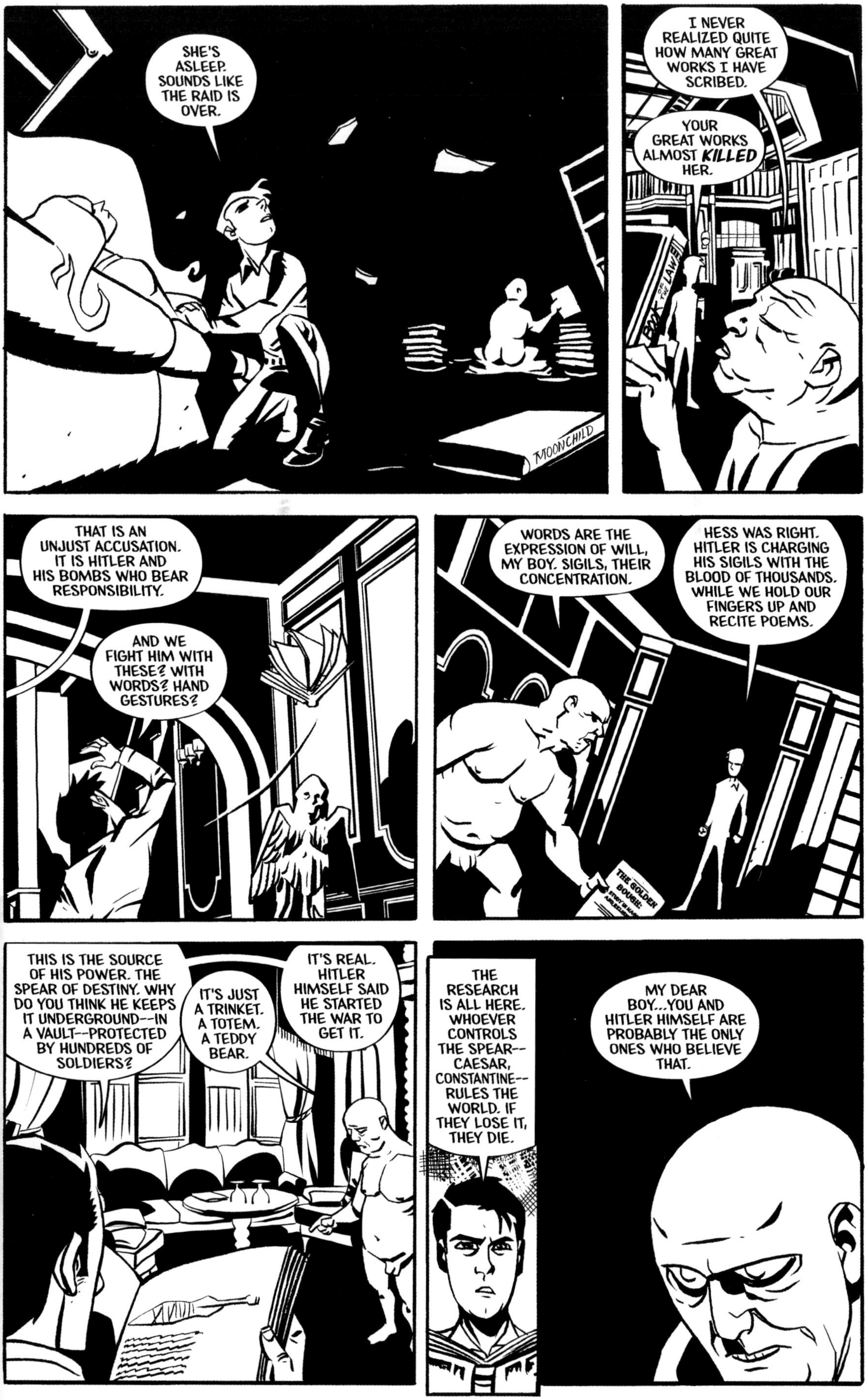
SHE'S ASLEEP. SOUNDS LIKE THE RAID IS OVER.
MOONCHILD
I NEVER REALIZED QUITE HOW MANY GREAT WORKS I HAVE SCRIBED.
YOUR GREAT WORKS ALMOST KILLED HER.
BOOK OF THE LAW
THAT IS AN UNJUST ACCUSATION. IT IS HITLER AND HIS BOMBS WHO BEAR RESPONSIBILITY.
AND WE FIGHT HIM WITH THESE? WITH WORDS? HAND GESTURES?
WORDS ARE THE EXPRESSION OF WILL, MY BOY. SIGILS, THEIR CONCENTRATION.
HESS WAS RIGHT. HITLER IS CHARGING HIS SIGILS WITH THE BLOOD OF THOUSANDS. WHILE WE HOLD OUR FINGERS UP AND RECITE POEMS.
THE GOLDEN BOUGH:
THIS IS THE SOURCE OF HIS POWER. THE SPEAR OF DESTINY. WHY DO YOU THINK HE KEEPS IT UNDERGROUND--IN A VAULT--PROTECTED BY HUNDREDS OF SOLDIERS?
IT'S JUST A TRINKET. A TOTEM. A TEDDY BEAR.
IT'S REAL. HITLER HIMSELF SAID HE STARTED THE WAR TO GET IT.
THE RESEARCH IS ALL HERE. WHOEVER CONTROLS THE SPEAR--CAESAR, CONSTANTINE--RULES THE WORLD. IF THEY LOSE IT, THEY DIE.
MY DEAR BOY... YOU AND HITLER HIMSELF ARE PROBABLY THE ONLY ONES WHO BELIEVE THAT.

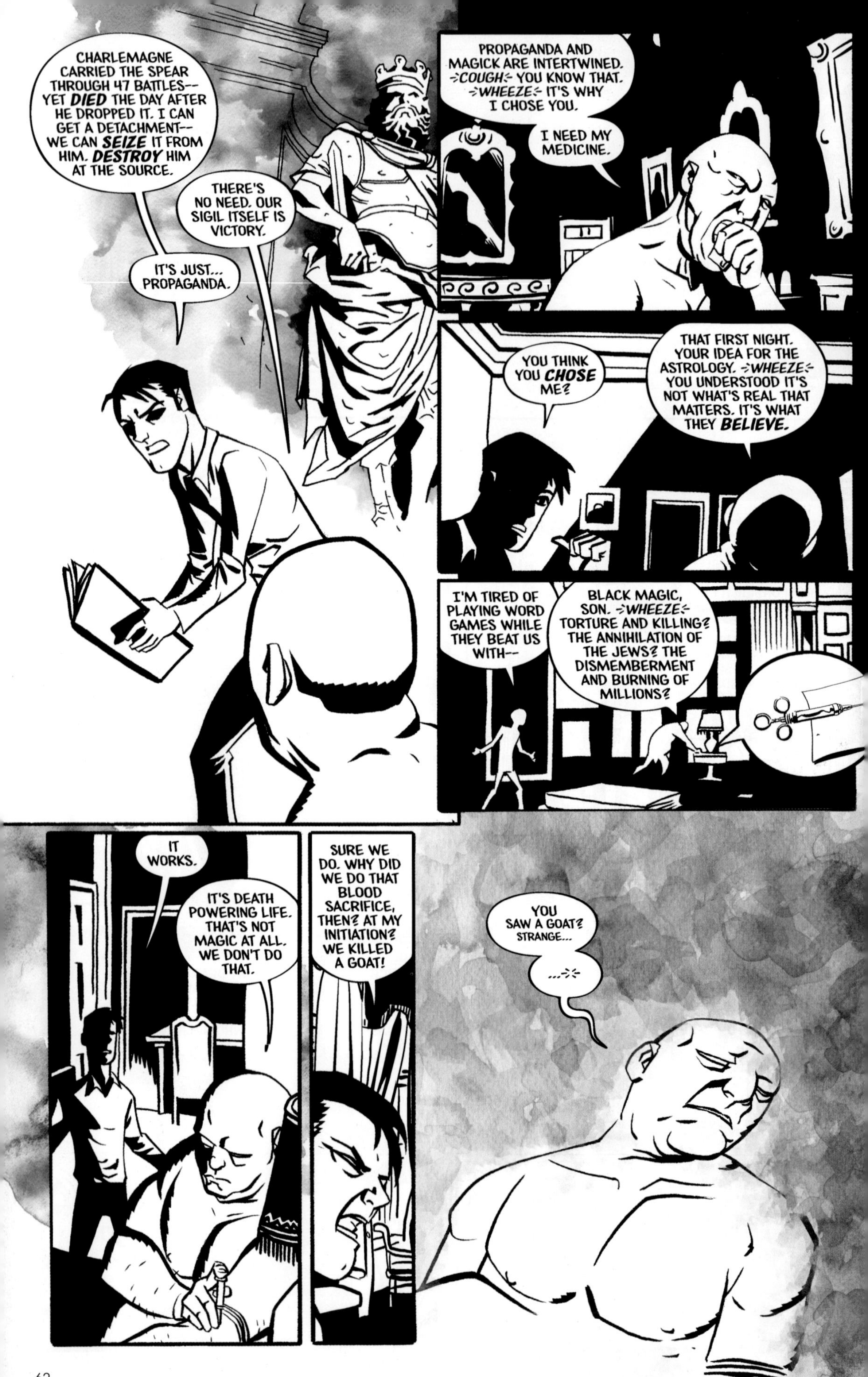
CHARLEMAGNE CARRIED THE SPEAR THROUGH 47 BATTLES-- YET DIED THE DAY AFTER HE DROPPED IT. I CAN GET A DETACHMENT-- WE CAN SEIZE IT FROM HIM. DESTROY HIM AT THE SOURCE.
THERE'S NO NEED. OUR SIGIL ITSELF IS VICTORY.
IT'S JUST... PROPAGANDA.
PROPAGANDA AND MAGICK ARE INTERTWINED. -COUGH- YOU KNOW THAT. -WHEEZE- IT'S WHY I CHOSE YOU.
I NEED MY MEDICINE.
YOU THINK YOU CHOSE ME?
THAT FIRST NIGHT. YOUR IDEA FOR THE ASTROLOGY. -WHEEZE- YOU UNDERSTOOD IT'S NOT WHAT'S REAL THAT MATTERS. IT'S WHAT THEY BELIEVE.
I'M TIRED OF PLAYING WORD GAMES WHILE THEY BEAT US WITH--
BLACK MAGIC, SON. -WHEEZE- TORTURE AND KILLING? THE ANNIHILATION OF THE JEWS? THE DISMEMBERMENT AND BURNING OF MILLIONS?
IT WORKS.
IT'S DEATH POWERING LIFE. THAT'S NOT MAGIC AT ALL. WE DON'T DO THAT.
SURE WE DO. WHY DID WE DO THAT BLOOD SACRIFICE, THEN? AT MY INITIATION? WE KILLED A GOAT!
YOU SAW A GOAT? STRANGE...
...-:-

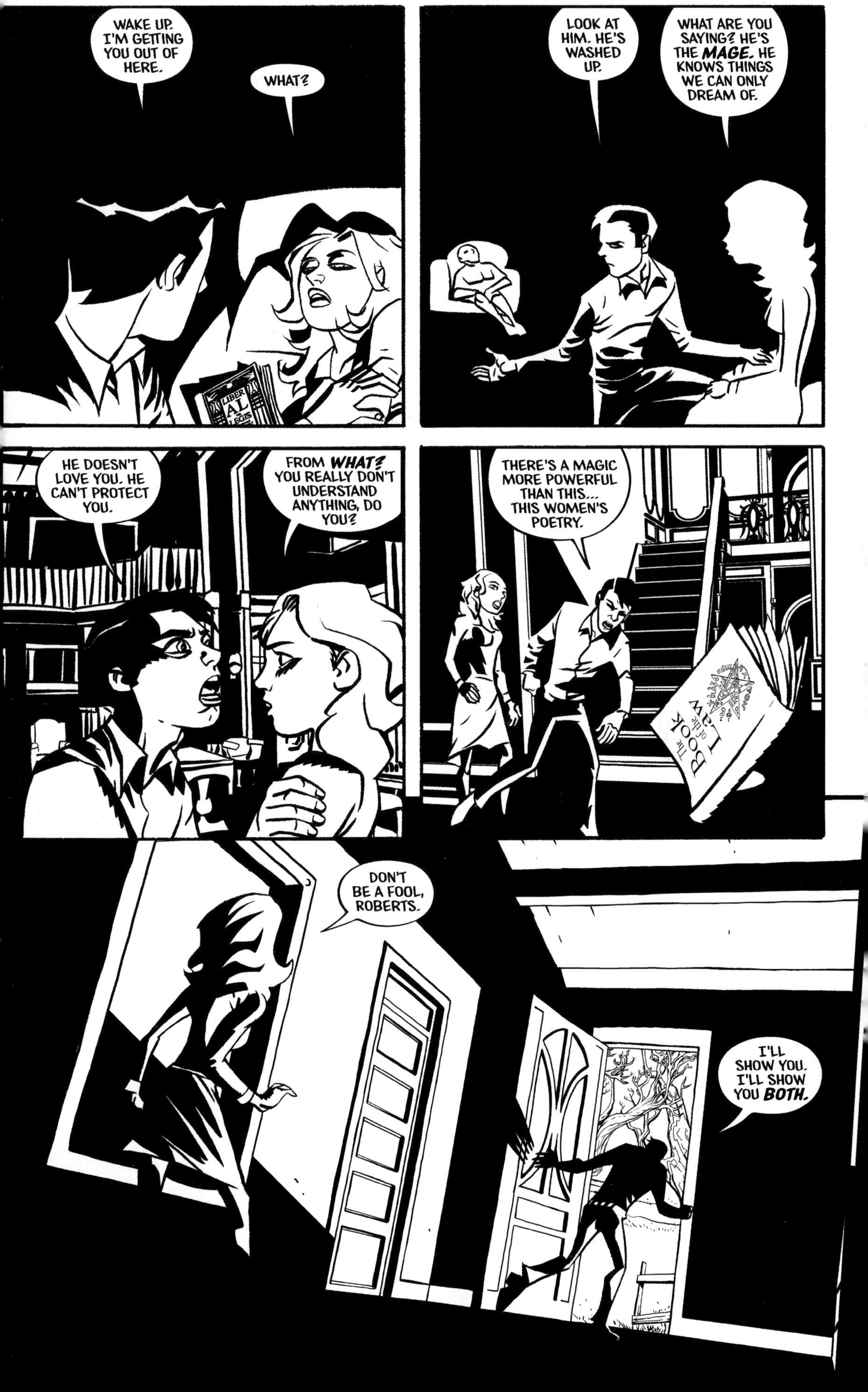
WAKE UP. I'M GETTING YOU OUT OF HERE.
WHAT?
LIBER AL LEGIS
LOOK AT HIM. HE'S WASHED UP.
WHAT ARE YOU SAYING? HE'S THE MAGE. HE KNOWS THINGS WE CAN ONLY DREAM OF.
HE DOESN'T LOVE YOU. HE CAN'T PROTECT YOU.
FROM WHAT? YOU REALLY DON'T UNDERSTAND ANYTHING, DO YOU?
THERE'S A MAGIC MORE POWERFUL THAN THIS... THIS WOMEN'S POETRY.
The BOOK of the LAW
DON'T BE A FOOL, ROBERTS.
I'LL SHOW YOU. I'LL SHOW YOU BOTH.

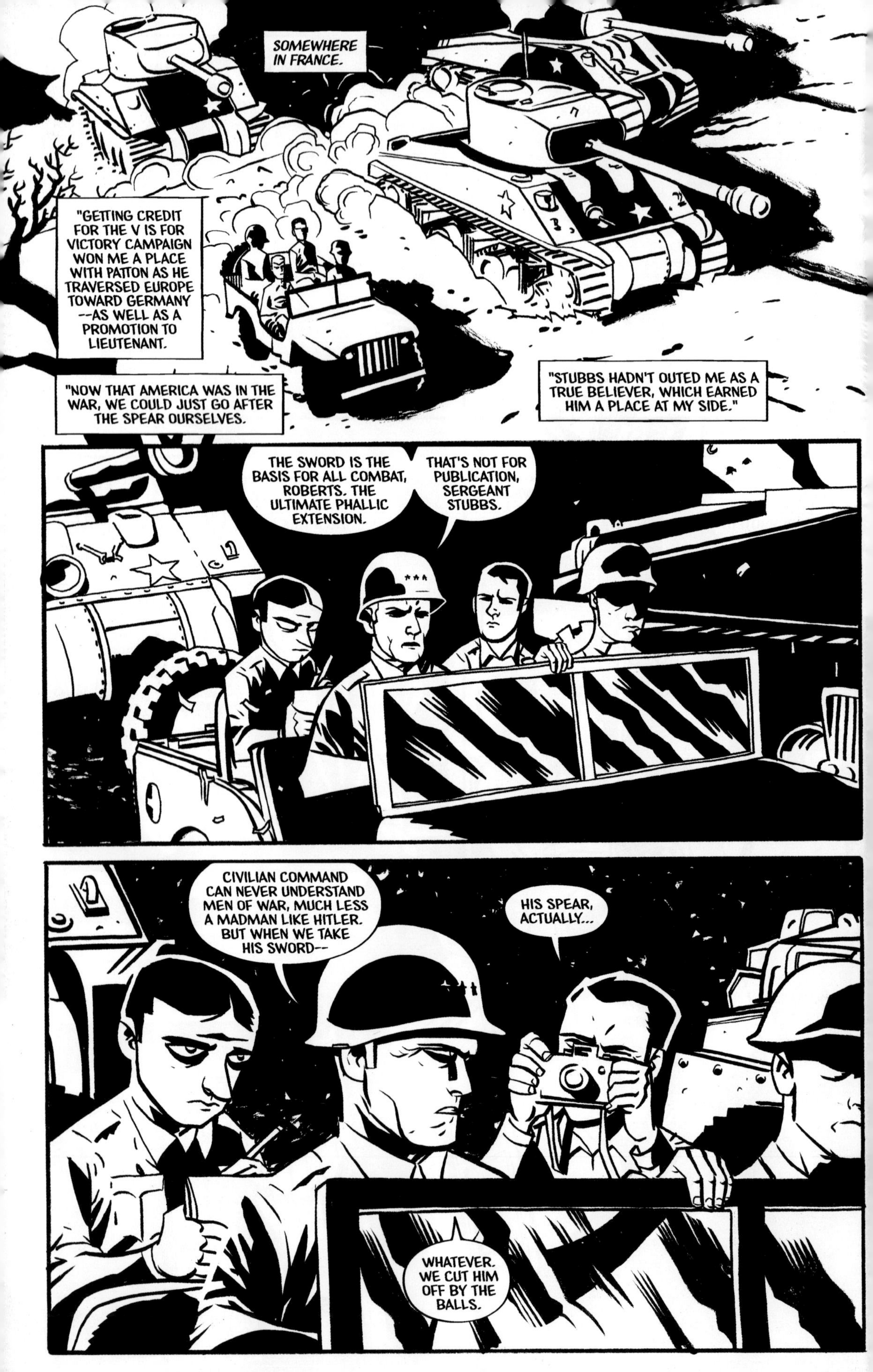
SOMEWHERE IN FRANCE.
"GETTING CREDIT FOR THE V IS FOR VICTORY CAMPAIGN WON ME A PLACE WITH PATTON AS HE TRAVERSED EUROPE TOWARD GERMANY --AS WELL AS A PROMOTION TO LIEUTENANT.
"NOW THAT AMERICA WAS IN THE WAR, WE COULD JUST GO AFTER THE SPEAR OURSELVES.
"STUBBS HADN'T OUTED ME AS A TRUE BELIEVER, WHICH EARNED HIM A PLACE AT MY SIDE."
THE SWORD IS THE BASIS FOR ALL COMBAT, ROBERTS. THE ULTIMATE PHALLIC EXTENSION.
THAT'S NOT FOR PUBLICATION, SERGEANT STUBBS.
CIVILIAN COMMAND CAN NEVER UNDERSTAND MEN OF WAR, MUCH LESS A MADMAN LIKE HITLER. BUT WHEN WE TAKE HIS SWORD--
HIS SPEAR, ACTUALLY...
WHATEVER. WE CUT HIM OFF BY THE BALLS.

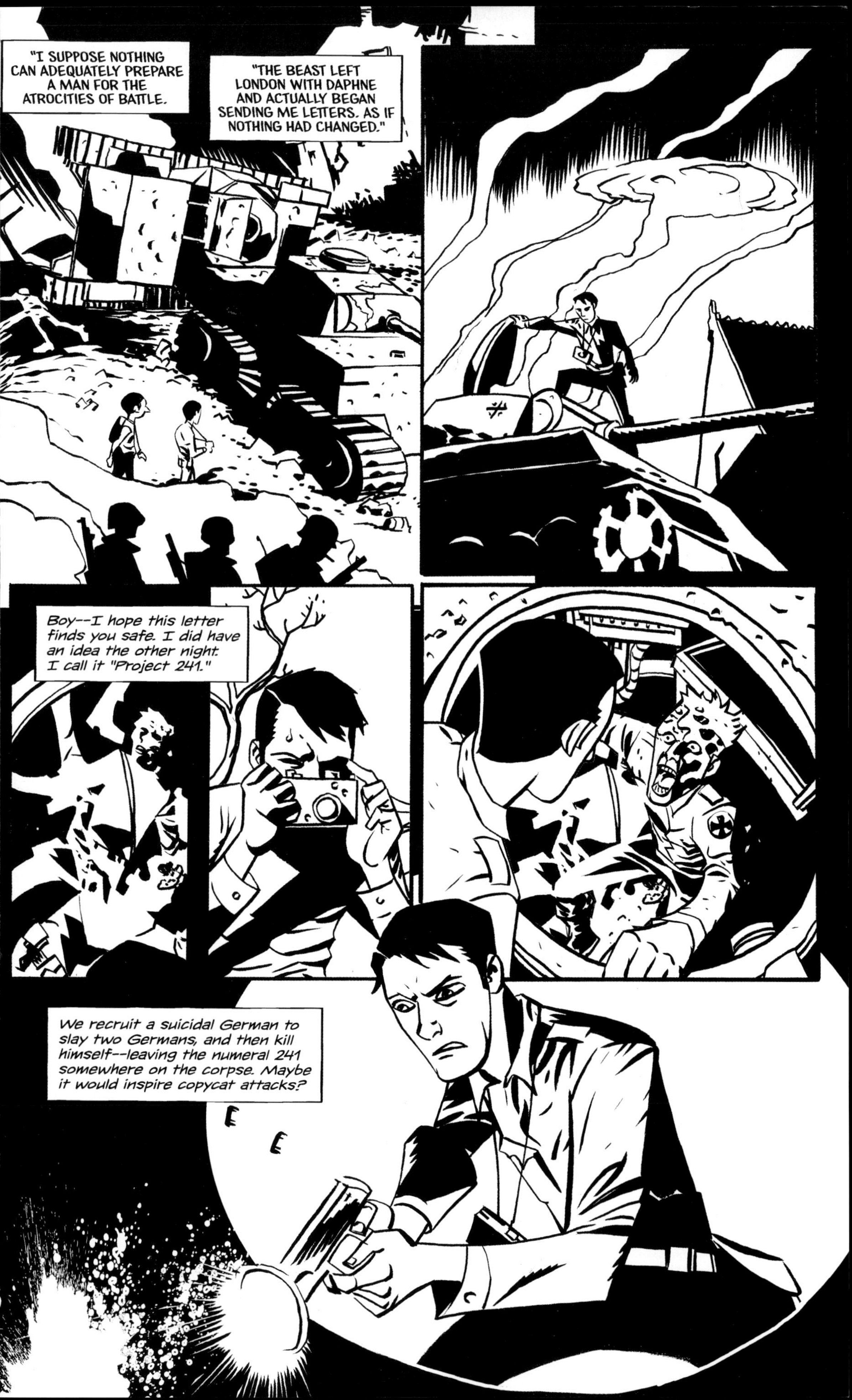
"I SUPPOSE NOTHING CAN ADEQUATELY PREPARE A MAN FOR THE ATROCITIES OF BATTLE.
"THE BEAST LEFT LONDON WITH DAPHNE AND ACTUALLY BEGAN SENDING ME LETTERS. AS IF NOTHING HAD CHANGED."
Boy--I hope this letter finds you safe. I did have an idea the other night. I call it "Project 241."
We recruit a suicidal German to slay two Germans, and then kill himself--leaving the numeral 241 somewhere on the corpse. Maybe it would inspire copycat attacks?
E
E

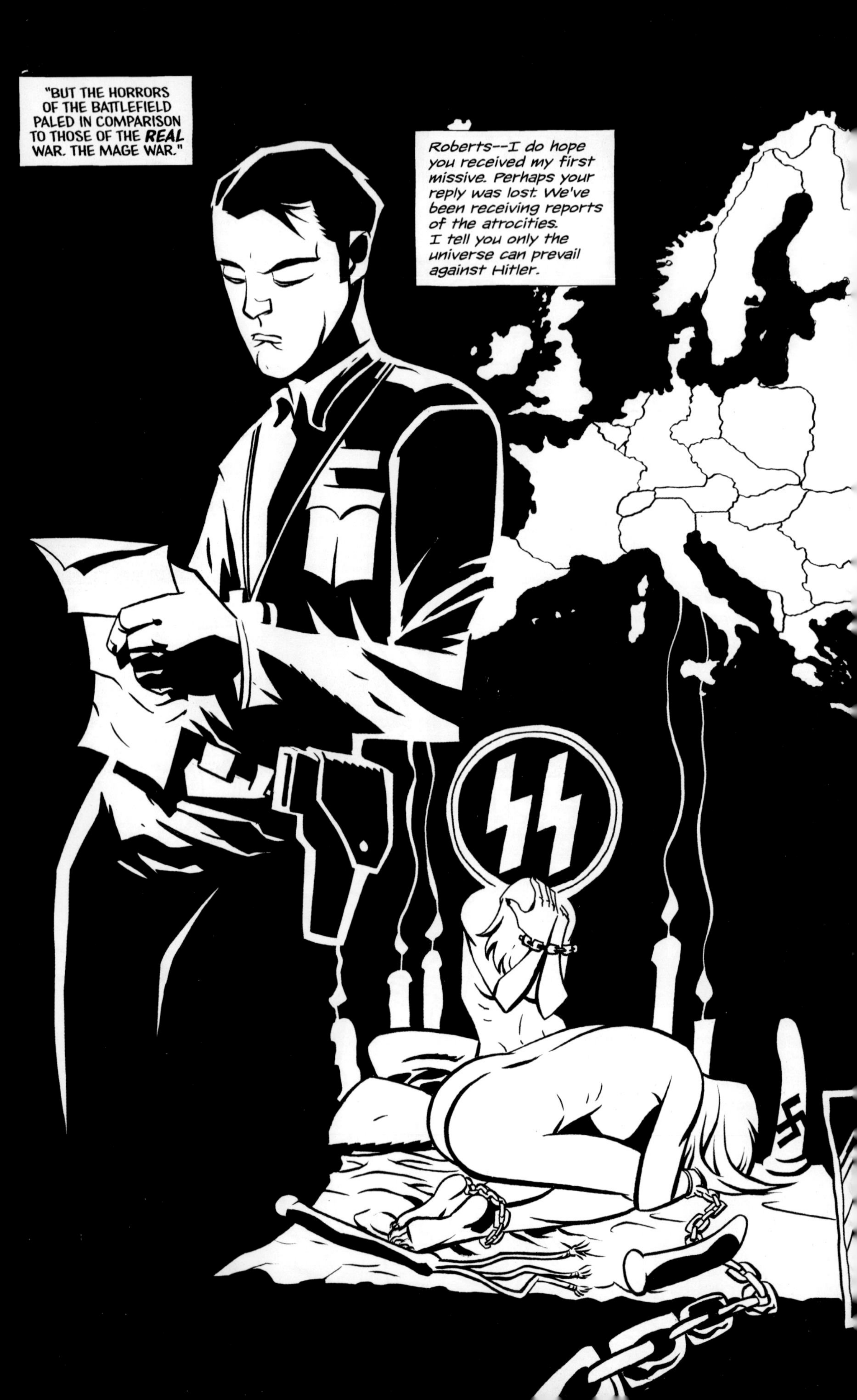
"BUT THE HORRORS OF THE BATTLEFIELD PALED IN COMPARISON TO THOSE OF THE REAL WAR. THE MAGE WAR."
Roberts--I do hope you received my first missive. Perhaps your reply was lost. We've been receiving reports of the atrocities. I tell you only the universe can prevail against Hitler.

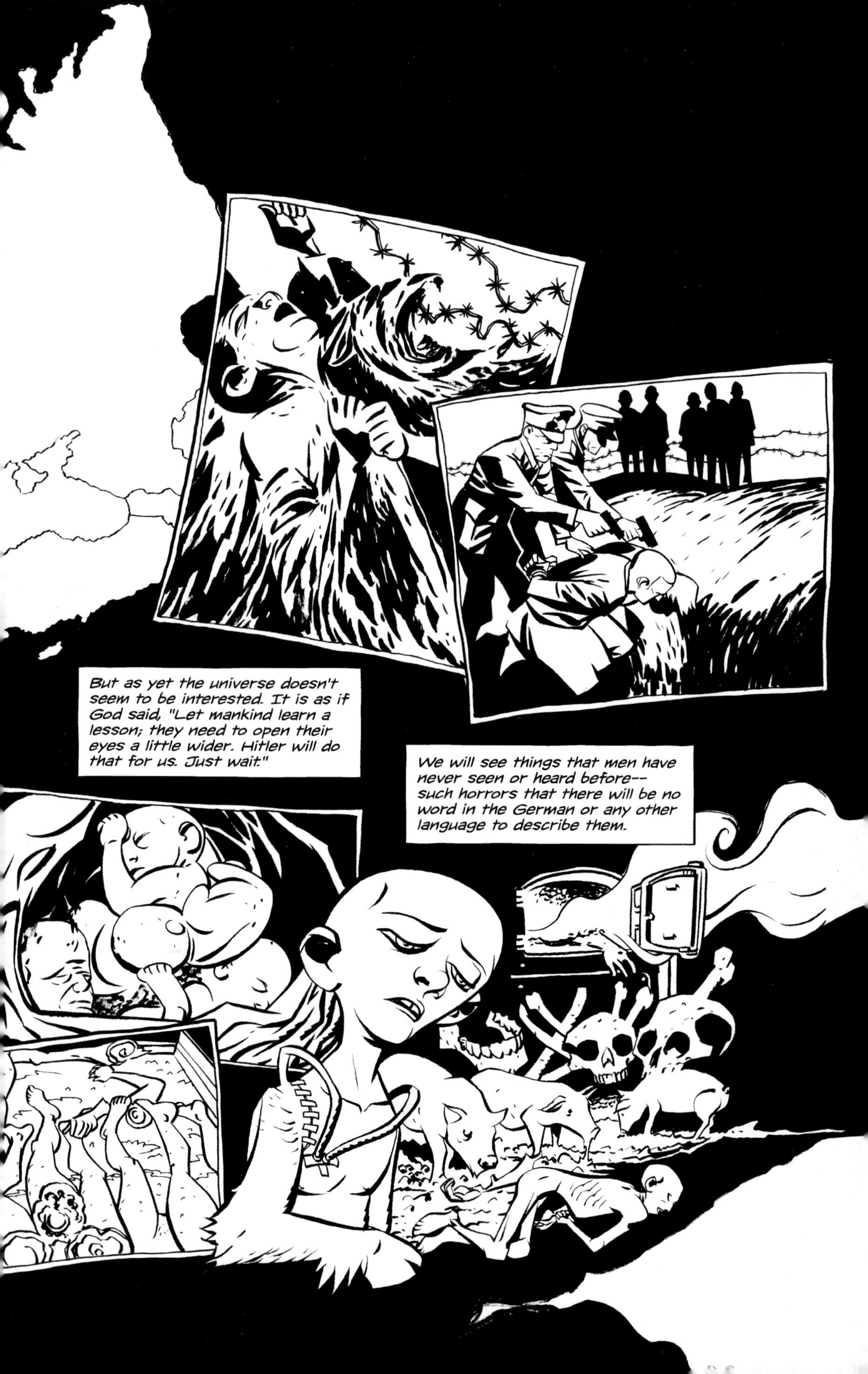
But as yet the universe doesn't seem to be interested. It is as if God said, "Let mankind learn a lesson; they need to open their eyes a little wider. Hitler will do that for us. Just wait."
We will see things that men have never seen or heard before-- such horrors that there will be no word in the German or any other language to describe them.

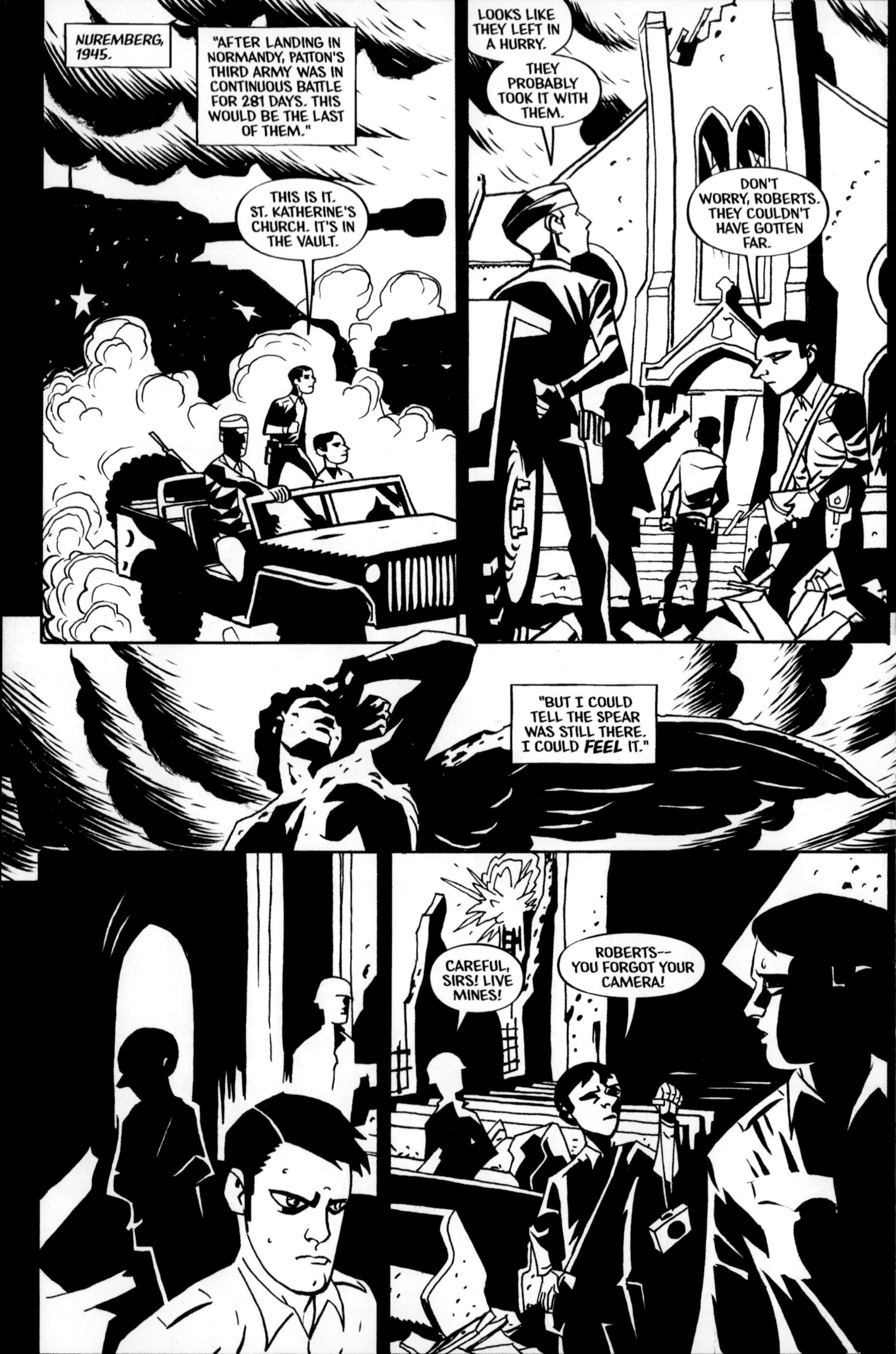
NUREMBERG, 1945.
"AFTER LANDING IN NORMANDY, PATTON'S THIRD ARMY WAS IN CONTINUOUS BATTLE FOR 281 DAYS. THIS WOULD BE THE LAST OF THEM."
THIS IS IT. ST. KATHERINE'S CHURCH. IT'S IN THE VAULT.
LOOKS LIKE THEY LEFT IN A HURRY.
THEY PROBABLY TOOK IT WITH THEM.
DON'T WORRY, ROBERTS. THEY COULDN'T HAVE GOTTEN FAR.
"BUT I COULD TELL THE SPEAR WAS STILL THERE. I COULD FEEL IT."
CAREFUL, SIRS! LIVE MINES!
ROBERTS-- YOU FORGOT YOUR CAMERA!

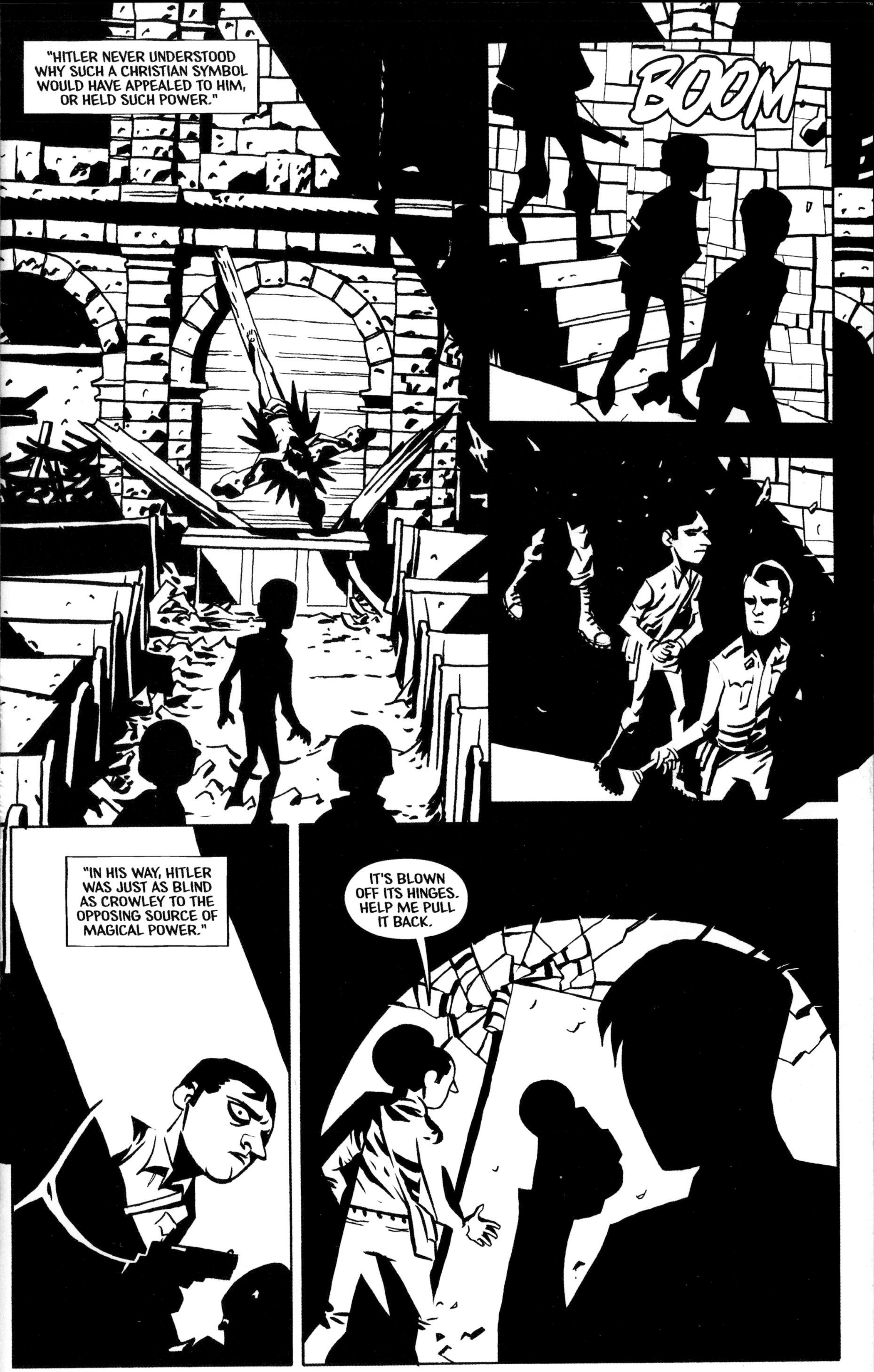
"HITLER NEVER UNDERSTOOD WHY SUCH A CHRISTIAN SYMBOL WOULD HAVE APPEALED TO HIM, OR HELD SUCH POWER."
BOOM
"IN HIS WAY, HITLER WAS JUST AS BLIND AS CROWLEY TO THE OPPOSING SOURCE OF MAGICAL POWER."
IT'S BLOWN OFF ITS HINGES. HELP ME PULL IT BACK.

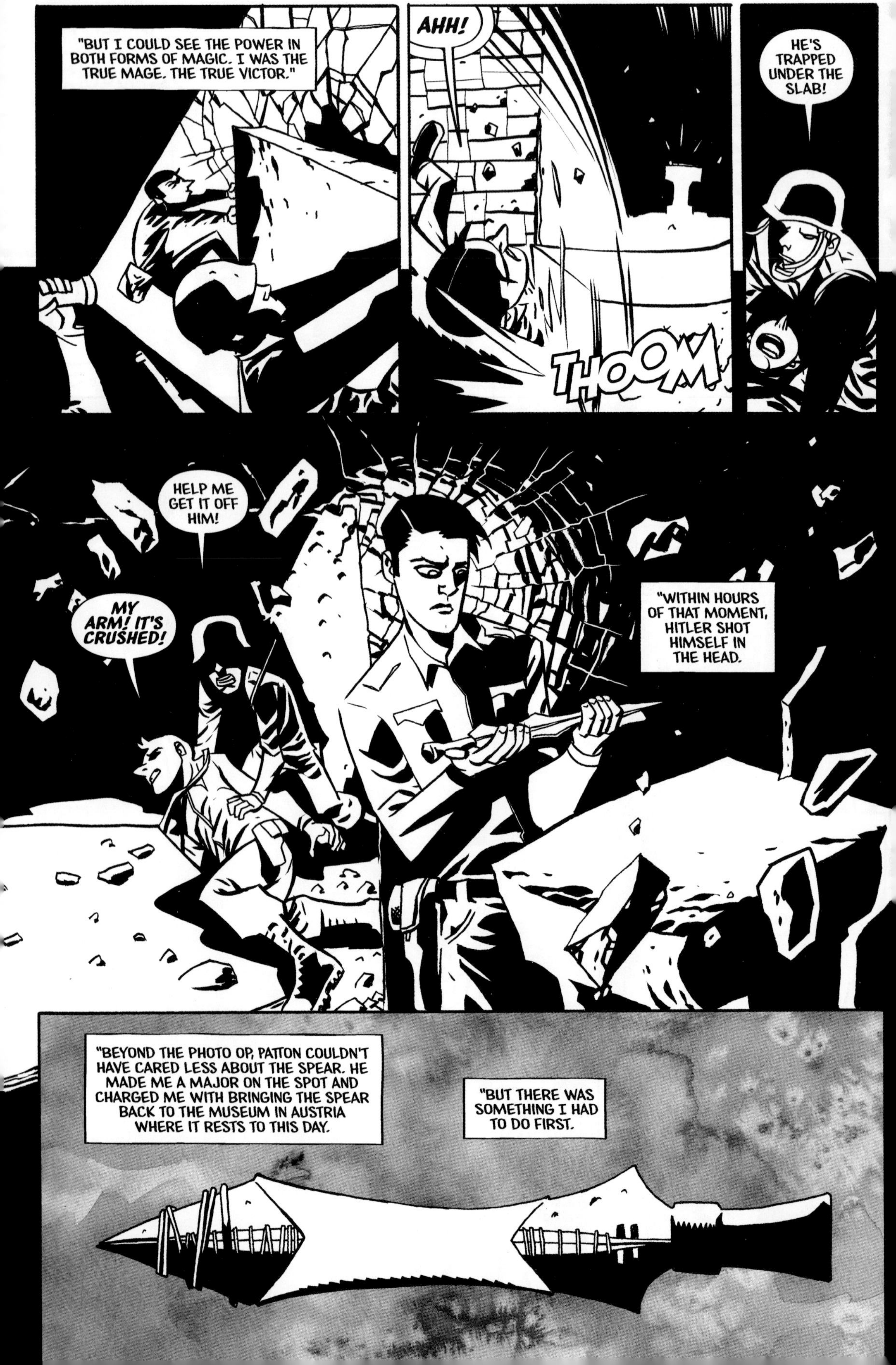
"BUT I COULD SEE THE POWER IN BOTH FORMS OF MAGIC. I WAS THE TRUE MAGE. THE TRUE VICTOR."
AHH!
THOOM
HE'S TRAPPED UNDER THE SLAB!
HELP ME GET IT OFF HIM!
MY ARM! IT'S CRUSHED!
"WITHIN HOURS OF THAT MOMENT, HITLER SHOT HIMSELF IN THE HEAD.
"BEYOND THE PHOTO OP, PATTON COULDN'T HAVE CARED LESS ABOUT THE SPEAR. HE MADE ME A MAJOR ON THE SPOT AND CHARGED ME WITH BRINGING THE SPEAR BACK TO THE MUSEUM IN AUSTRIA WHERE IT RESTS TO THIS DAY.
"BUT THERE WAS SOMETHING I HAD TO DO FIRST.

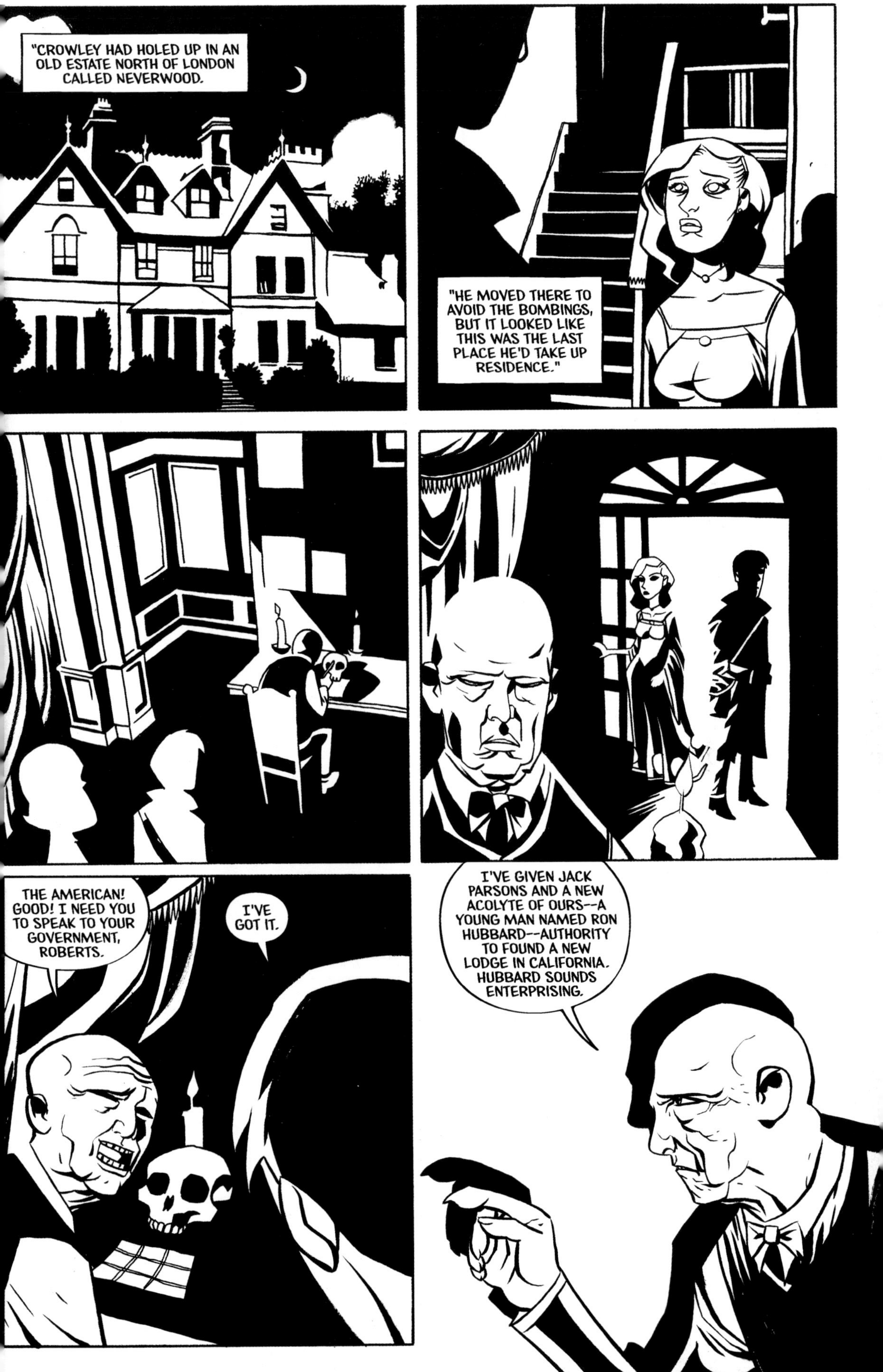
"CROWLEY HAD HOLED UP IN AN OLD ESTATE NORTH OF LONDON CALLED NEVERWOOD.
"HE MOVED THERE TO AVOID THE BOMBINGS, BUT IT LOOKED LIKE THIS WAS THE LAST PLACE HE'D TAKE UP RESIDENCE."
THE AMERICAN! GOOD! I NEED YOU TO SPEAK TO YOUR GOVERNMENT, ROBERTS.
I'VE GOT IT.
I'VE GIVEN JACK PARSONS AND A NEW ACOLYTE OF OURS--A YOUNG MAN NAMED RON HUBBARD--AUTHORITY TO FOUND A NEW LODGE IN CALIFORNIA. HUBBARD SOUNDS ENTERPRISING.

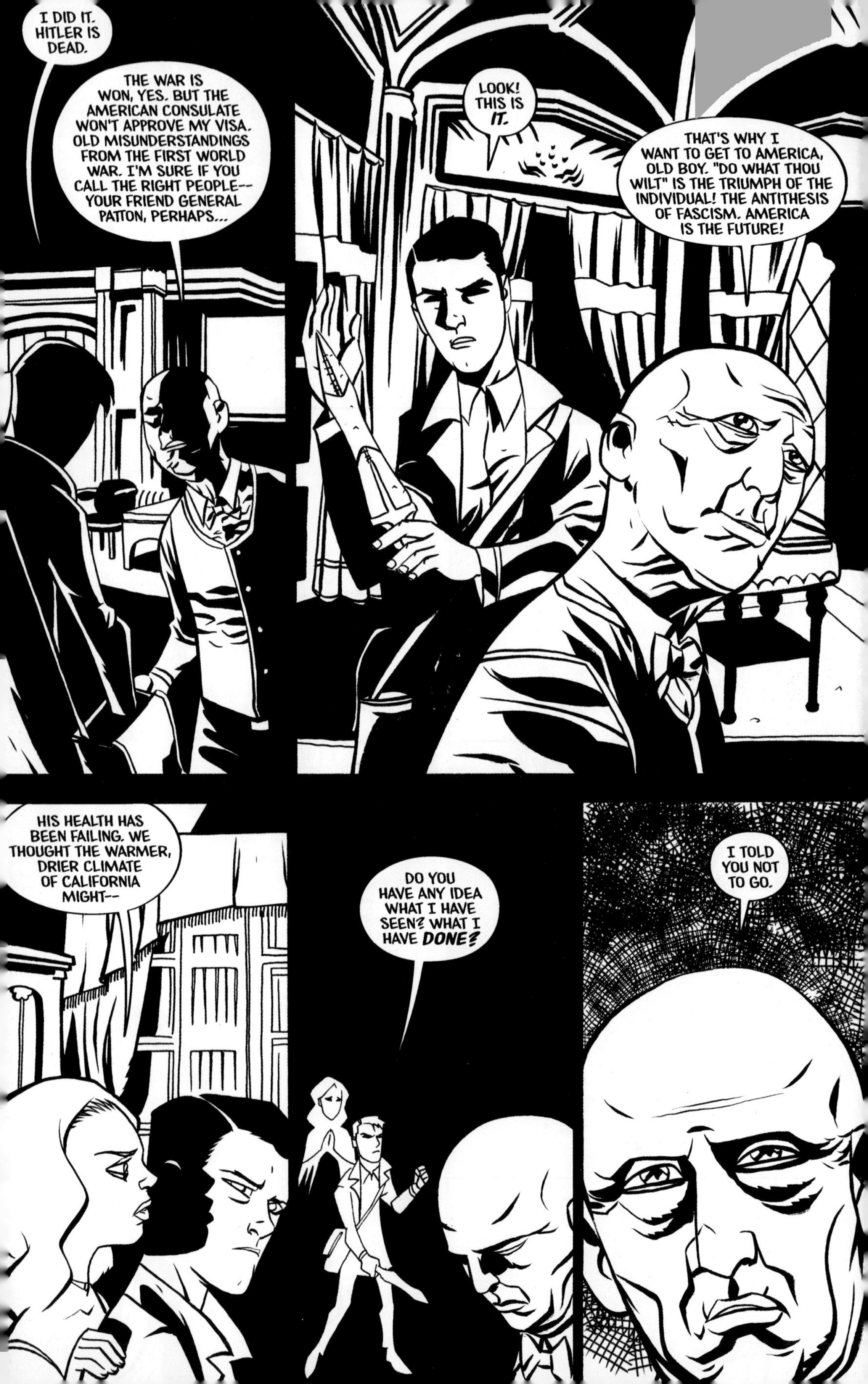
I DID IT. HITLER IS DEAD.
THE WAR IS WON, YES. BUT THE AMERICAN CONSULATE WON'T APPROVE MY VISA. OLD MISUNDERSTANDINGS FROM THE FIRST WORLD WAR. I'M SURE IF YOU CALL THE RIGHT PEOPLE-- YOUR FRIEND GENERAL PATTON, PERHAPS...
LOOK! THIS IS *IT.*
THAT'S WHY I WANT TO GET TO AMERICA, OLD BOY. "DO WHAT THOU WILT" IS THE TRIUMPH OF THE INDIVIDUAL! THE ANTITHESIS OF FASCISM. AMERICA IS THE FUTURE!
HIS HEALTH HAS BEEN FAILING. WE THOUGHT THE WARMER, DRIER CLIMATE OF CALIFORNIA MIGHT--
DO YOU HAVE ANY IDEA WHAT I HAVE SEEN? WHAT I HAVE **DONE?**
I TOLD YOU NOT TO GO.

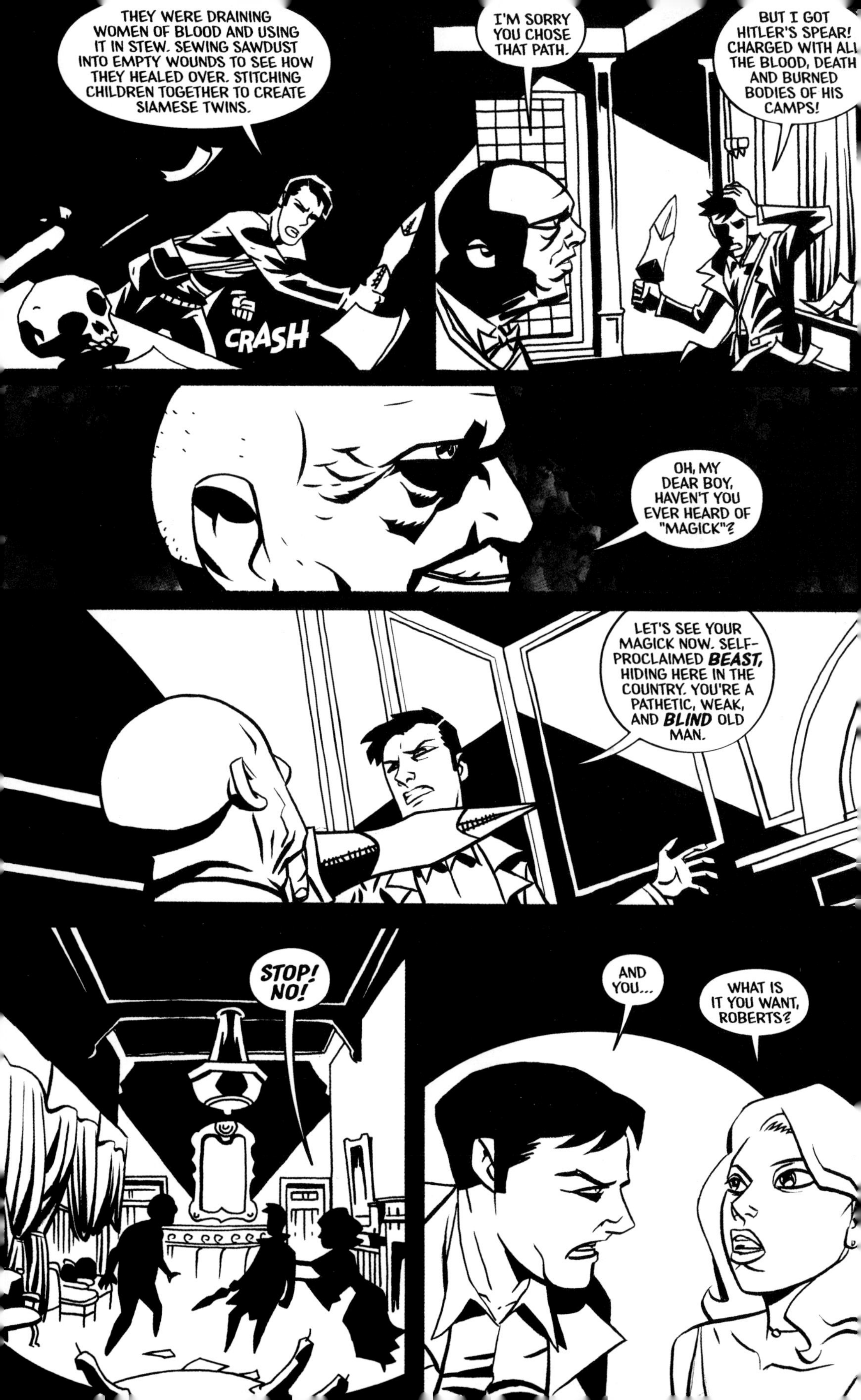
THEY WERE DRAINING WOMEN OF BLOOD AND USING IT IN STEW. SEWING SAWDUST INTO EMPTY WOUNDS TO SEE HOW THEY HEALED OVER. STITCHING CHILDREN TOGETHER TO CREATE SIAMESE TWINS.
CRASH
I'M SORRY YOU CHOSE THAT PATH.
BUT I GOT HITLER'S SPEAR! CHARGED WITH ALL THE BLOOD, DEATH AND BURNED BODIES OF HIS CAMPS!
OH, MY DEAR BOY, HAVEN'T YOU EVER HEARD OF "MAGICK"?
LET'S SEE YOUR MAGICK NOW. SELF-PROCLAIMED ***BEAST,*** HIDING HERE IN THE COUNTRY. YOU'RE A PATHETIC, WEAK, AND ***BLIND*** OLD MAN.
STOP! NO!
AND YOU...
WHAT IS IT YOU WANT, ROBERTS?

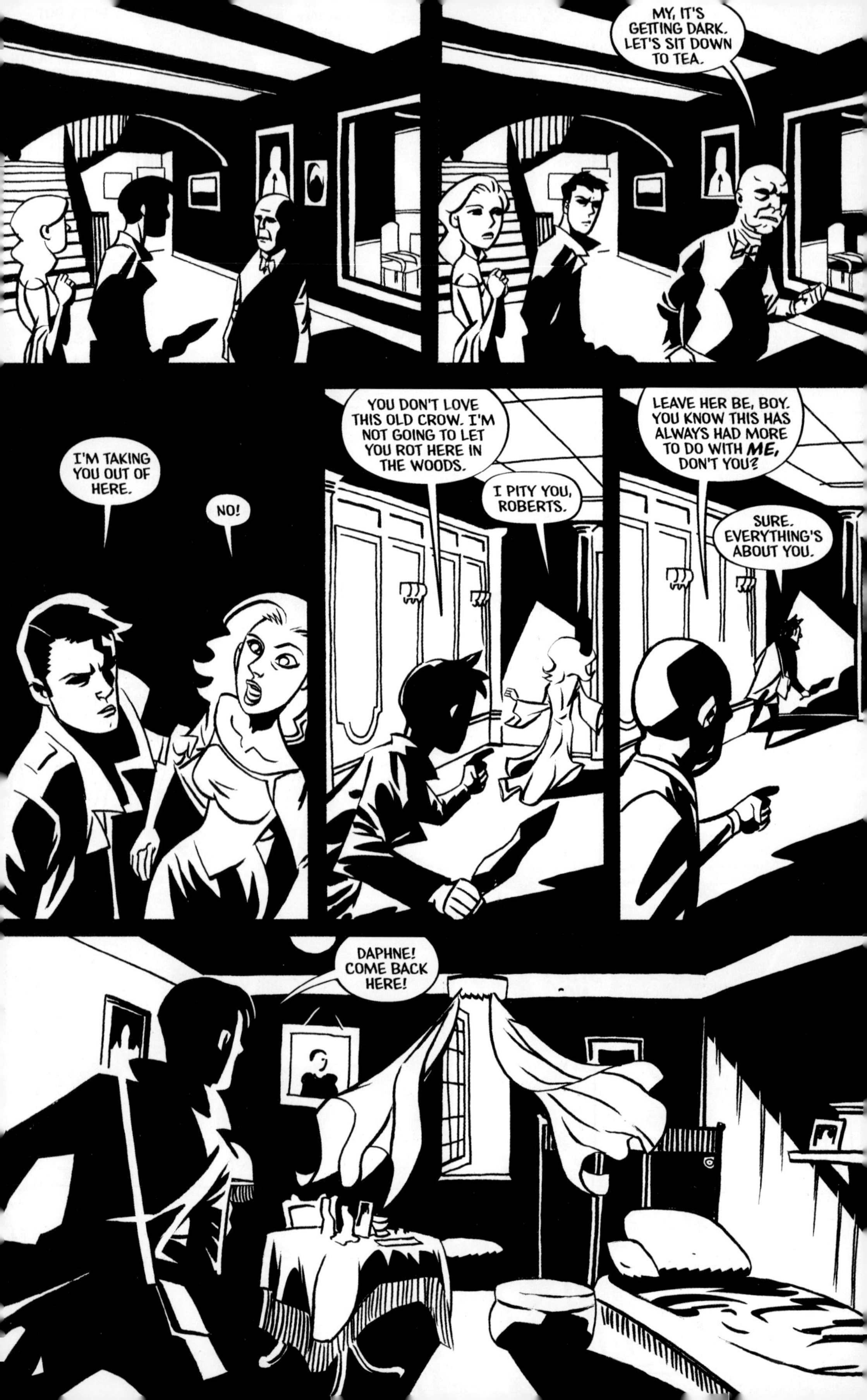
MY, IT'S GETTING DARK. LET'S SIT DOWN TO TEA.
I'M TAKING YOU OUT OF HERE.
NO!
YOU DON'T LOVE THIS OLD CROW. I'M NOT GOING TO LET YOU ROT HERE IN THE WOODS.
I PITY YOU, ROBERTS.
LEAVE HER BE, BOY. YOU KNOW THIS HAS ALWAYS HAD MORE TO DO WITH ME, DON'T YOU?
SURE. EVERYTHING'S ABOUT YOU.
DAPHNE! COME BACK HERE!

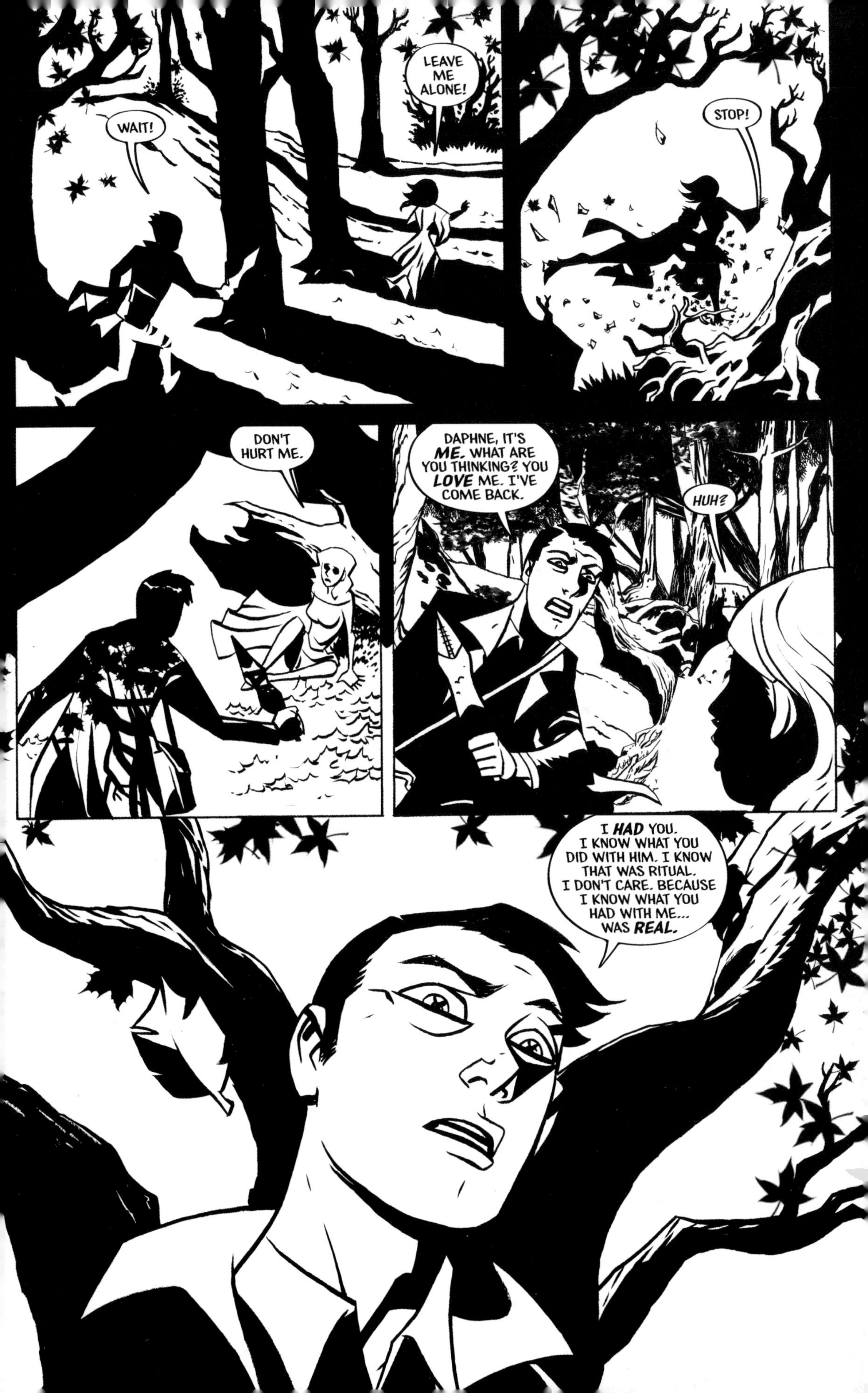
WAIT!
LEAVE ME ALONE!
STOP!
DON'T HURT ME.
DAPHNE, IT'S ME. WHAT ARE YOU THINKING? YOU LOVE ME. I'VE COME BACK.
HUH?
I HAD YOU. I KNOW WHAT YOU DID WITH HIM. I KNOW THAT WAS RITUAL. I DON'T CARE. BECAUSE I KNOW WHAT YOU HAD WITH ME... WAS REAL.

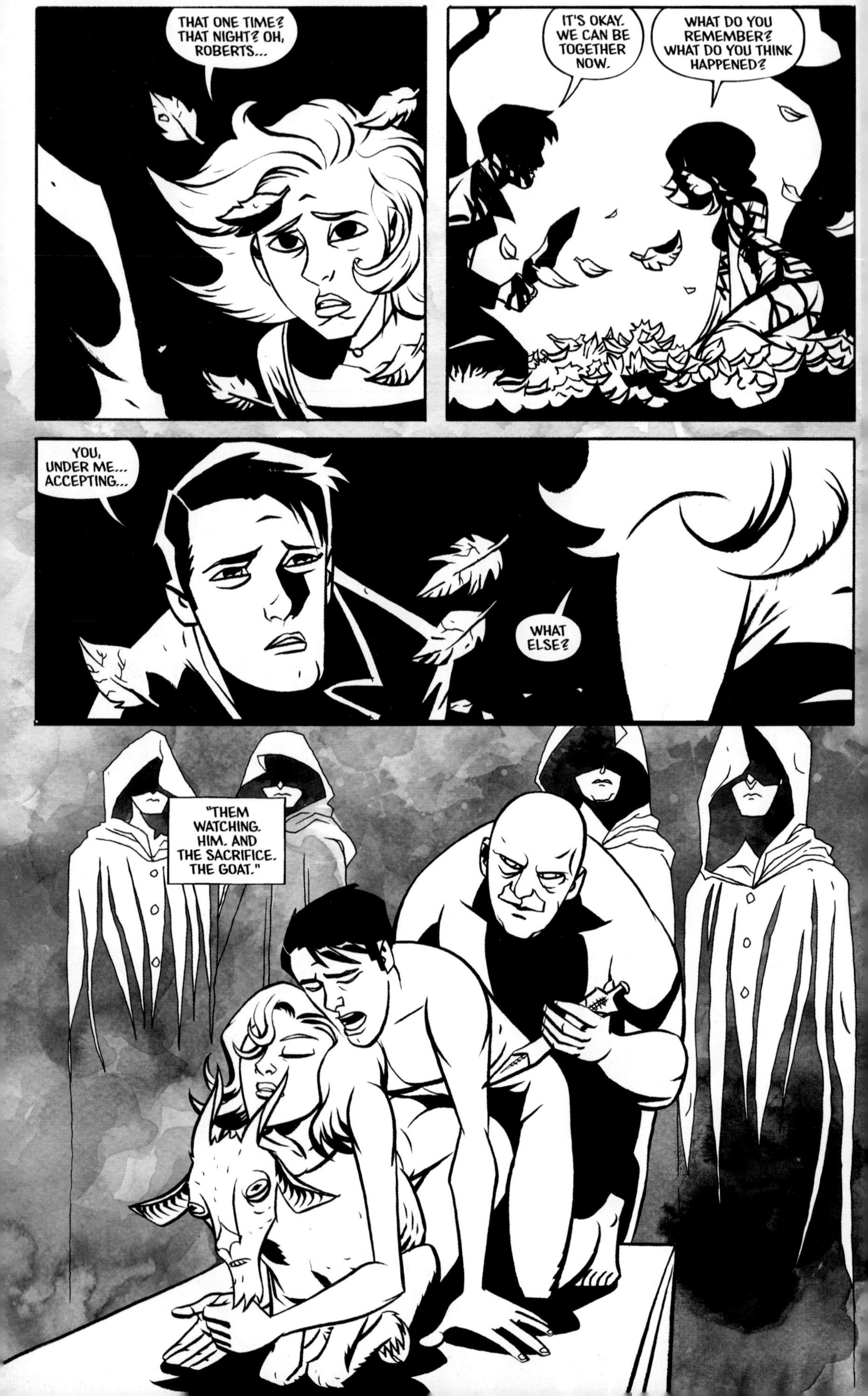
THAT ONE TIME? THAT NIGHT? OH, ROBERTS...
IT'S OKAY. WE CAN BE TOGETHER NOW.
WHAT DO YOU REMEMBER? WHAT DO YOU THINK HAPPENED?
YOU, UNDER ME... ACCEPTING...
WHAT ELSE?
"THEM WATCHING. HIM. AND THE SACRIFICE. THE GOAT."

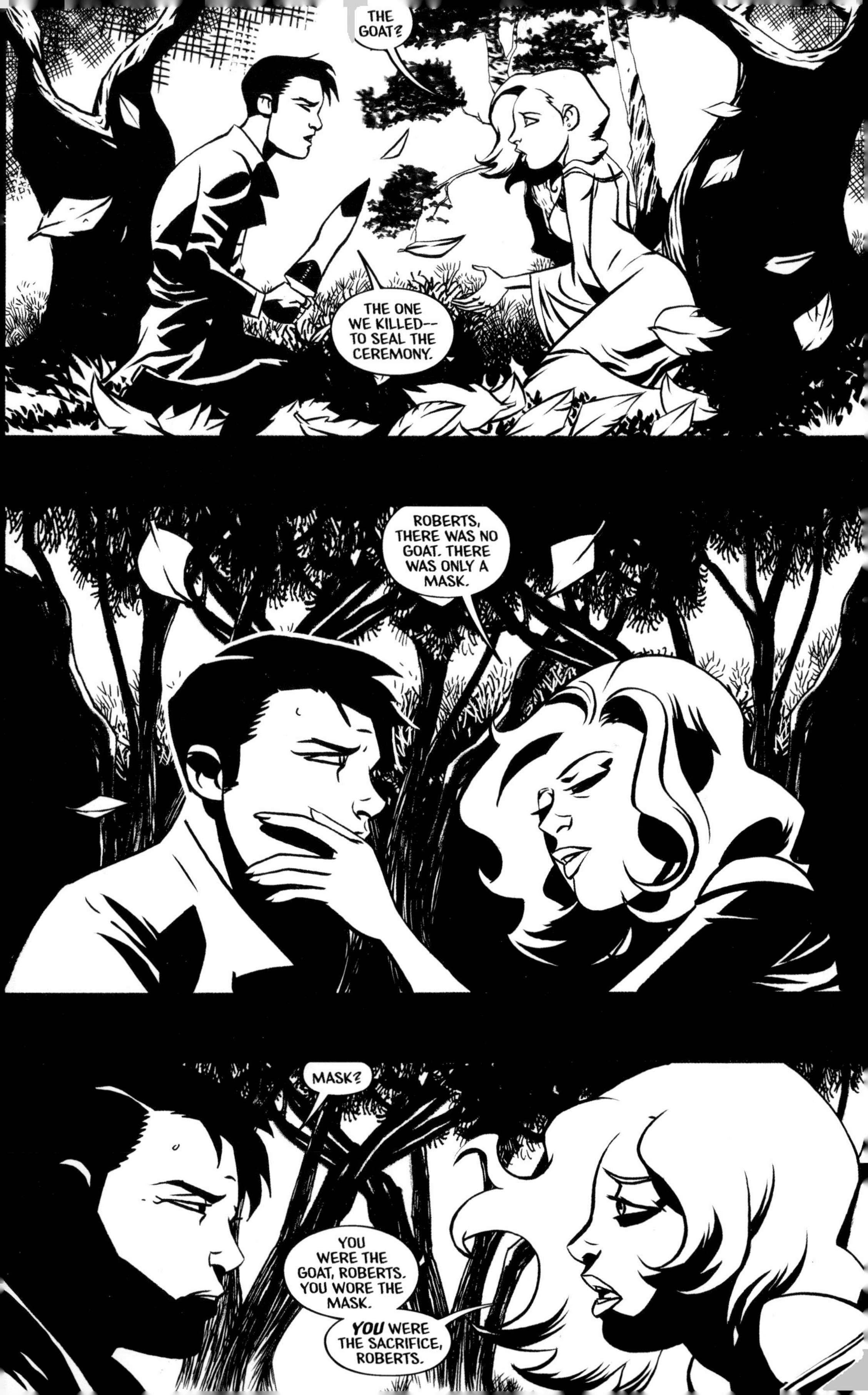
THE GOAT?
THE ONE WE KILLED-- TO SEAL THE CEREMONY.
ROBERTS, THERE WAS NO GOAT. THERE WAS ONLY A MASK.
MASK?
YOU WERE THE GOAT, ROBERTS. YOU WORE THE MASK.
*YOU* WERE THE SACRIFICE, ROBERTS.

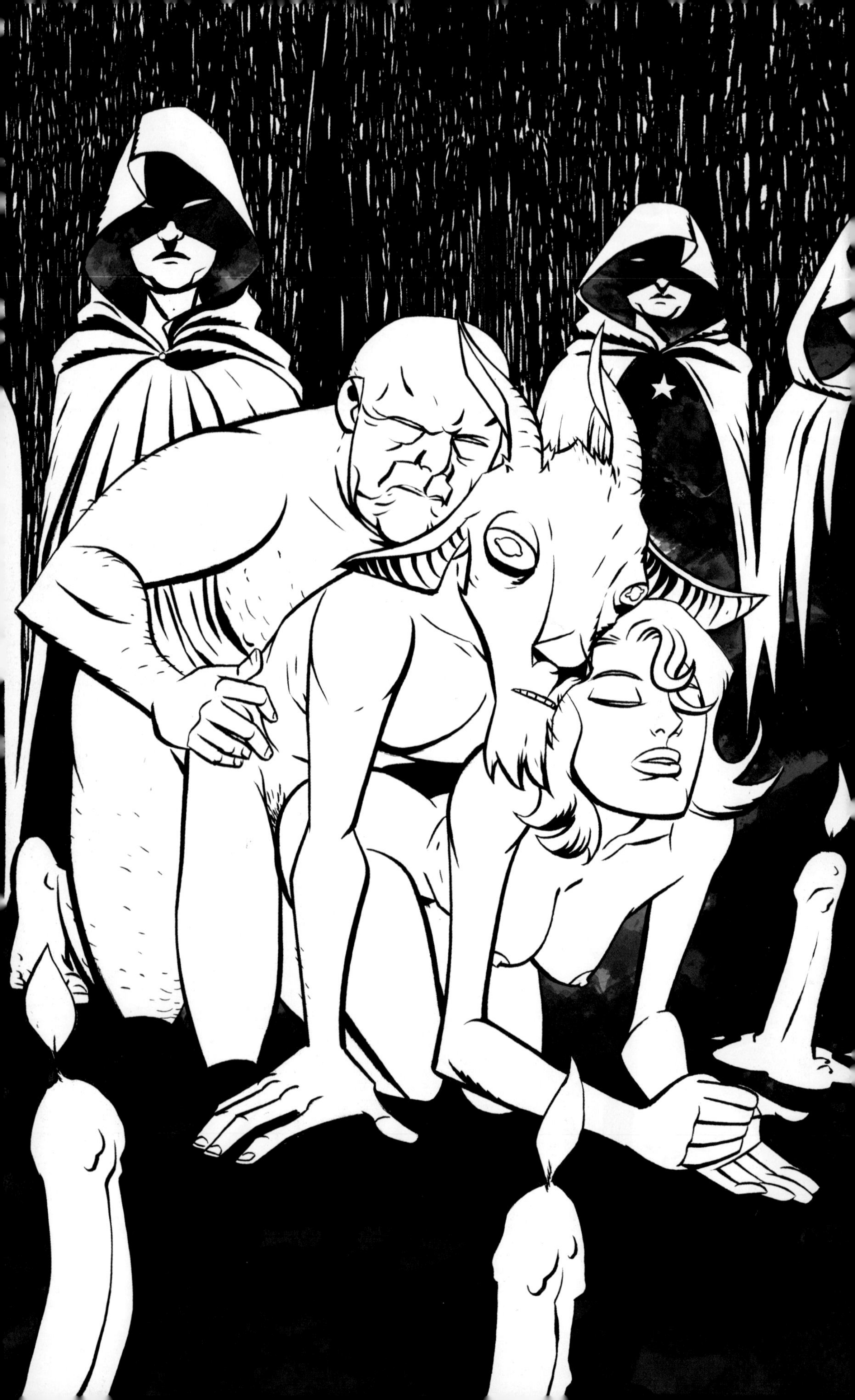

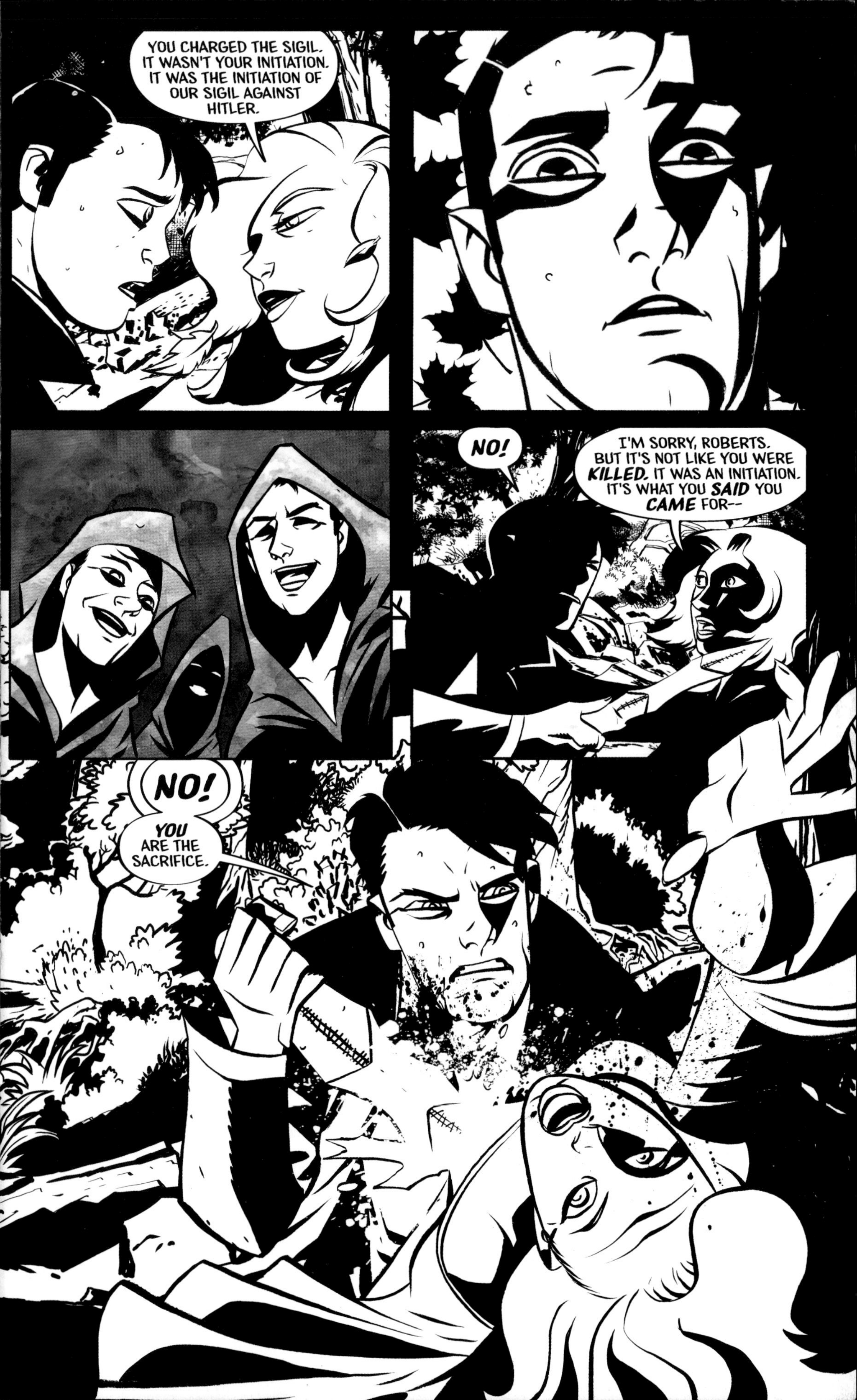
YOU CHARGED THE SIGIL. IT WASN'T YOUR INITIATION. IT WAS THE INITIATION OF OUR SIGIL AGAINST HITLER.
NO!
I'M SORRY, ROBERTS. BUT IT'S NOT LIKE YOU WERE KILLED. IT WAS AN INITIATION. IT'S WHAT YOU SAID YOU CAME FOR--
NO!
YOU ARE THE SACRIFICE.

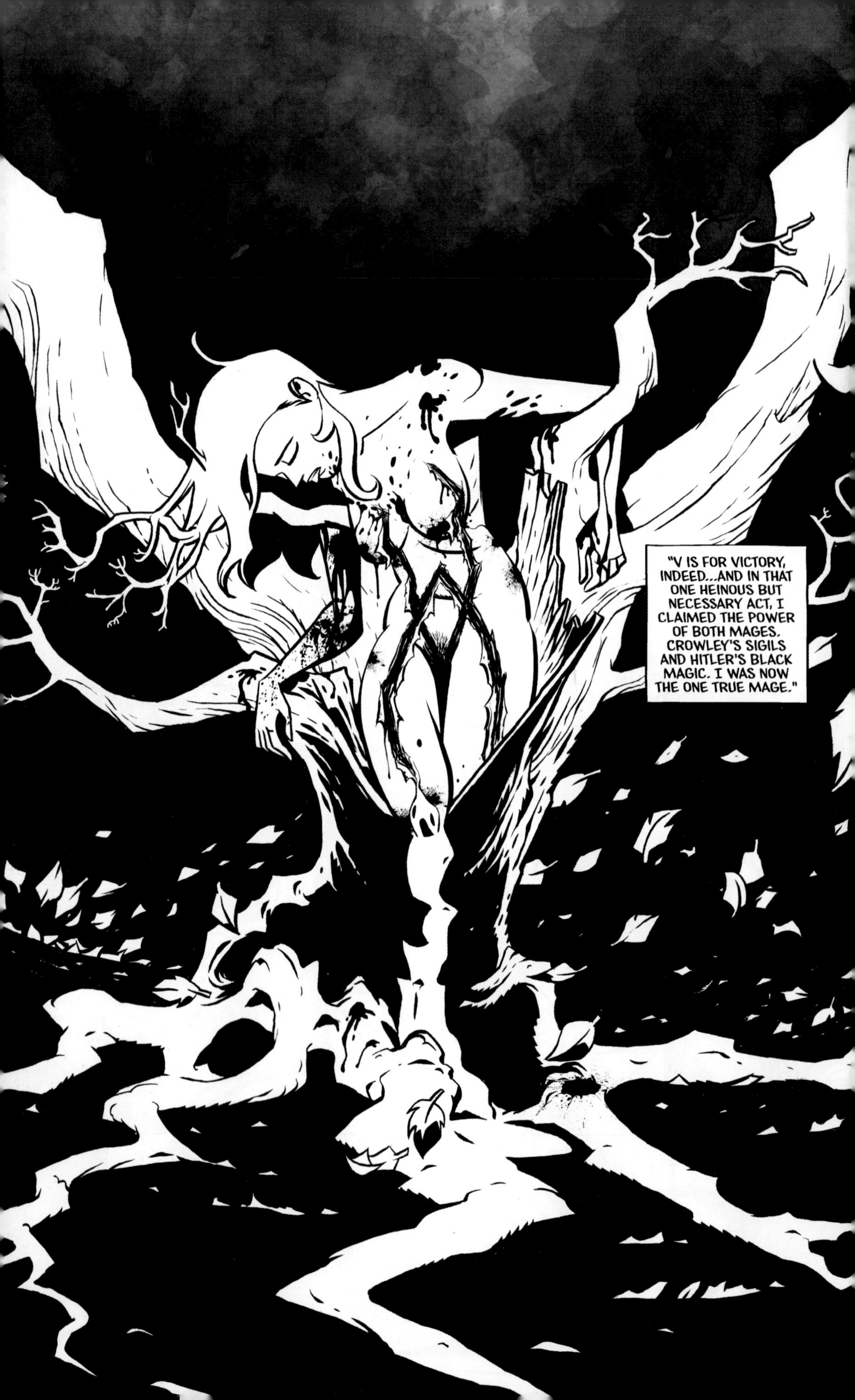
"V IS FOR VICTORY, INDEED...AND IN THAT ONE HEINOUS BUT NECESSARY ACT, I CLAIMED THE POWER OF BOTH MAGES. CROWLEY'S SIGILS AND HITLER'S BLACK MAGIC. I WAS NOW THE ONE TRUE MAGE."

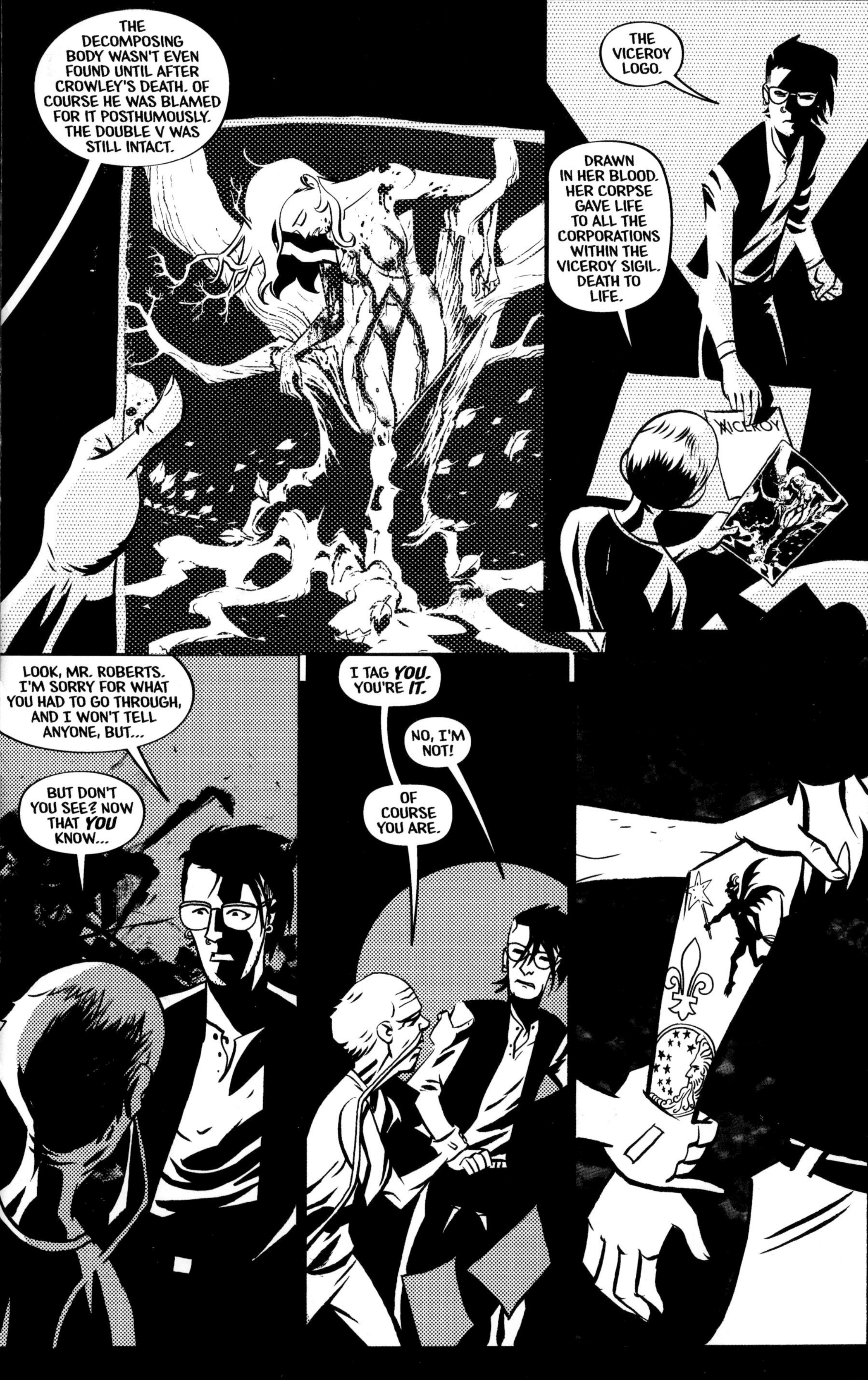
THE DECOMPOSING BODY WASN'T EVEN FOUND UNTIL AFTER CROWLEY'S DEATH. OF COURSE HE WAS BLAMED FOR IT POSTHUMOUSLY. THE DOUBLE V WAS STILL INTACT.
THE VICEROY LOGO.
DRAWN IN HER BLOOD. HER CORPSE GAVE LIFE TO ALL THE CORPORATIONS WITHIN THE VICEROY SIGIL. DEATH TO LIFE.
VICEROY
LOOK, MR. ROBERTS. I'M SORRY FOR WHAT YOU HAD TO GO THROUGH, AND I WON'T TELL ANYONE, BUT...
BUT DON'T YOU SEE? NOW THAT *YOU* KNOW...
I TAG *YOU*. YOU'RE *IT*.
NO, I'M NOT!
OF COURSE YOU ARE.

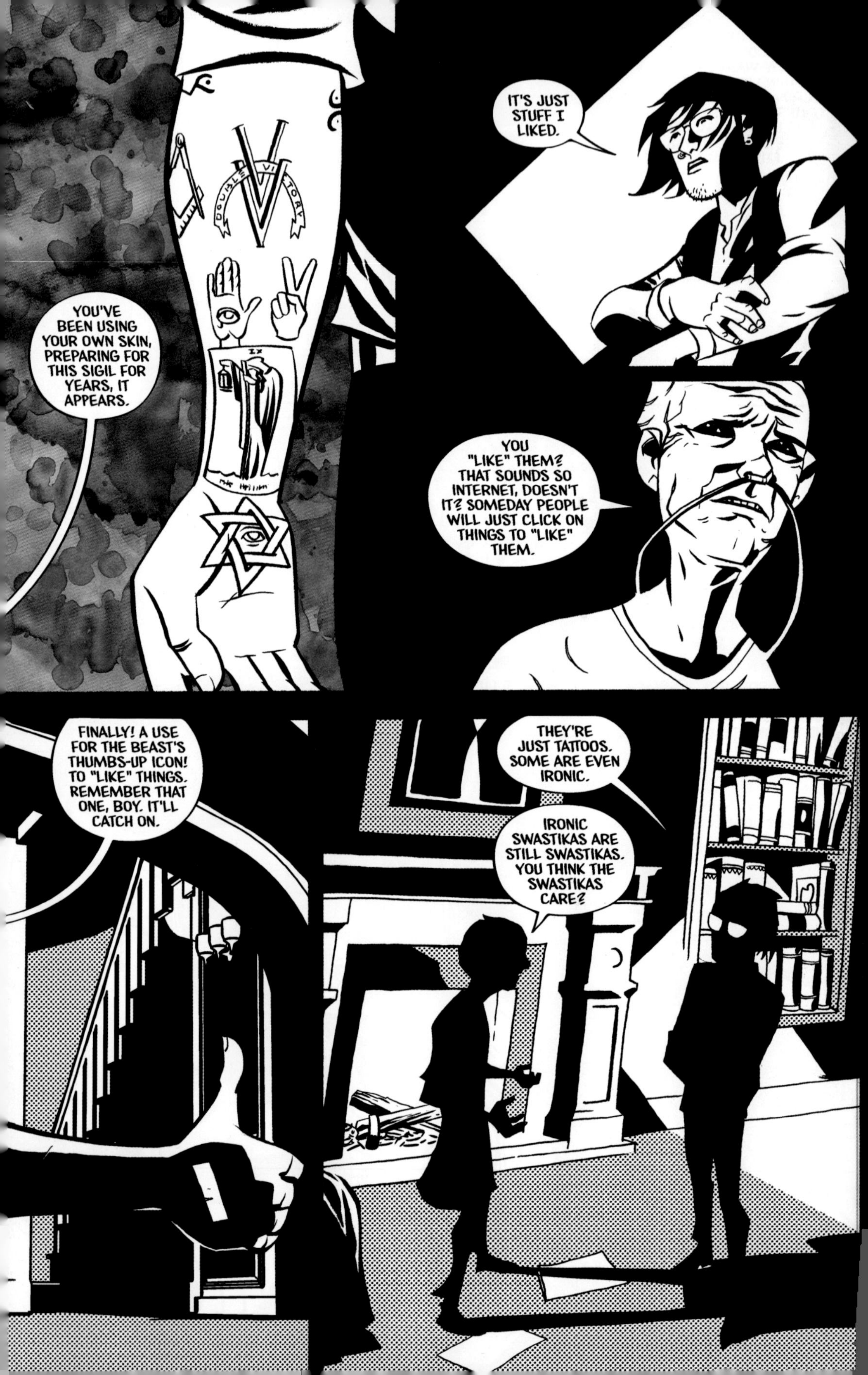
YOU'VE BEEN USING YOUR OWN SKIN, PREPARING FOR THIS SIGIL FOR YEARS, IT APPEARS.
DOUBLE VICTORY
IT'S JUST STUFF I LIKED.
YOU "LIKE" THEM? THAT SOUNDS SO INTERNET, DOESN'T IT? SOMEDAY PEOPLE WILL JUST CLICK ON THINGS TO "LIKE" THEM.
FINALLY! A USE FOR THE BEAST'S THUMBS-UP ICON! TO "LIKE" THINGS. REMEMBER THAT ONE, BOY. IT'LL CATCH ON.
THEY'RE JUST TATTOOS. SOME ARE EVEN IRONIC.
IRONIC SWASTIKAS ARE STILL SWASTIKAS. YOU THINK THE SWASTIKAS CARE?

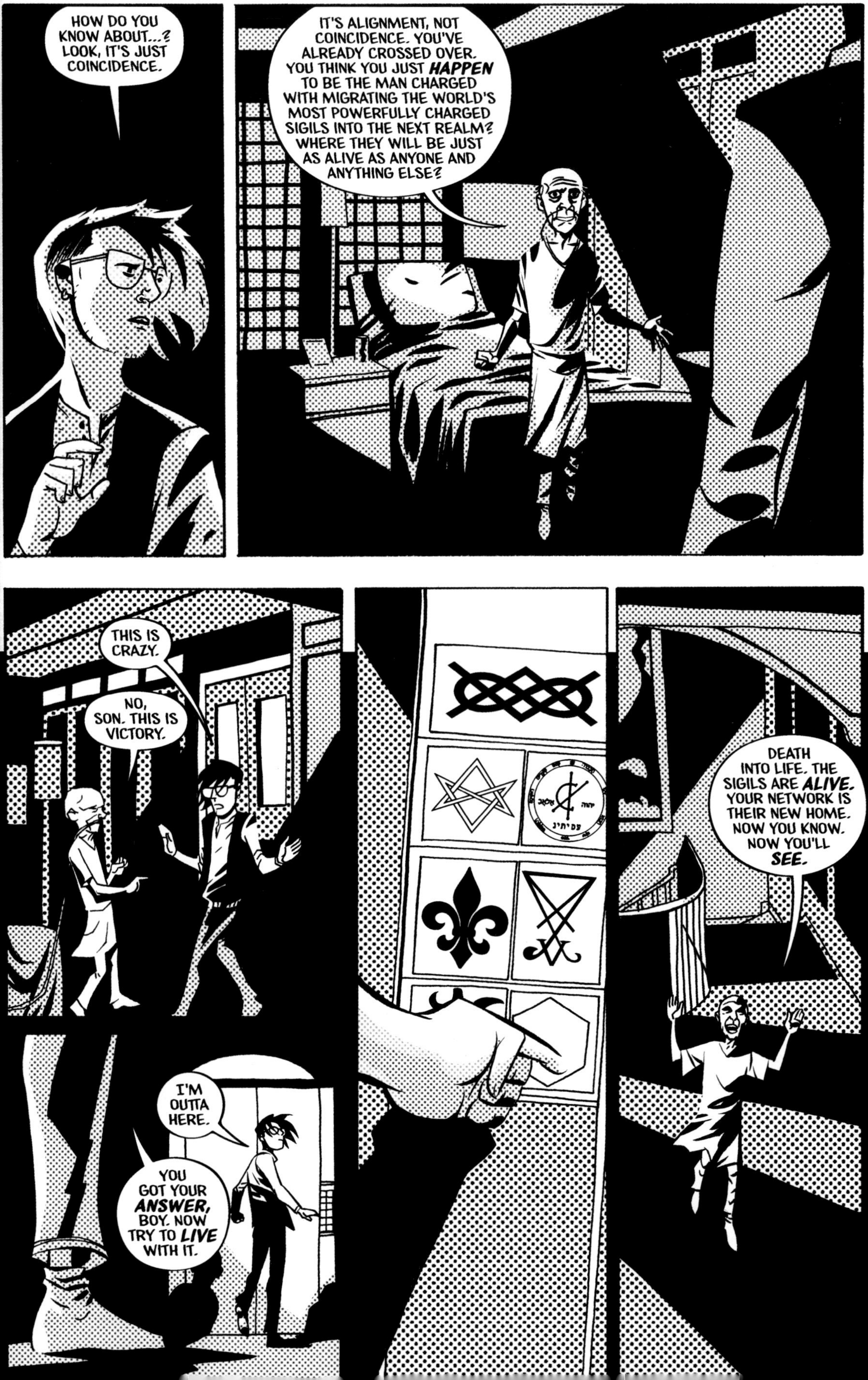
HOW DO YOU KNOW ABOUT...? LOOK, IT'S JUST COINCIDENCE.
IT'S ALIGNMENT, NOT COINCIDENCE. YOU'VE ALREADY CROSSED OVER. YOU THINK YOU JUST HAPPEN TO BE THE MAN CHARGED WITH MIGRATING THE WORLD'S MOST POWERFULLY CHARGED SIGILS INTO THE NEXT REALM? WHERE THEY WILL BE JUST AS ALIVE AS ANYONE AND ANYTHING ELSE?
THIS IS CRAZY.
NO, SON. THIS IS VICTORY.
I'M OUTTA HERE.
YOU GOT YOUR ANSWER, BOY. NOW TRY TO LIVE WITH IT.
DEATH INTO LIFE. THE SIGILS ARE ALIVE. YOUR NETWORK IS THEIR NEW HOME. NOW YOU KNOW. NOW YOU'LL SEE.

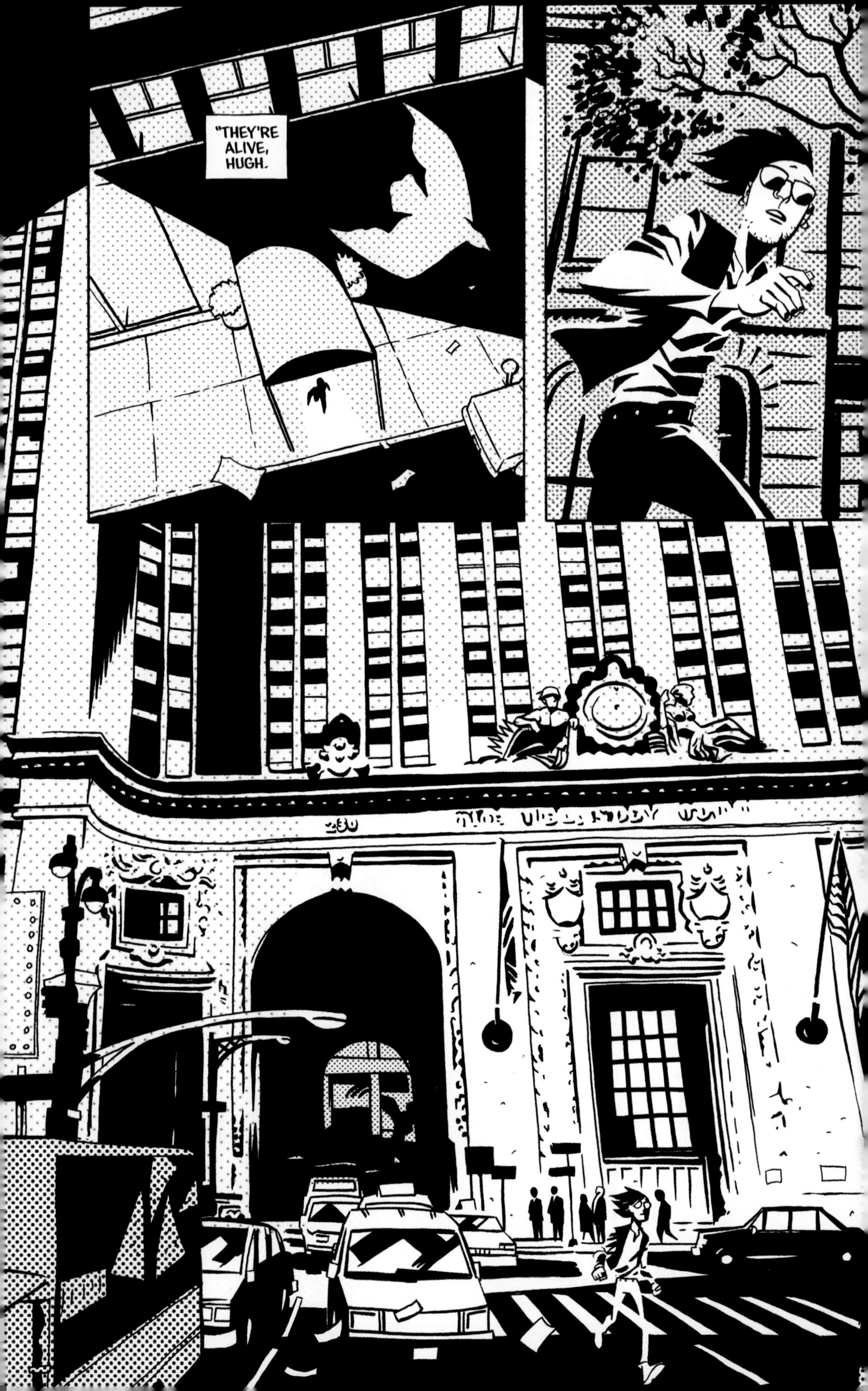
"THEY'RE ALIVE, HUGH.

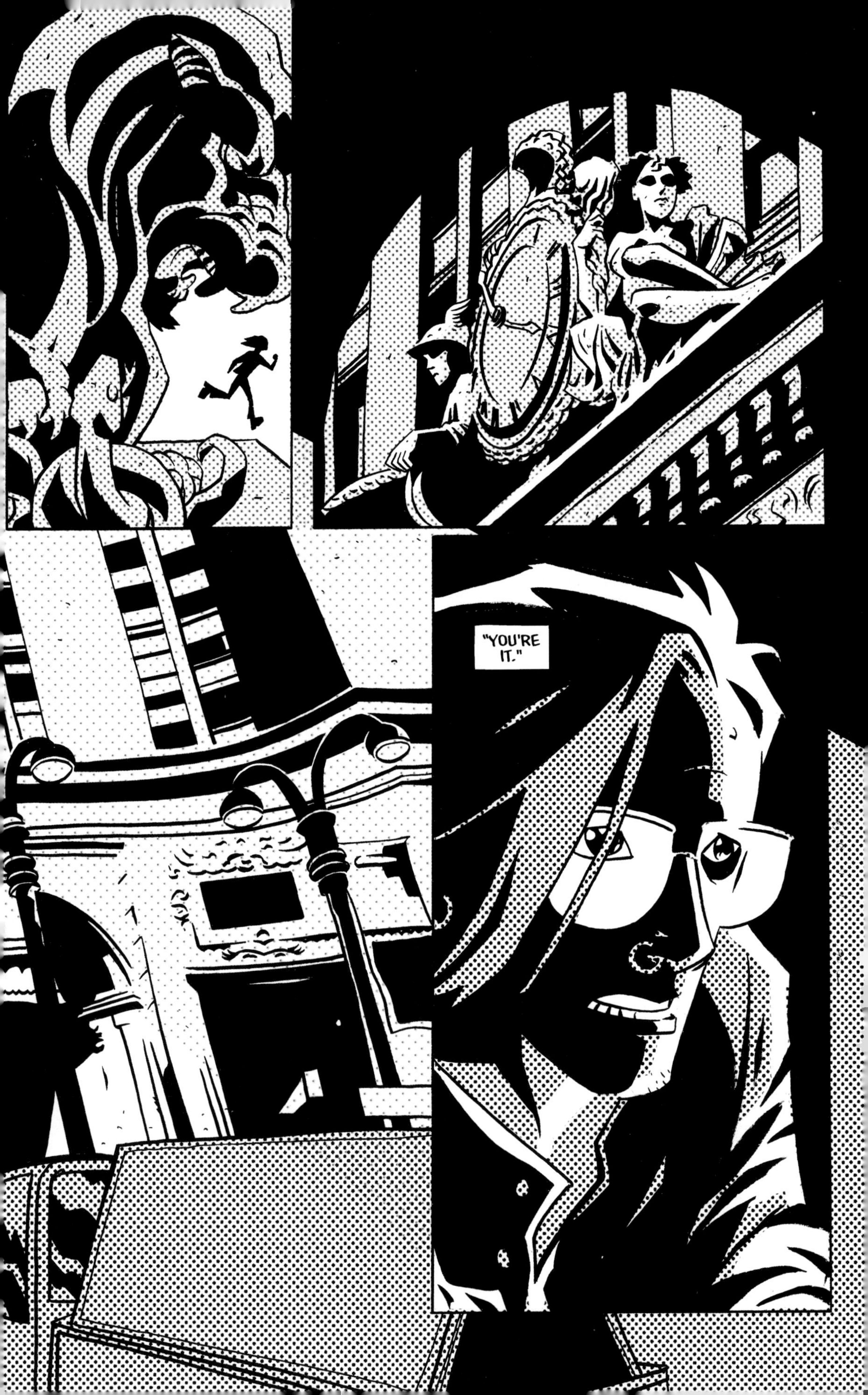
"YOU'RE IT."

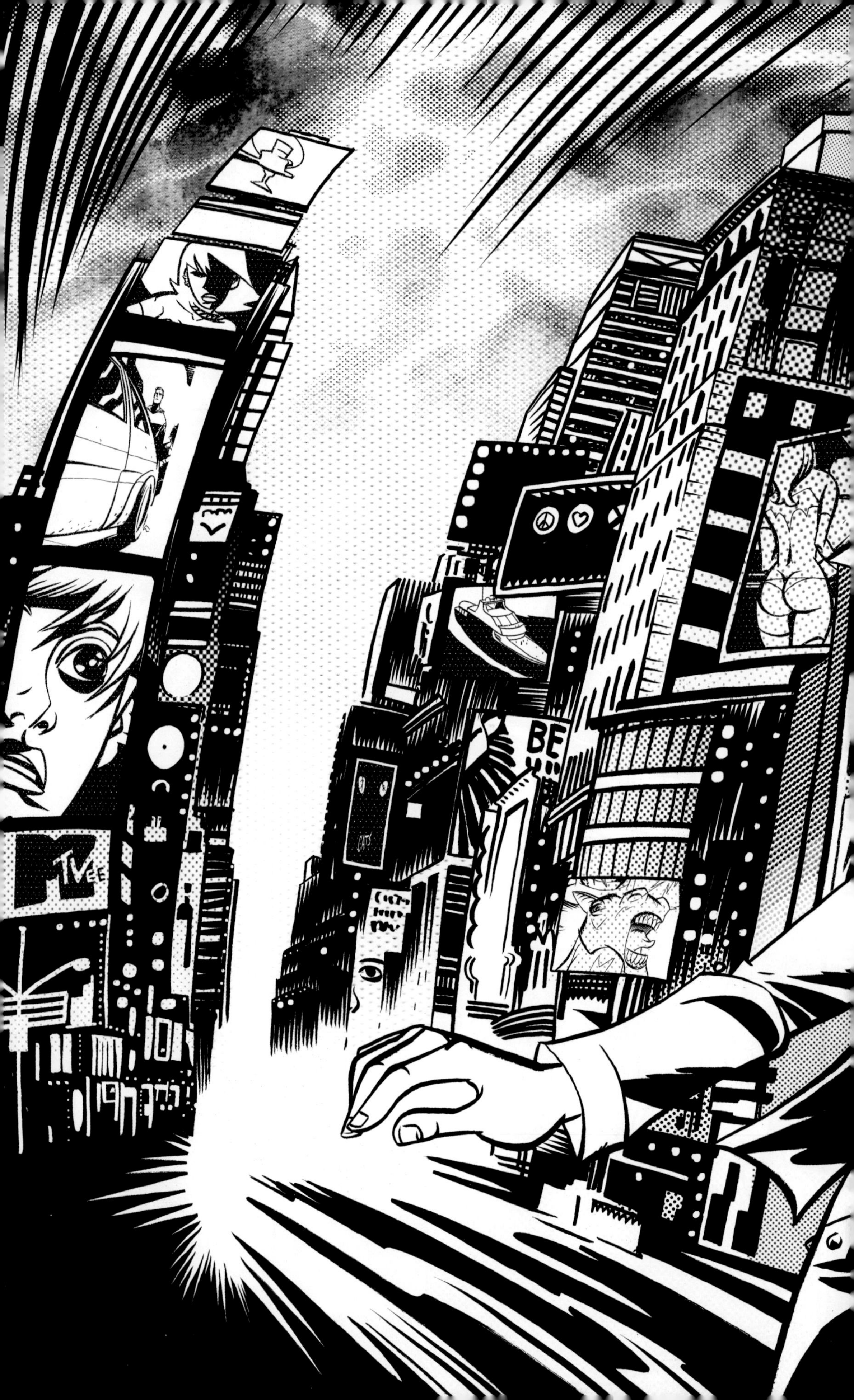
BE

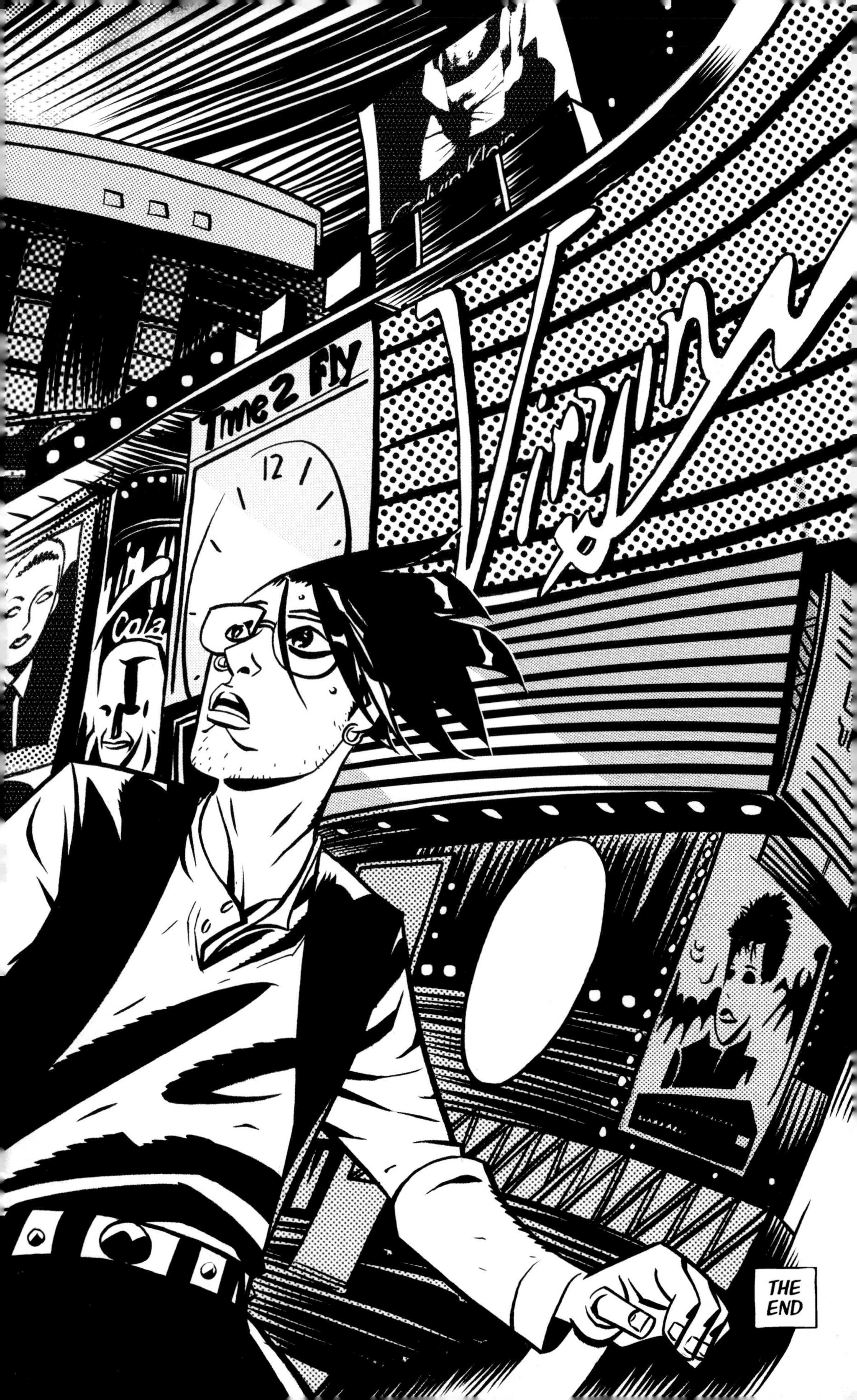
Calvin Klein
Time 2 Fly
12
Virgin
Cola
THE END

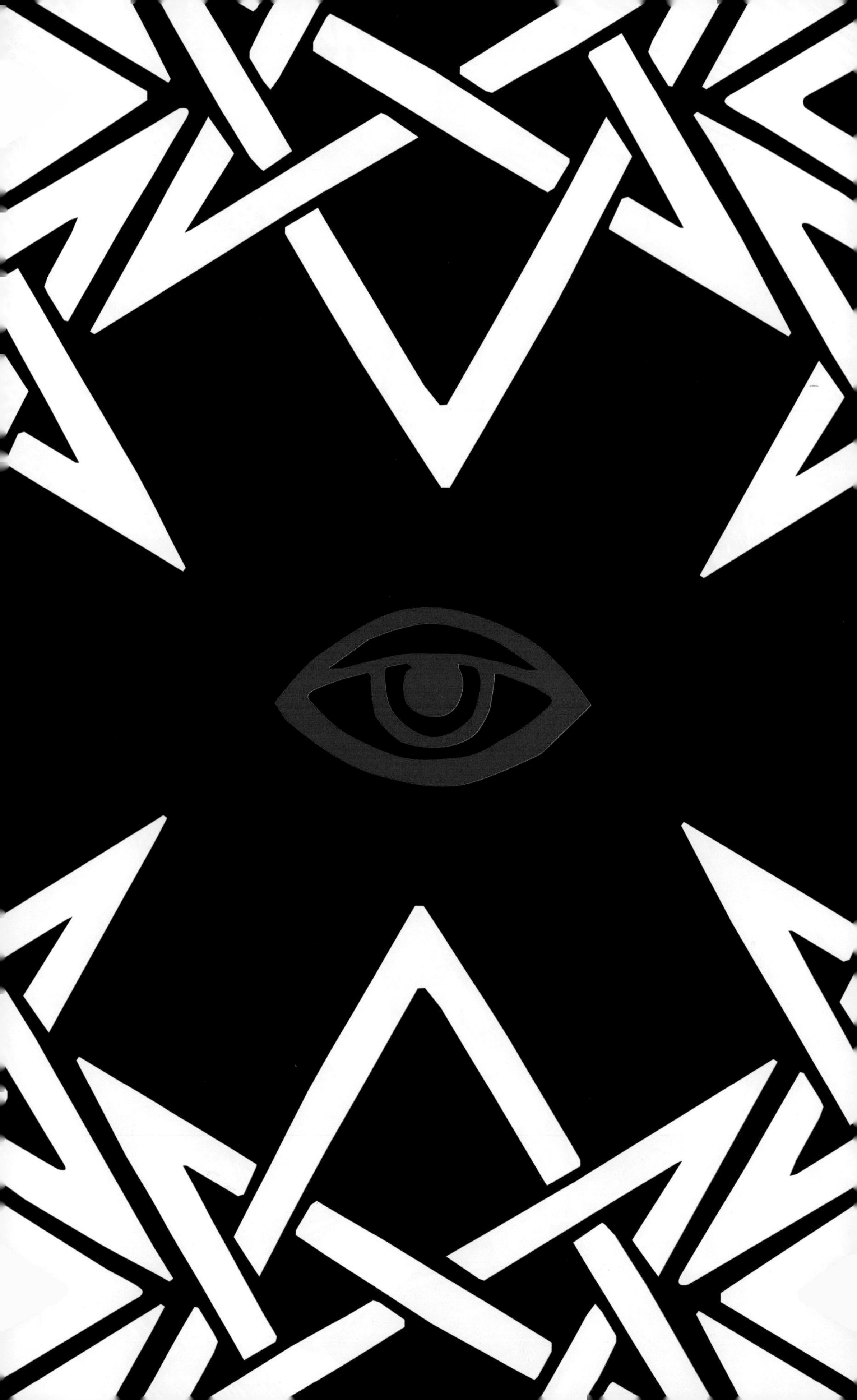

# ALEISTER & ADOLF

## SKETCHBOOK

Notes by Michael Avon Oeming

Here is an early sketch of Roberts. He went through several different looks. I was looking at a lot of actors from the '40s and '50s. I looked at a lot of Howard Hughes (especially with his occult and conspiracy ties), but eventually we landed on a sort of young Cary Grant as a direction.

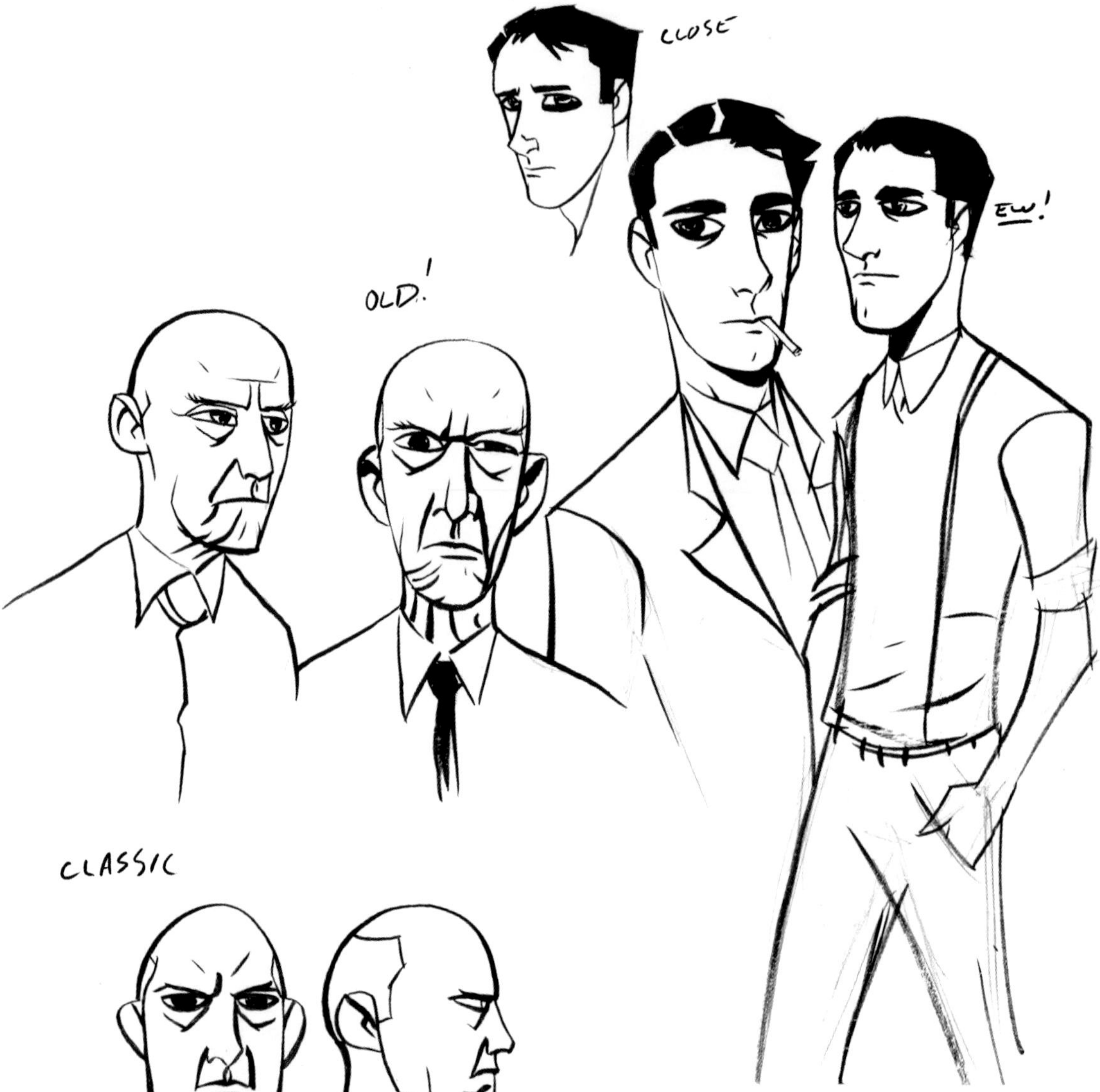
CLOSE
EW!
OLD!

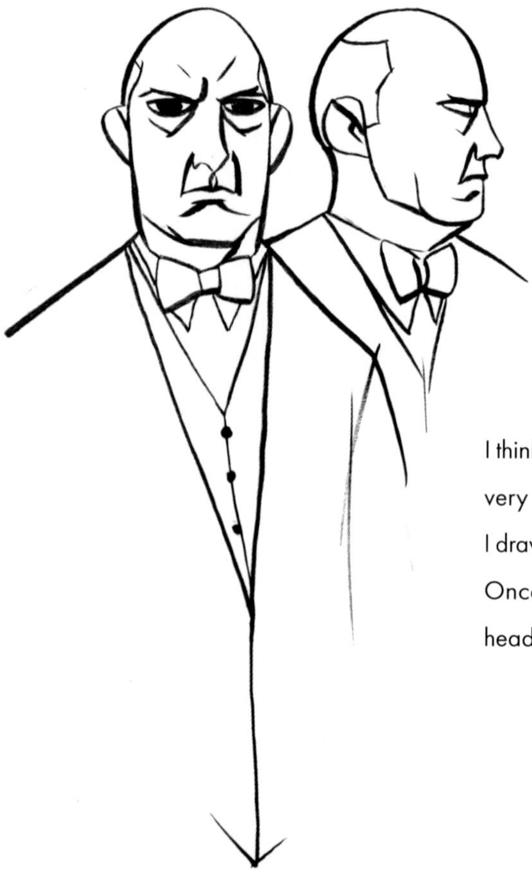
CLASSIC

I think I figured out eventually that I kept drawing his face very long. I also discovered I do that with a lot of noses I draw; most noses, even prominent ones, are pretty short. Once I figured Crowley had a sort of bullet-shaped head, I knew I was on to something. He's so fun to draw.

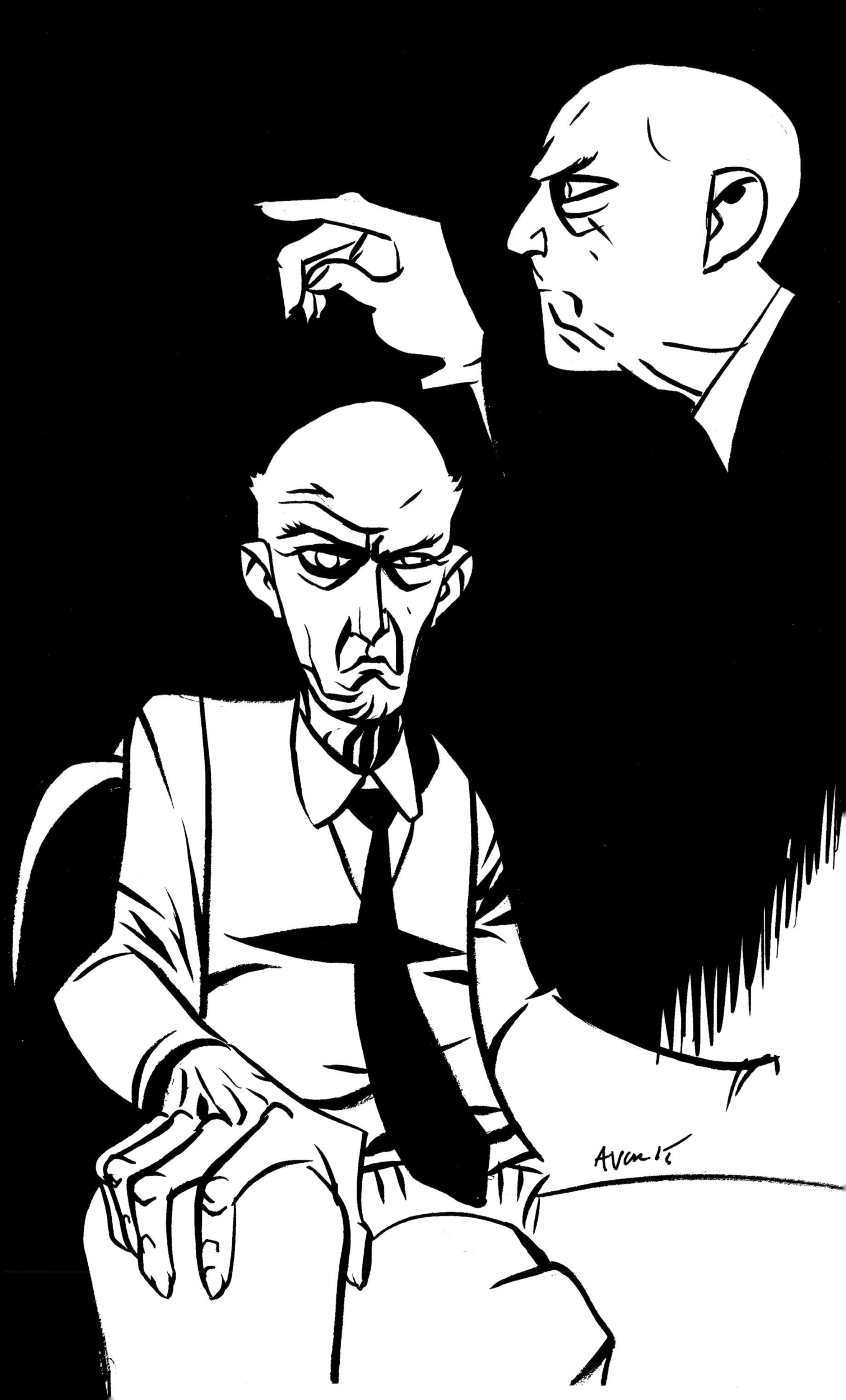

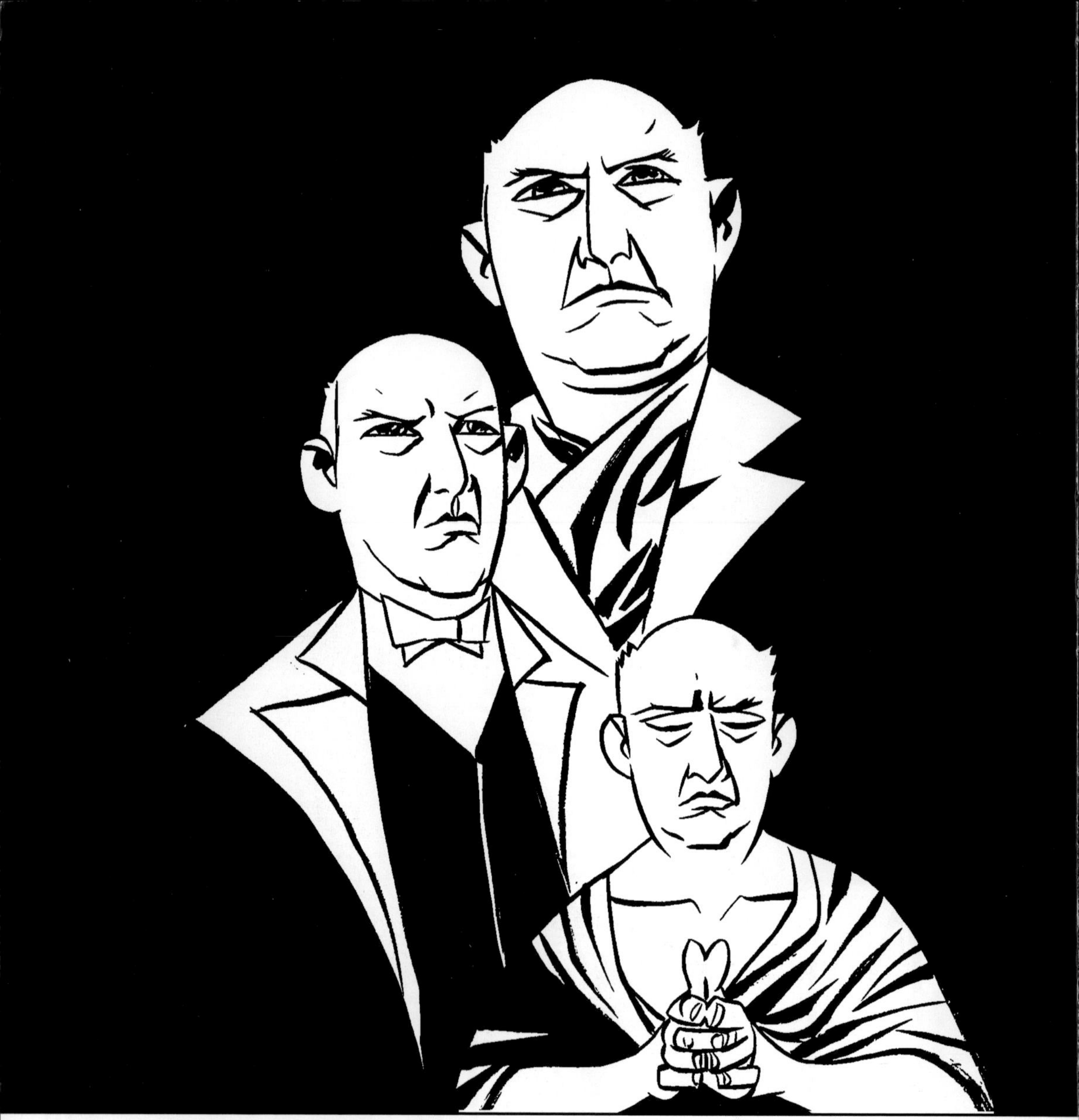

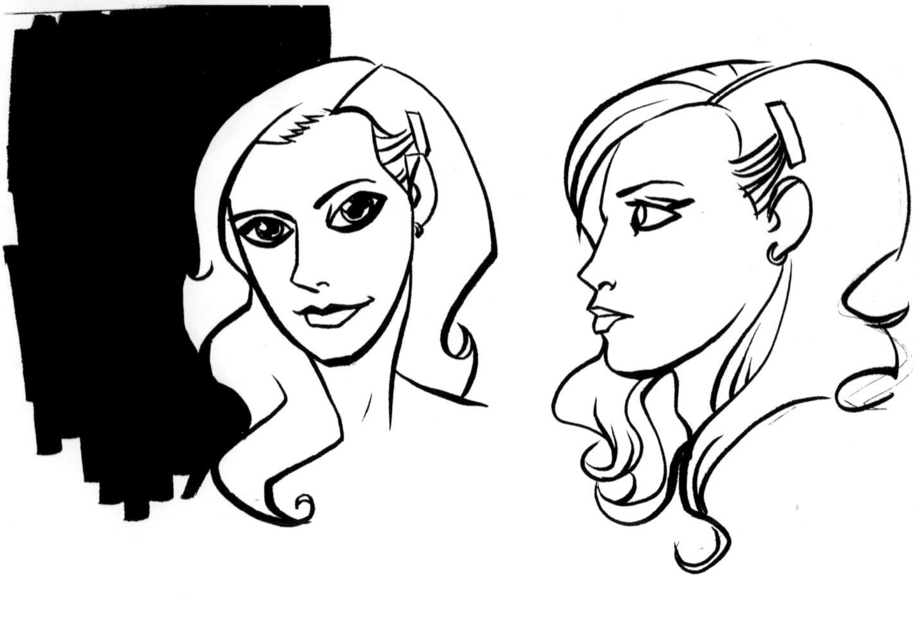

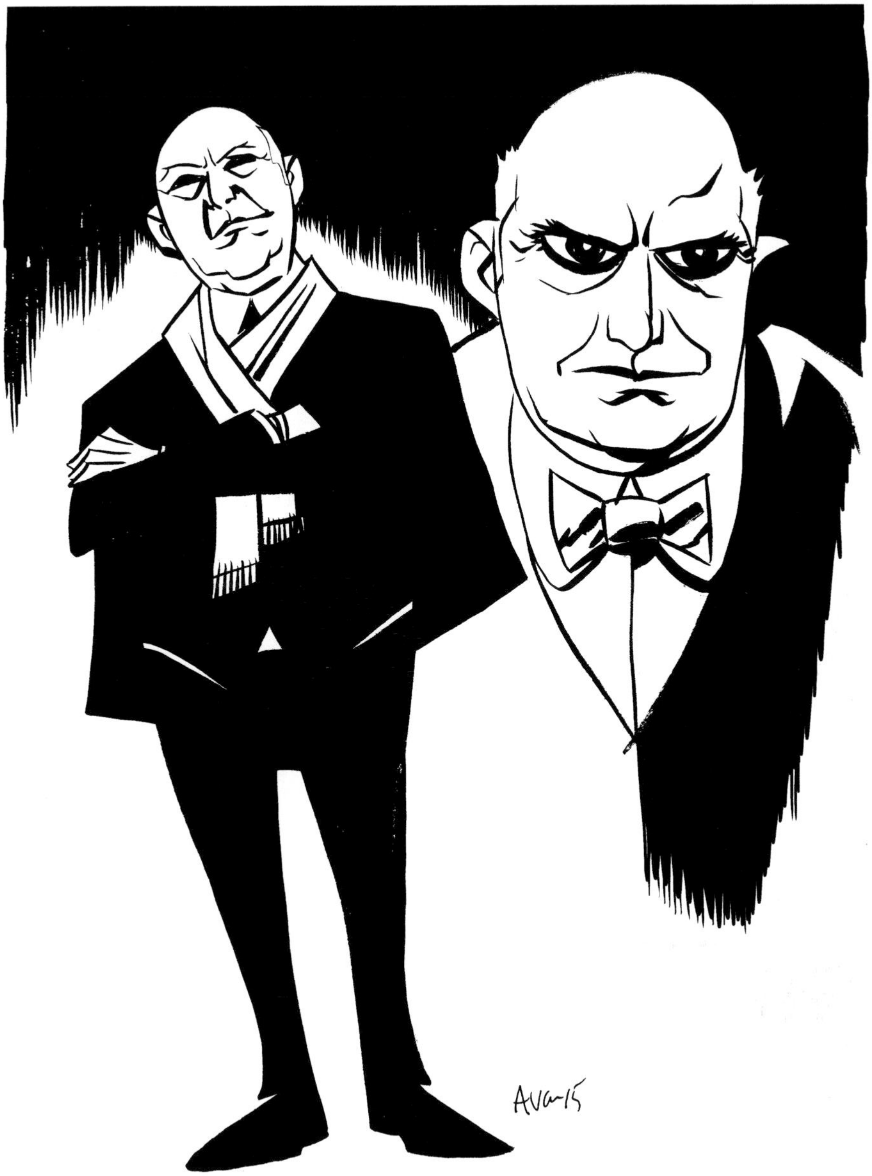

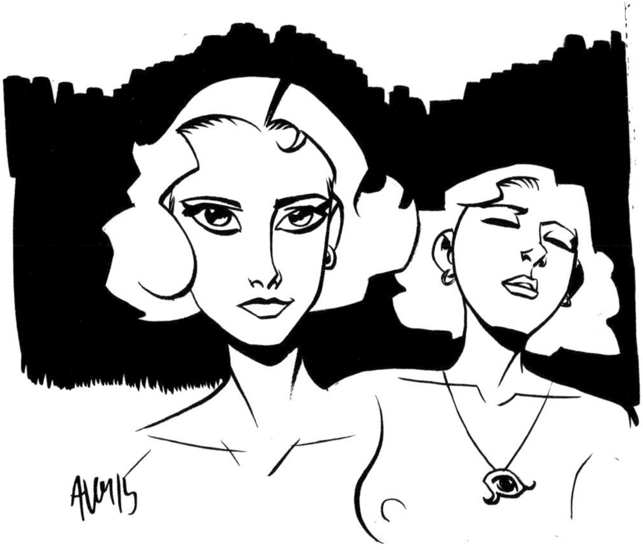

Daphne. Oh, Daphne. She is the heart of the book. Caught between whatever the truth of Crowley is and her feelings for a young, naive man she could have loved. I'm not one for drawing glamour women, but once I got her hair, that was the key.

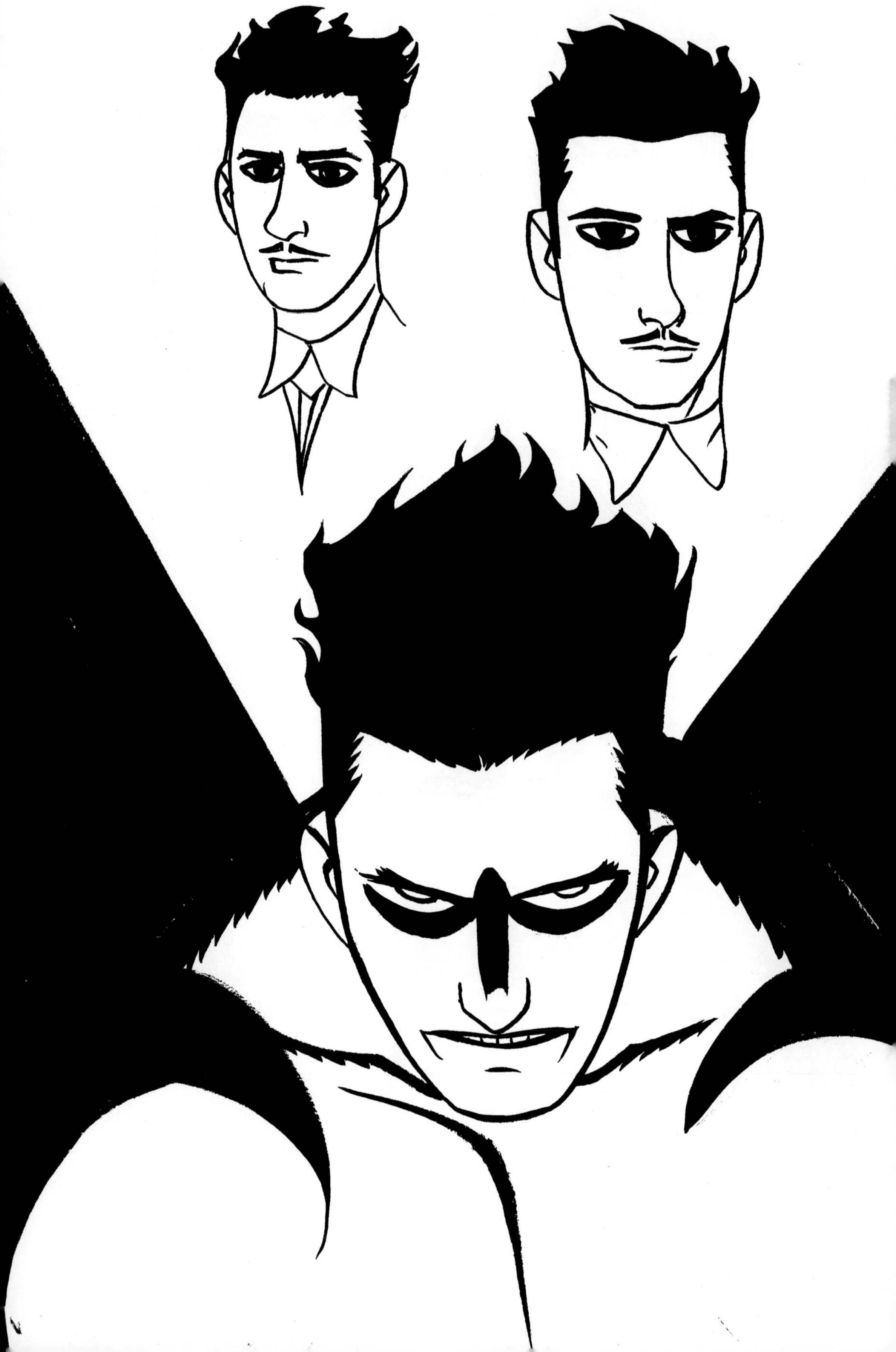

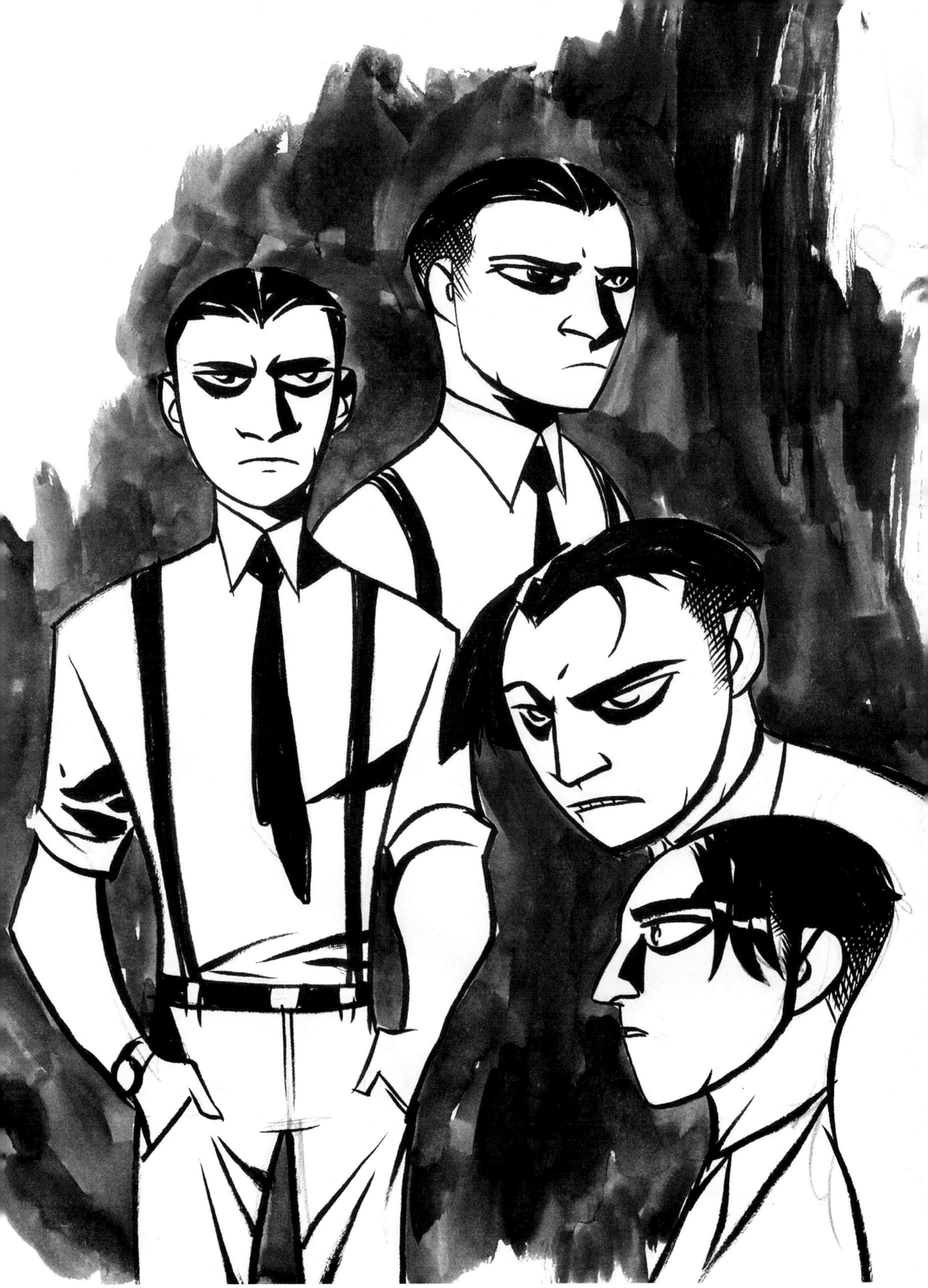

Early version of Roberts. Previous page was Jack Parsons, my most favorite bizarre and strange person of modern times. Read all about his evil occult plans and how they formed JPL and NASA. It all grew out of the occult. I believe there may still be some secret cult within NASA that believes this shit, because like it or not, the founder of JPL worshiped demons, and that is a fact.

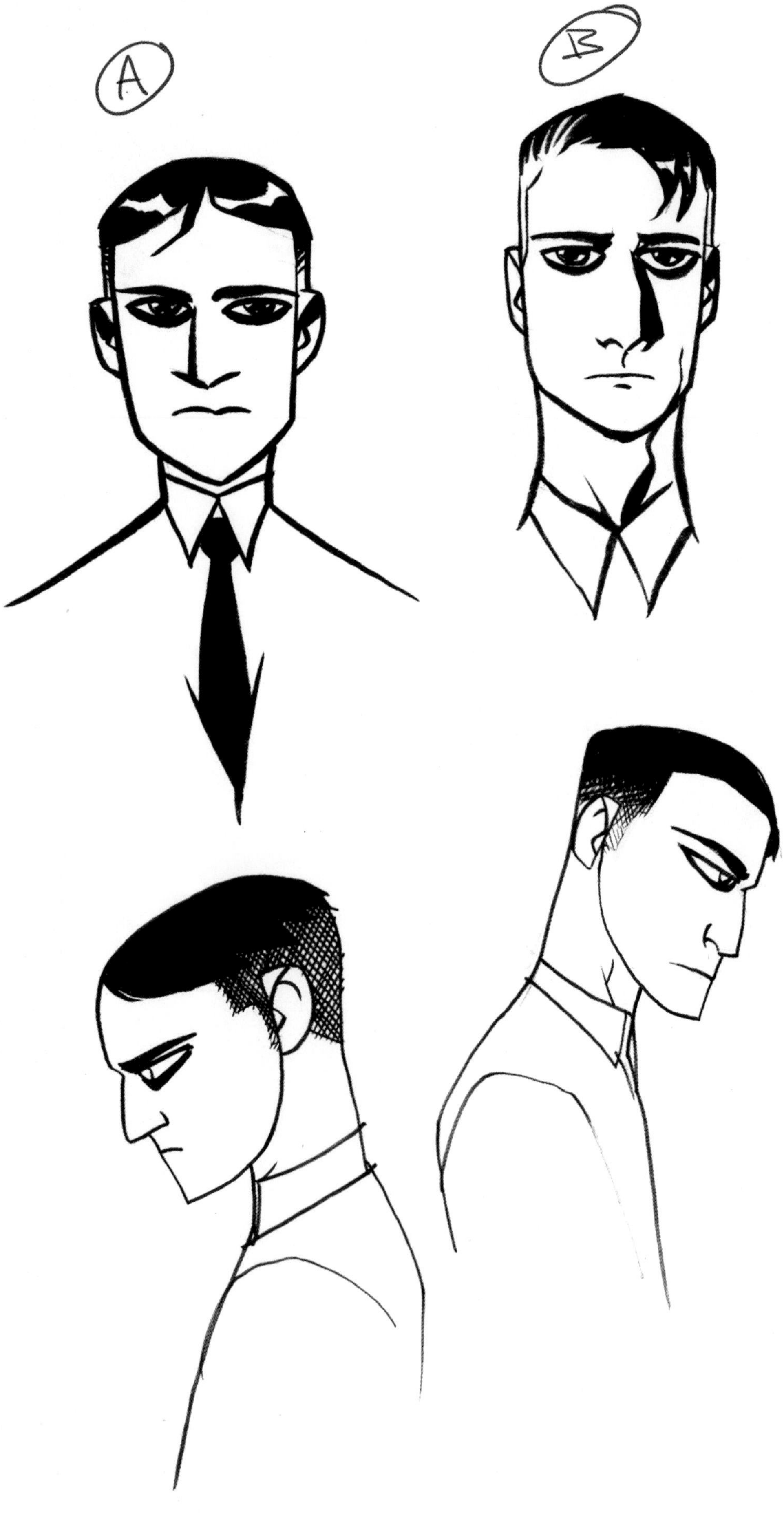
A
B

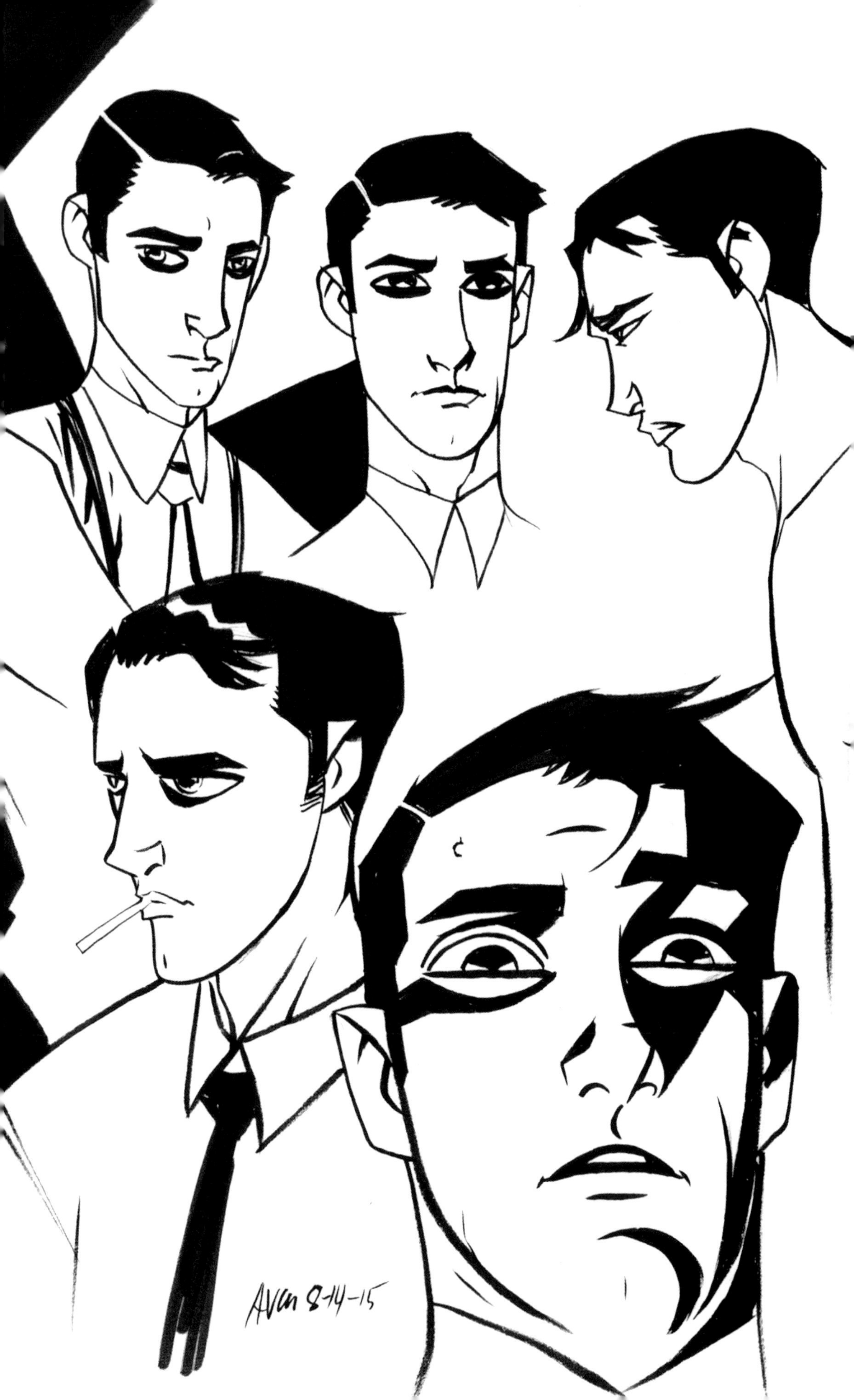
Avon 8-14-15

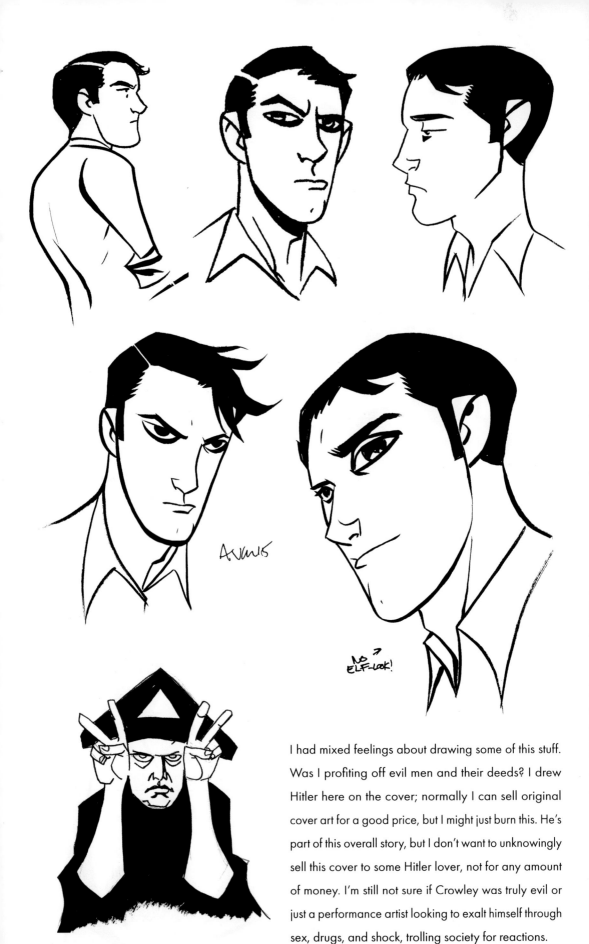

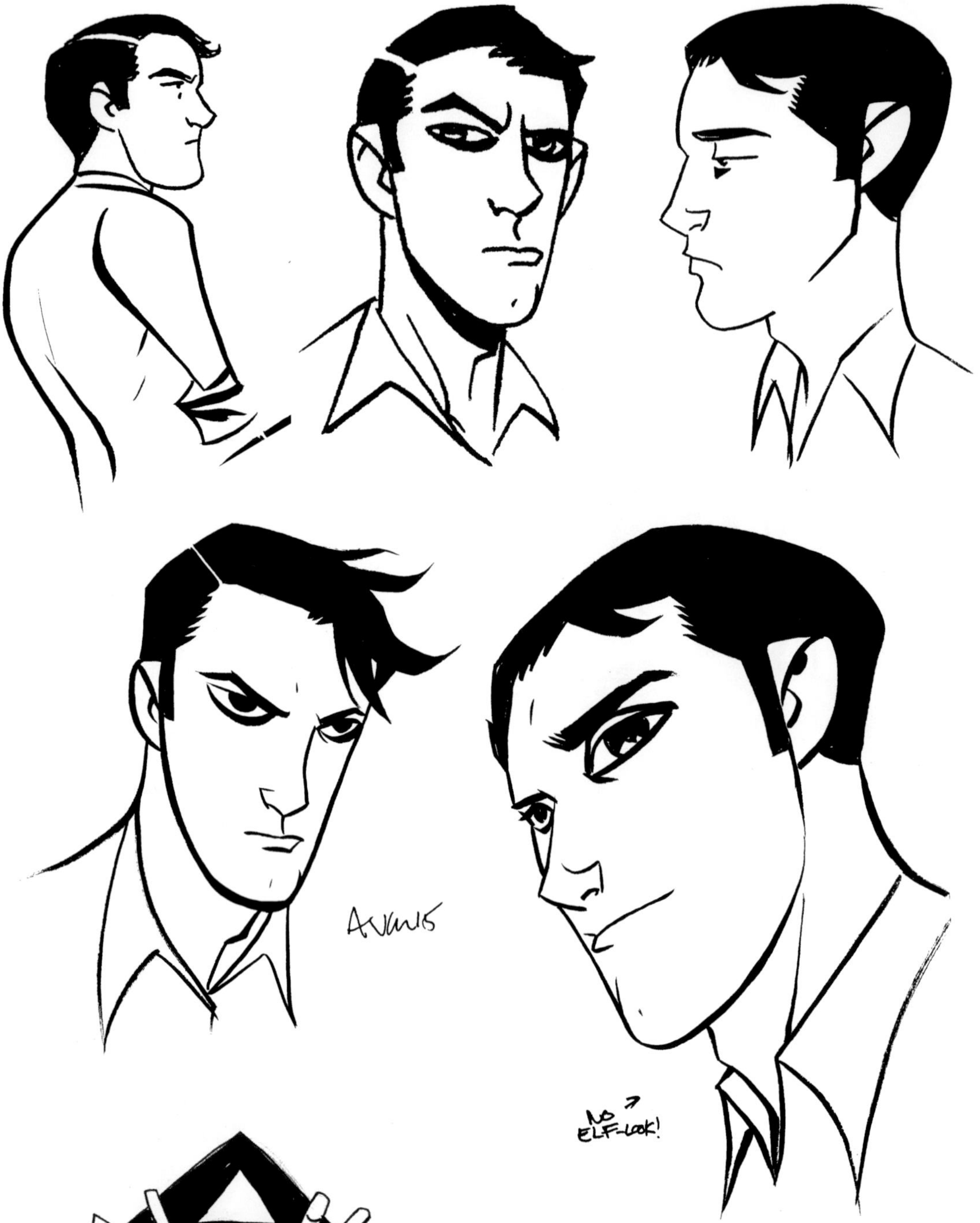
NO ELF-LOOK!

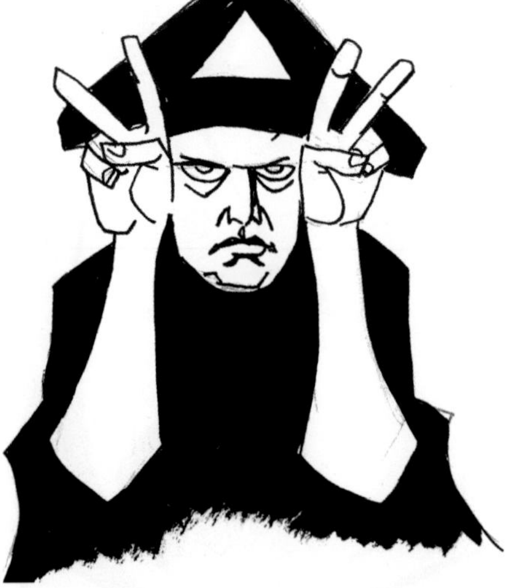

I had mixed feelings about drawing some of this stuff. Was I profiting off evil men and their deeds? I drew Hitler here on the cover; normally I can sell original cover art for a good price, but I might just burn this. He's part of this overall story, but I don't want to unknowingly sell this cover to some Hitler lover, not for any amount of money. I'm still not sure if Crowley was truly evil or just a performance artist looking to exalt himself through sex, drugs, and shock, trolling society for reactions.

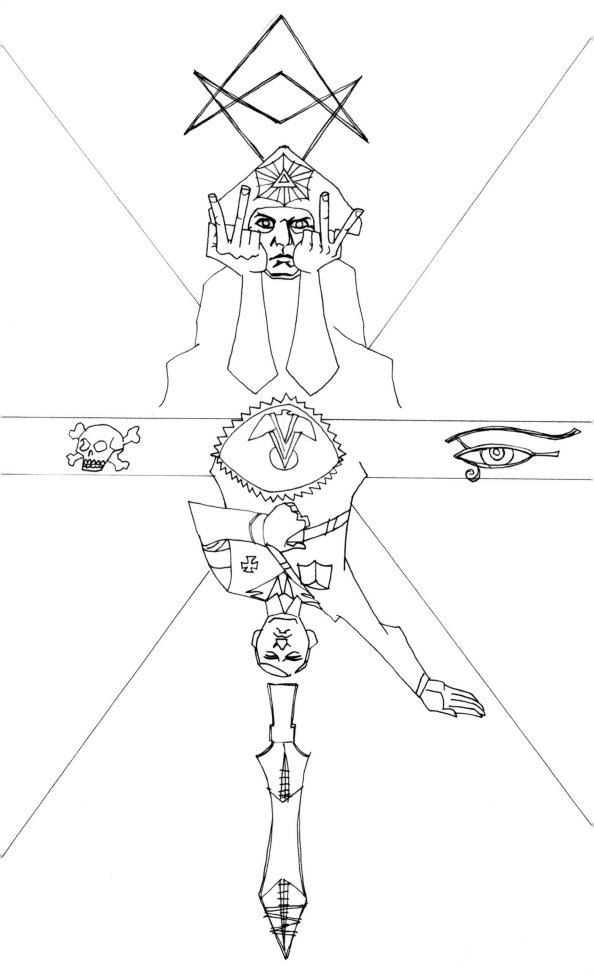

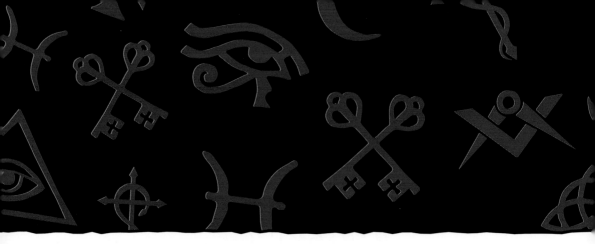

## DOUGLAS RUSHKOFF

Douglas Rushkoff writes comics when he wants to tell the truth. The renowned author of books about media and technology including *Cyberia*, *Media Virus*, *Program or Be Programmed*, *Present Shock*, and *Throwing Rocks at the Google Bus*, Rushkoff is the winner of both the Marshall McLuhan and Neil Postman Awards and was named by MIT as one of the world's ten most influential intellectuals. Rushkoff also makes television documentaries for PBS, including *Merchants of Cool* and *Generation Like*, appears on shows from *NBC Nightly News* to *The Colbert Report*, and hosts the podcast *Team Human*.

But when Rushkoff wants to get serious about something, he turns to comics. He created the Harvey Award–nominated Vertigo series *Testament*, in which gods live outside the panels, influencing action from the gutter. He also wrote the graphic novels *A.D.D.* (Vertigo) and *Club Zero-G* (Disinformation), which both explore teens, media, and cultural mutation.

With *Aleister & Adolf*, Rushkoff risks his psyche and those of his readers by contemplating the real lesson of Aleister Crowley, the magickal intent of the Holocaust, and—perhaps worst of all—the true origins of brand iconography.

## MICHAEL AVON OEMING

Michael Avon Oeming began his career in comics at the age of fourteen. Dedicated to his craft, Mike was eventually kicked out of high school for skipping class to stay home and draw. His first big break was as an inker on *Daredevil*, and shortly after he was hired as a penciler/inker on DC's version of *Judge Dredd*, then *Foot Soldiers* and *Bulletproof Monk*, which became a film. Michael was nominated for an Eisner for his work on *Powers* with Brian Michael Bendis. Other notable titles involve his love of mythology, such as *Thor*, *Hammer of the Gods*, and *The Mice Templar* with Bryan J. L. Glass. He has worked on several works with his wife, Taki Soma, such as *Rapture*, *Sinergy*, and *United States of Murder Inc.*, written by Bendis. Michael is an executive producer on the *Powers* TV series from Sony/PlayStation. His interests in mythology, the occult, and conspiracies have led him to the book you currently hold in your hands. Yes, we can see you.

DARK HORSE HORROR

drawing on your nightmares

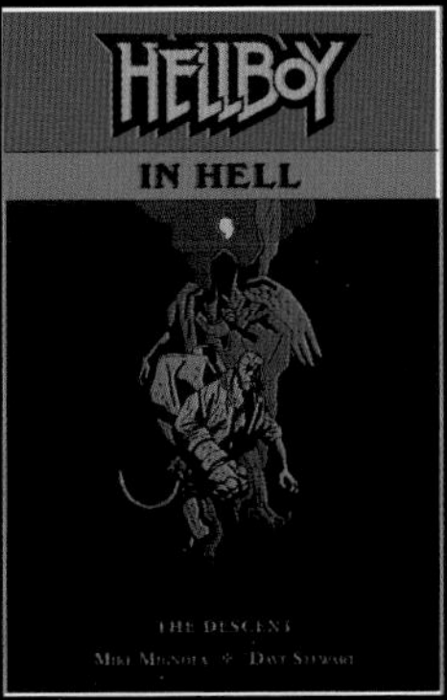
HELLBOY
IN HELL
THE DESCENT

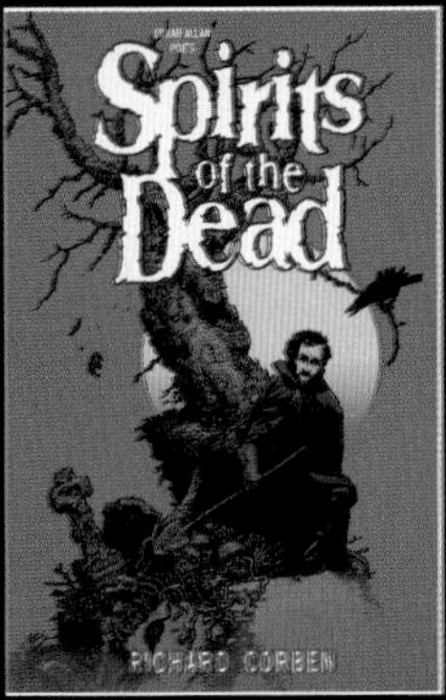
Spirits of the Dead
RICHARD CORBEN

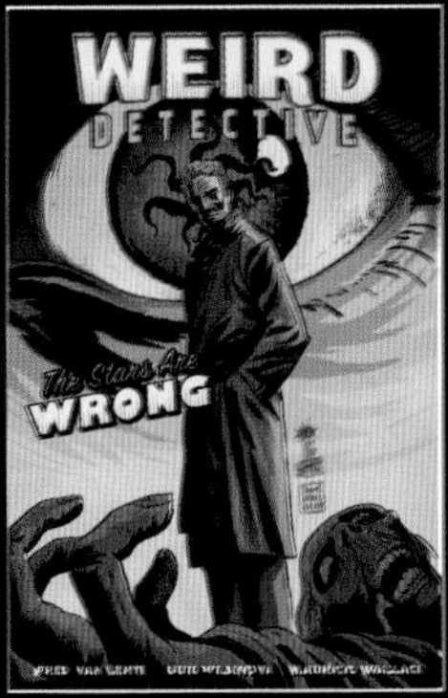
WEIRD DETECTIVE
The Stars Are WRONG

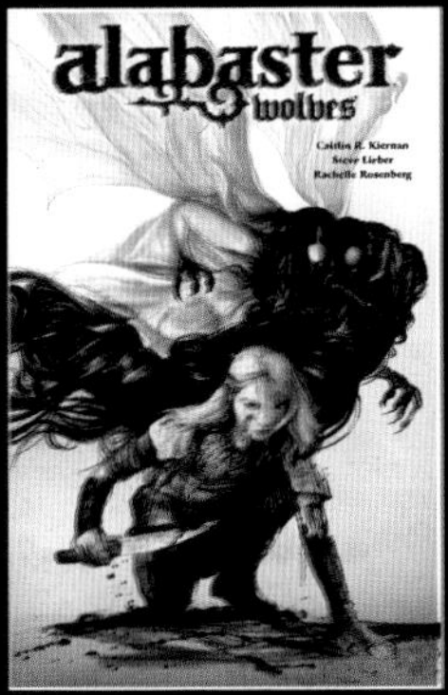
alabaster
wolves

**HELLBOY IN HELL VOLUME 1: THE DESCENT**
*Mike Mignola*
ISBN 978-1-61655-444-6 | $17.99

**EDGAR ALLAN POE'S SPIRITS OF THE DEAD**
*Richard Corben*
ISBN 978-1-61655-356-2 | $24.99

**GRINDHOUSE: DOORS OPEN AT MIDNIGHT DOUBLE FEATURE VOLUME 1**
*Alex de Campi, Chris Peterson, and Simon Fraser*
ISBN 978-1-61655-377-7 | $17.99

**HARROW COUNTY VOLUME 1: COUNTLESS HAINTS**
*Tyler Crook and Cullen Bunn*
ISBN 978-1-61655-780-5 | $14.99

**ALABASTER: WOLVES**
*Caitlín R. Kiernan and Steve Lieber*
ISBN 978-1-61655-025-7 | $19.99

**DEATH FOLLOWS**
*Cullen Bunn, A. C. Zamudio, and Çarlos Nicolas Zamudio*
ISBN 978-1-61655-951-9 | $17.99

**HOUSE OF PENANCE**
*Peter J. Tomasi and Ian Bertram*
ISBN 978-1-50670-033-5 | $19.99

**JOE GOLEM: OCCULT DETECTIVE - THE RAT CATCHER & THE SUNKEN DEAD**
*Mike Mignola, Christopher Golden, and Patric Reynolds*
ISBN 978-1-61655-964-9 | $24.99

**WEIRD DETECTIVE: THE STARS ARE WRONG**
*Fred Van Lente, Guiu Vilanova, and Mauricio Wallace*
ISBN 978-1-50670-038-0 | $17.99

**H.P. LOVECRAFT'S THE HOUND AND OTHER STORIES**
*Gou Tanabe*
ISBN 978-1-50670-312-1 | $12.99

**GARY GIANNI'S MONSTERMEN AND OTHER SCARY STORIES**
*Gary Gianni*
ISBN 978-1-50670-480-7 | $19.99

AVAILABLE AT YOUR LOCAL COMICS SHOP OR BOOKSTORE! • To find a comics shop in your area, visit comicshoplocator.com.
For more information or to order direct visit DarkHorse.com or call 1-800-862-0052 Mon.–Fri. 9 AM to 5 PM Pacific Time. Prices and availability subject to change without notice.

SPECULATIVE FICTION FROM

# darkhorse originals

"Unique creators with unique visions."—MIKE RICHARDSON, PUBLISHER

Sabertooth Swordsman

## SABERTOOTH SWORDSMAN

*Damon Gentry and Aaron Conley*

Granted the form of the Sabertooth Swordsman by the Cloud God of Sasquatch Mountain, a simple farmer embarks on a treacherous journey to the Mastodon's fortress!

ISBN 978-1-61655-176-6 | $17.99

Pixu
The Mark of Evil
Gabriel Bá Becky Cloonan
Vasilis Lolos Fábio Moon

## PIXU: THE MARK OF EVIL

*Gabriel Bá, Becky Cloonan, Vasilis Lolos, and Fábio Moon*

This gripping tale of urban horror follows the lives of five lonely strangers who discover a dark mark scrawled on the walls of their building. As the walls come alive, everyone is slowly driven mad, stripped of free will, leaving only confusion, chaos, and eventual death.

ISBN 978-1-61655-813-0 | $14.99

SACRIFICE

## SACRIFICE

*Sam Humphries, Dalton Rose, Bryan Lee O'Malley, and others*

What happens when a troubled youth is plucked from modern society and sent on a psychedelic journey into the heart of the Aztec civilization—one of the greatest and most bloodthirsty times in human history?

ISBN 978-1-59582-985-6 | $19.99

MIND MGMT
The Mind Management
Comprehensive Report 1 of 3
Psychic warfare and its effect on the individual.
Includes field reports on you and your misguided paranoia.
Matt Kindt

## DE:TALES

*Fábio Moon and Gabriel Bá*

Brimming with all the details of human life, Moon and Bá's charming stories move from the urban reality of their home in São Paulo to the magical realism of their Latin American background. Named by *Booklist* as one of the 10 Best Graphic Novels of 2010.

ISBN 978-1-59582-557-5 | $19.99

## MIND MGMT OMNIBUS

*Matt Kindt*

This globe-spanning tale of espionage explores the adventures of a journalist investigating the mystery of a commercial flight where everyone aboard loses their memories. Each omnibus volume collects two volumes of the Eisner Award–winning series!

**VOLUME 1: THE MANAGER AND THE FUTURIST**
ISBN 978-1-50670-460-9 | $24.99

**VOLUME 2: THE HOME MAKER AND THE MAGICIAN**
ISBN 978-1-50670-461-6 | $24.99

**VOLUME 3: THE ERASER AND THE IMMORTALS**
ISBN 978-1-50670-462-3 | $24.99

AVAILABLE AT YOUR LOCAL COMICS SHOP OR BOOKSTORE

To find a comics shop near you, visit comicshoplocator.com • For more information or to order direct, visit DarkHorse.com

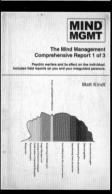